PRAGMATIC RURAL DEVELOPMENT FOR POVERTY ALLEVIATION

Dr. K. A. Jalihal, (born on 3rd April 1927), B.Sc. (Agri.), M.Sc (USA), Ph.D., S/o. Anantarao Jalihal comes from a Freedom Fighters family in Gadag of Gadag district, Karnataka. He started his service as lecturer in agronomy, Agricultural College, Dharwad in 1947 and has subsequently worked as (a) Superintendent of Agricultural School, (b) Assistant Professor of Agronomy in Pune Agricultural College, (c) Head of the Tobacco Research Station at Nippani, Belgaum district, (d) Professor of Agronomy and Extension in the Bangalore Agricultural College. He was the first Registrar of UAS, Bangalore in 1965 and then worked as Professor and Head, Department of Agricultural Extension from 1966 to 1975. For a period of 12 years he worked as Director of Extension and he was responsible for adoption of many new innovations in Agriculture by farmers in Karnataka. He was also incharge of Dean's post in the U.A.S. Bangalore before bifurcation in 1987. He has publised more than 100 research papers and guided eight Ph.D. and 16 M.Sc. students in Agricultural Extension.

Dr. M. Shivamurthy (born on 10th June 1957) is the son of Sri H. B. Murudaiah and Smt Sarvamangala belongs to the farming family situated in a remote village in Tumkur district, Karnataka. He did his B.Sc. (Horticulture), M.Sc. (Agri.) and Ph.D. in Agricultural Extension from University of Agricultural Sciences, Bangalore. He has also completed two Diploma courses— Post-graduate Diploma in Intensive Crop Production at Regional Research Station, Mandya and Diploma in Rural Development from Indira Gandhi National Open University (IGNOU), New Delhi. He started his career as grassroots level extension worker in the University of Agricultural Sciences, as Extension Guide for 9 years from 1982 to 1991. He has published 40 research articles, 20 popular articles and 3 books for the benefit of farming community. One of his book Kushki Thotagarike (Dryland Horticulture) published in 1995 has received the State level "Best Book Award". He has visited Cairo University, Cairo, Egypt to present his research paper. He has guided five M.Sc. students.

PRAGMATIC RURAL DEVELOPMENT FOR POVERTY ALLEVIATION
A Pioneering Paradigm

K.A. JALIHAL
Director of Extension & Dean (Retd.),
University of Agricultural Sciences,
Bangalore

and

M. SHIVAMURTHY
Associate Professor,
Department of Agricultural Extension
UAS, GKVK, Bangalore - 560065

CONCEPT PUBLISHING COMPANY, NEW DELHI-110059

ISBN 81-8069-030-X

First Published 2003

Published and Printed by

Ashok Kumar Mittal
Concept Publishing Company
A/15-16, Commercial Block, Mohan Garden,
New Delhi-110059 (India)

Phones: 25351460, 25351794
Fax: 091-(11) - 25357103
Email : publishing@conceptpub.com

ACKNOWLEDGEMENTS

It is my first and foremost duty to acknowledge persons and experiences, which motivated me to write this book. It was in early nineteen eighties when I was incharge of implementing a village-oriented lab to land programme by involving poor farmers. In the initial years of implementing this programme different experiences acted as motivating forces for encouraging me to take up writing for the upliftment of the rural poor. Some of these experiences are described as follows.

Experience 1: One of the requirements in implementing the lab to land programme was to prepare a list of rural poor families as found on the records in the revenue departments. To our surprise no comprehensive list of poor families was prepared by the rural development section, although it was more than ten years since the rural development programme was initiated in the Fourth Five-Year Plan. On enquiry it was learnt that the district authorities used to prepare only a list of such poor farmers to whom subsidy was to be given. Thus providing subsidy to only few had come in the way of preparing the list of all poor farmers.

Experience 2: In one of the villages of Bangalore district the university staff had organised a meeting of poor farmers to discuss about starting dairying as a subsidiary enterprise to increase the income of the poor families. The meeting was also attended by a Bank Manager, who was supposed to provide loans to poor farmers who were interested. When the question of maintaining cross-bred cows *v/s* buffalo was discussed in the meeting, most of the farmers showed their interest to maintain only buffaloes due to the high cost of cross-bred cows. The Bank Manager was also happy, since, he had provided a small amount for the programme. Before sanctioning the loans, the interested farmers were taken on a field trip to Melur and Mallur villages of Kolar district, which were trip to Melur and Mallur villages of Kolar district, which were recognised as Denmark of Karnataka, since these two villages had hundreds of cross-bred cows maintained by poor farmers. After Bangalore district farmers returned from their field trip, they started making request for maintaining cross-bred cows. They had developed achievement motivation due to the field visit.

Experience 3: A nationalised bank in Kolar district had revised the working hours and announced the bank business from 8.00 A.M. till 8.00 P.M. The bank manager organised a public function to give wide publicity about new bank timings. When he announced this in the meeting, an old small farmer stood up in the meeting and complained that the poor farmers from neighbouring villages are not getting the assistance to take advantage of the loan provided by the bank thus highlighting the need for providing specialised assistance, which is now known as management, services for small farmers.

Experience 4: In one of the villages in Dharwad district a meeting was organised involving tribal farmers to discuss the possibility of starting additional enterprises for improving their economy. Most of the farmers in the meeting told that no such meetings were ever organised in their village so far. After the discussion, a number of them agreed to take up additional enterprises.

Experience 5: While implementing the whole farm demonstration programme, by the university extension service a small farmer from Kanakapura taluk of Bangalore district, was enrolled as a whole farm demonstrator. He had only two hectares of dry land with an average yield of 12 – 15 quintals of ragi per hectare. We persuaded him to dig a well for irrigation with the loan provided by a Swedish based non-government organisation MYRADA. When the well was completed and pumpset installed, it transformed the economy of the farmer due to irrigation, which was more than adequate for his entire area of four acres. He could now grow three crops per year and his farm income had increased fifteen times when compared to his earlier dry cropping system. In two years his name had to be removed from the list of small farmers, which was prepared earlier.

These above mentioned experiences motivated this author that some useful literature should be developed for implementing effective rural development programme. The author is thus highly grateful to all those small farmers who participated in the experiences for motivating him to write this book.

Since the time I decided to write this book during late nineteen nineties, I have been a patient of Parkinson disease which affected my handwriting ability. The only course left was to dictate my ideas to a steno typist. At this crucial stage I was lucky to get the assistance of Smt. K.R. Dinamani who was working as a steno typist, when I was Director of Extension in the university. Due to devotion of old association, she readily agreed to walk to my house after office hours and volunteered to provide free stenographing assistance. I really do not know how to acknowledge this kind help provided by this great lady.

Dr. M. Shivamurthy, the second author of the book agreed to assist me in this book writing, primarily as a person to help me in getting the required references from the libraries and to correct the typed material. His association continued for a period of more than five years. He also became the second author by contributing his part to some chapters pertaining to empowerment of poor rural women. I am extremely grateful to his devoted assistance provided to me in this book writing.

Three persons who worked as directors of extension in the university during the last seven years helped me in completing my book writing, by deputing their technical staff to help me after office hours in preparing fair copies of the draft material. These directors namely, Late Dr. M .B. Channegowda, Late Dr. K.T. Ramachandra, and the present director Dr. V. Veerabhadraiah were my students for their Ph.D. degrees. Due to their teacher devotion they were kind enough to provide this assistance, for which I am greatly indebted to them.

As the book was nearing completion, there was a need to collect the typed material and prepare a final fair copy for computer typing. In this task I had the privilege of getting voluntary services of Mr. Ranganath Mangalvedker, Assistant Professor Extension in the Agricultural University. He used to walk to my residence and assist me in completion of this work. His devotion requires to be recognised with a sense of gratitude.

During the process of writing this book, an outline of the book was prepared. I used to discuss this outline with some of my close friends and relatives. During my visit to Dharwad, two of my friends namely Dr. K.C. Hiremath retired Professor of Agricultural Economics, University of Agricultural Sciences Bangalore, and Dr. K. Ragavendra Rao, retired Professor of Political Science, Mangalore University, showed keen interest on the outline of the book and suggested few modifications, to make the book more useful. When the draft book was ready, they went through the entire material and suggested some additions, especially to the topic dealing with objectives of rural development as visualised by pioneers. Their timely assistance is greatly appreciated.

Mr. K.S. Deshpande, retired librarian of Karnataka University Dharwad and an authority on library movement in the country showed active interest in my book writing and provided me continued moral support in completing the book inspite of my physical handicaps.. After the final draft was ready, he voluntarily took the responsibility of editing the book by spending a lot of time in reading the book. As a result of his editing the presentation became more readable. I gratefully acknowledge for his help in editing the book.

There were number of occasions when fair copies of the drafts had to be written legibly for the use of typists. This responsibility was shared in my house by the four persons. My daughter Nandini Deshpande and my grand-daughter Shruthi Deshpande helped me in this work when I went to Dharwad to stay with them, and also when they came to Bangalore in holidays. Similarly, my another daughter Vayjayanthi Kulahalli and my grand-son Anirudha Kulahalli also assisted me in this work when they visited Bangalore and also when I went to Bombay to stay with them. Due to their help I was able to complete the book in the scheduled time. I am highly grateful to them for this work.

My book writing became an interesting topic in my family due to the long time it took for completing. However, it did not become a bore to my family members. My wife Mandakini always co-operated in this work and never complained regarding inconvenience in assisting to alleviate rural poverty, part of the credit must go to the co-operation extended by my wife to this work.

Mr. N. Govindappa, the stenographer and computer typist took up the responsibility of computer typing of the book inspite of his very busy schedule with student's thesis typing. He was kind enough to provide revised typed copies three times to suit my requirements. My grateful thanks are to him.

During the last phases of this book work there was a need for using computer with a copier to prepare the final draft on the floppy. In this crucial work Mr. Raghavendra Kulahalli architect and relative of mine and his wife Seema came to my help and spared their computer for a number of days whenever we needed it. Similarly, one of my neighbour friend Sudhindra Kalghatgi and his wife Anju and their daughter Meera spared their computer whenever we requested inspite of inconveniences caused to them. I gratefully acknowledge their help.

I fail in my duty if I do not recognise the support given by the Concept Publishing Company, New Delhi, for taking up publication of this book. This company is in the field of academic publications for the last three decades and has great concern for social science publications, which prompted them to take up publishing this book dealing with rural poverty alleviation. The publisher in his very first letter recognised the value of the book by stating "We have gone through the details on the contents of the proposed book Pragmatic Rural Development for Poverty Alleviation—A Handbook, and find its usefulness for academicians, policy makers and those who are interested in poverty reduction in India. We would like to consider it for publication." Keeping to their word, this publishing company completed printing of the book very quickly, our grateful thanks for this kind support provided.

Dr. K.A. Jalihal
Dr. M. Shivamurthy

CONTENTS

LIST OF TABLES

PART I

RURAL POVERTY

1

INTRODUCTION

A majority of the world's poor people, are located in the rural South Asia, to which belong the largest countries of the sub-continent, namely India, Pakistan and Bangladesh. The rural poor are mostly agricultural labourers, artisans, tenants and small farmers, who own some land but most of whom, are also tenants with cultivated holdings of less than two hectares. Thus any programme aimed at the eradication of rural poverty must cover development programmes of these categories. The subject matter of development of the rural poor is not only vast but also equally complicated.

Perpetuation of India's Rural Poverty has become proverbial. The first Prime Minister of India Jawaharlal Nehru's pledge to solve the problems of the poor and starving, remains even now unfulfilled and his daughter's later call for *"Garibi Hatao"* still remains as a slogan without the required action in eradicating rural poverty. Even after 50 years of Independence, the percentage of the rural poor continues to remain high.

The International Year for Eradication of Poverty, which was earmarked as 1996, has already closed 5 years ago and now the UN Decade, dedicated to Poverty Eradication (1997-2006), has completed four years. Both the UN and India have now celebrated the 50th year of their existence and independence respectively. Both these are now being criticised for not yet succeeding in translating their grandiloquent platitudes, into effective real gains for the disadvantaged millions. Half a century after independence we have today the largest population of poor people in the world; one-fourth of our rural population is below poverty line and inspite of UN Agencies' massive aid projects, the gap between the rich and the poor has actually doubled in the last three decades.

The UN Economic and Social Survey conducted in 1997 has noted that India provided a substantial Rs. 64.4 billion for poverty alleviation in its 1996-97 budget, but it was not effective enough as design, organization, financing and targetting of such programmes needed to be sharpened further. Regarding the poverty alleviation programmes, this survey commented that "the programmes were agency driven and unresponsive to the real needs of the poor and lacked co-ordination among the multiple agencies which led to friction, duplication and unutilized synergies".[1]

In view of these circumstances, an important question raised is : What needs to be done to accelerate the alleviation of rural poverty in India?

The main reason for this unfortunate situation is that there is a lack of clear understanding of what pragmatic rural development is and how to implement poverty alleviation programmes in an effective way. This is observed at all levels from the top downwards. Even the top most level, Planning Commission is no exception to this. A Government of India High Powered Committee on Agricultural Policies and Programmes constituted in 1990, has pointed out that the most important requirement for the success of alleviation of rural poverty is agricultural development and Indian Planners have not even thought of this requirement seriously[2].

The World Bank (1975), has pointed out that a major requirement for the successful operation of co-operative groups and for regional and local government is the provision of trained manpower. Thus, training facilities are needed to prepare full time staff and to improve the effectiveness of community leaders, school teachers, religious leaders and other agents of change[3].

Hence, there is a need to see that training materials should be developed which will give a clear understanding of what causes rural poverty and how to design pragmatic rural development in order to accelerate poverty alleviation. To help in this task, it is necessary that simple and meaningful information on pragmatic rural development is compiled and made available.

Although, number of books have been published in recent years on the topic of rural development and poverty alleviation, no concerted efforts have been made to bring out an integrated readily usable information tool on what is pragmatic rural development and how to implement rural development programmes effectively.

Lot of information on this aspect is however available in scattered literature, both theoretical and practical. As pleaded by Robert Chambers, a practical theory of rural development and simple literature on this aspect is the need of the day[4].

The present book is an attempt to fill up this lacuna and make available some basic information relating to practical theory of rural development required for accelerating poverty alleviation. We have named this practical theory as 'Pragmatic Rural Development'. The book is divided into two parts. Part-I deals with the concept of rural poverty, causes of rural poverty, poverty related situational facts and some of the results of efforts made so far in alleviating rural poverty. Part-II of the book has the following components.

1. Some basic concepts of pragmatic rural development.
2. Issues important in pragmatic rural development.
3. Models of economic growth and their effect on rural poverty alleviation.
4. Strategies to be used for accelerating poverty alleviation.
5. Methods and techniques for promoting welfare of the rural poor.
6. Programme objectives of Rural Development for poverty alleviation.
7. Need for developing programme areas from programme objectives for easy and effective implementation.

The book closes with a last chapter where an inventory of priority programme areas under the programme objectives of pragmatic rural development, have been listed with a brief situational statement and suggested actions including innovative measures wherever available.

It is hoped that this book would be of some help for all those who are interested in the field of rural development for accelerating poverty alleviation.

We are also planning to bring out another book which will include some useful readings on some selected topics which are part of this pragmatic rural development which will provide some more detailed information on the various points dealt with in this book.

REFERENCES

1. UN Economic and Social Commission for Asia and Pacific, Annual Survey, 1997, Released on April 16, 1997, Published by the *Deccan Herald* on April 17, 1997.

2. Government of India, Report of the High Powered Committee on Agricultural Policies and Programmes, 1990.

3. World Bank, 1975—Rural Development—Sector Policy Paper.

4. Chambers Robert, 1993, *Rural Development—putting the last first*. Longman Scientific and Technical, New York, p. 44.

2

THE RURAL POOR

2.1 PREAMBLE

Rural poverty has been an unfortunate bane in the so-called third world countries since long. India is no exception. It is estimated that in India, even after 50 years of independence and 47 years of planned growth, alleviation of rural poverty is not satisfactorily progressing.

The Government of India has formally admitted to the World Bank in November 2000 that the country's poverty ratio has not declined to the targetted extent notwithstanding average growth levels in the post-reforms period being higher than that in the prereforms era[1].

India's Planning Commission official keepers of poverty estimates and progress on the poverty alleviation programme burnt the mid night oil to come out with the presentation to the World Bank, President James D. Wolfensohn on 13th November, 2000 to show that 26.10 per cent (1999 figures) of the country's population was poor[2], which included 23.62 per cent in the urban areas and 27.0 per cent in rural areas[2].

2.2 RURAL POVERTY MANIFESTATIONS

The publication "Platform for Action and the Beijing Declaration[3], published by the United Nations, Department of Public Information has described rural poverty manifestations in the following words.

"Rural poverty has various manifestations, including lack of income and productive resources sufficient to ensure a sustainable livelihood; hunger and malnutrition ; ill health; limited or lack of access to education and other basic services; increasing morbidity and mortality from illness; homelessness and inadequate housing; unsafe environments; and social discrimination and exclusion. It is also characterised by lack of participation in decision making and in civil, social and cultural life. It occurs in all countries — as mass poverty in many developing countries and as pockets of poverty amidst wealth in developed countries[3]".

United Nations ESCAP publication 'The Rural Poor'[4] adds the following :

"The rural poor may not be all starving but more often they are malnourished and frequently suffer from diseases. These rural poors are mostly illiterate or not much educated. They are insufficiently clothed, mostly bare footed and often live in temporary houses roofed with grass and located in unsanitary conditions. This section of the poor further lacks sufficient resources to purchase food and other necessities of life are forbidden to enjoy the living conditions which are customary in their societies. Their purchasing power is very low as a result of which, they are excluded from normal living pattern, customs and other activities[4]".

Rural poverty is also a multi-dimensional phenomenon. At least 30-40 per cent of the rural population is estimated to be poor in food consumption, poor by health standards, stay in mud or kutcha houses, mostly illiterate, rather ignorant and generally suppressed and further found exploited by the elite sector of the rural communities. Under employment and unemployment are common and their per capita income precarious, so also their per capita intake of calories. Worst of all, such rural poor staying below the poverty line rather unfortunately, are multiplying at a higher rate inspite of high infant mortality and death rate[2]. Even after the commencement of our liberal economic policies of the 90s, a gap between the rich and the rural poor is seen widening[4].

2.3 PROFILES OF THE RURAL POOR

We have heard of the famous adage "If you want to teach John Latin, you must not only know Latin but also John". This is true in case of the rural poor also. If you want to develop rural poor, you should not only know the methods and techniques of helping the rural poor but you must also know, the characteristics of the rural poor which will enable us to use the required methods and techniques judiciously. Keeping this in mind, in the following paragraphs the profiles of the rural poor are being spelled out.

Economic characteristics of the rural poor farmers

FAO publication has identified the following characteristics[5]:

1. A high proportion of the land is devoted to food crops in order to meet family subsistence needs.
2. A high proportion of output that is retained for home consumption or inversely a lower ratio of marketed surplus to output.
3. Rural poor resort to distress selling immediately after harvest in order to meet their debt or other obligations.
4. A diverse mixture of crops that allows them to hedge rationally against both agro-climatic and market risks.
5. A higher degree of risk aversions, faced with either new or rapidly changing market, technology or policy conditions.
6. Very low operative capital turnover in production coupled with a higher debt burden in relation to their resources.
7. Labour is the most important input used for production as it is relatively abundant and most of it is supplied by the family.
8. They are poor and have little ready cash.

9. Loans are usually unavailable to these people.
10. They are conscious of an uncertain environment, shortage and of family responsibilities and therefore they are averse to risks.
11. They often suffer cyclic labour shortage and unemployment.
12. They live in areas where the infrastructure of market supplies and communications is often weak and not to be relied upon.

Proceedings of a National Conference summarises socio-personal, socio-psychological characteristics as well as economic behaviour of the rural poor as follows[6] :

Socio-personal characteristics of the rural poor

1. Mostly belong to low caste,
2. They have low education,
3. Social and institutional participation low,
4. Low adoption leadership,
5. Low socio-economic status, and
6. Low adoption level.

Socio-psychological characteristics of the rural poor

1. They have low knowledge about new technology,
2. They have favourable attitude towards land reforms,
3. Very low risk orientation,
4. High urban pull,
5. Low political knowledge,
6. Self-reliance ability medium,
7. Low aspiration level, and
8. Traditional value orientation.

Economic behaviour of the rural poor

1. Investment orientation low,

2. Degree of land consolidation low,
3. Low farm mechanization,
4. High tenant status,
5. Intensity of cropping high,
6. Low storage behaviour,
7. High market behaviour,
8. High credit orientation,
9. Number of enterprises more,
10. Very high utilization of family labour, and
11. Very high indebtedness[5].

2.4 IDENTIFICATION OF THE RURAL POOR

The rural poor mostly belong to the category of small farmers, tenants, share croppers, artisans and landless labourers. These are the people who suffer from hunger.

There are two classes of the rural poor people namely; (1) People who are in absolute poverty, whose family annual income (family with 5 persons) is less than the poverty line fixed by the government from time to time, and (2) people who are in relative poverty, — whose family income though higher than fixed by the government, is however, less than one-third of the national average per family income[7].

The rural poverty line in India

On a broad basis, it is generally accepted that the rural poverty line in India should be based on the minimum per capita amount required to provide the nutritive norm of 2400 calories per person per day in rural areas for family members. This amount naturally varies slightly for the rural areas and the urban areas. The poverty line was first estimated by a Working Group appointed by the Government of India in 1962. It was then found to be Rs. 20 per month per head in rural areas and Rs. 25 per person per month in urban areas. The poverty line has been changing according to the index of cost of living from year to year and from plan to plan. Table 2.1 and Fig. 2.1 gives information on the rural poverty line[8].

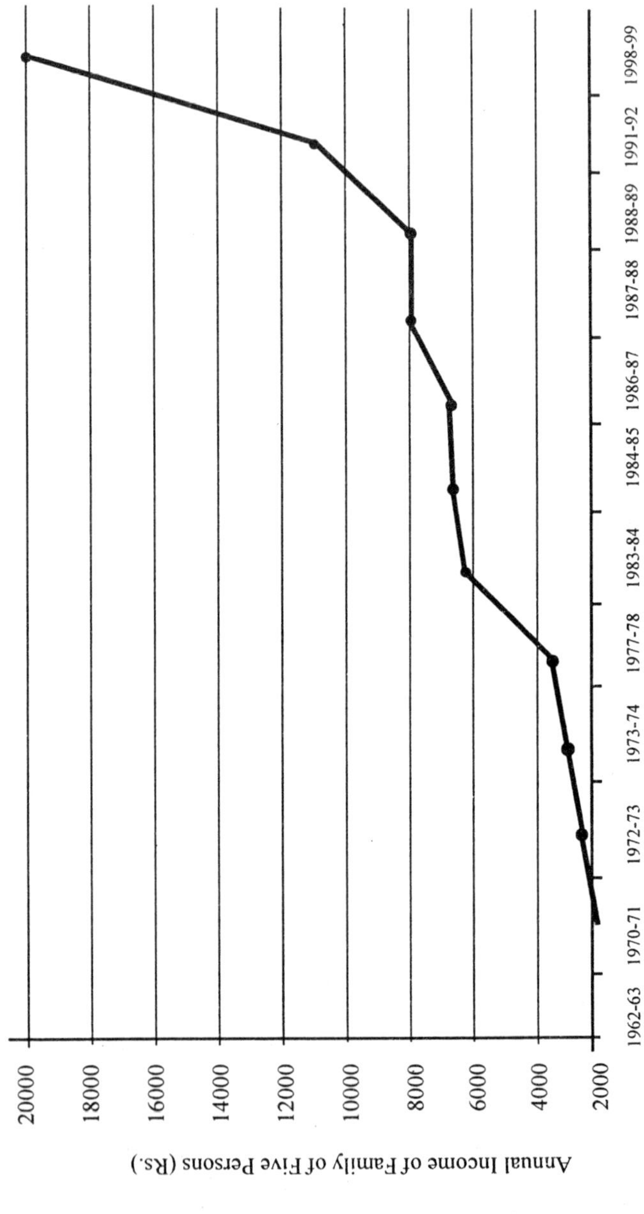

Fig. 2.1 : Rural Poverty Line in India

Table 2.1 : Rural poverty line in India

Year	Plan	Per capita per month income (Rs.)	Per family per year income of 5 members (Rs.)
1962-63	III Plan	20.00	1,200.00
1970-71	IV Plan	33.01	1,980.60
1972-73	IV Plan	40.24	2,414.40
1973-74	IV Plan	49.09	2,945.40
1977-78	V Plan	57.64	3,458.40
1983-84	VI Plan	101.80	6,108.00
1984-85	VI Plan	109.00	6,540.00
1986-87	VII Plan	110.75	6,645.00
1987-88	VII Plan	131.80	7,908.00
1988-89	VII Plan	132.79	7,967.40
1991-92	VIII Plan	183.00	11,000.00
1998-99	IX Plan	333.00	20,000.00

Source : Information furnished by Planning Commission from time to time.[8]

2.5 A GLIMPSE OF RURAL POVERTY IN INDIA

Extent of rural poverty in India over the years

The percentage of rural poor in India which was estimated at 56.4 per cent of the rural population in 1973-74 is now reported to be at 27.4 per cent in 1999-2000 as per following details[9].

Table 2.2 : Percentage of poor people in India 1999-2000

Rural sector		Urban sector		Combined all India	
Number in million	Poverty Ratio	Number in million	Poverty ratio	Number in million	Poverty ratio
193.20	27.09	67.00	23.62	260.20	26.10

Source: Information released by Govt. of India in February 2001, published by *Times of India* on 23-2-2001 (page 1 and 5).

Table 2.3 : Percentage of rural poor people in different States of India

Sl. No.	State	Percentage of rural poor		Percentage of poor (urban + rural)
		1973-74	1987-88	1999-2000
1.	Orissa	68.6	61.5	47.15
2.	Bihar	61.9	52.2	42.60
3.	Madhya Pradesh	67.6	46.6	37.43
4.	Uttar Pradesh	61.7	47.6	31.15
5.	West Bengal	61.4	33.4	27.02
6.	Karnataka	56.4	34.4	20.04
7.	Nagaland, Sikkim, Tripura and all Union territories	54.6	37.5	—
8.	Kerala	54.2	24.4	12.72
9.	Maharashtra	53.3	38.1	25.02
10.	Tamil Nadu	51.2	40.6	21.12
11.	Andhra Pradesh	47.7	19.5	15.77
12.	Jammu and Kashmir	42.9	23.6	3.48
13.	Rajasthan	41.9	29.2	5.28
14.	Assam	41.5	31.3	36.09
15.	Gujarat	35.8	17.2	14.07
16.	Manipur	38.1	7.5	7.50
17.	Haryana	31.0	15.6	15.60
18.	Punjab	24.2	11.7	6.16
19.	Himachal Pradesh	23.7	14.2	7.63
20.	Delhi	21.7	1.2	8.23
21.	Arunachal Pradesh	*	*	33.47
22.	Meghalaya	*	*	37.87
23.	Mizoram	*	*	19.47
24.	Nagaland	*	*	32.47
25.	Sikkim	*	*	36.55
26.	Tripura	*	*	34.44
27.	Andaman & Nicobar	*	*	20.99
28.	Chandigarh	*	*	5.75
29.	Dadra and Nagarhaveli	*	*	17.14
30.	Goa	*	*	4.40
31.	Daman and Diu	*	*	4.44
32.	Laxadweep	*	*	15.60
33.	Pondicherry	*	*	21.67
	All India	54.6	37.6	28.10

* Included in the serial No. 7

Source : (1) *Economic and Political Weekly* - Aug. 24, 1993[10], Table 8

(2) Estimates of poor, reported in *Times of India*, Dt. 23-2-2001[9]

Note : Since figures of 1999-2000 are available for total urban and rural constituted, it is estimated that rural poverty is higher by 2-3 per cent than the reported figure in the Table.

State-wise picture of rural poverty

Table 2.3 indicates comparative picture of rural poverty in the various States of India and the change taking place over the years. Table 2.4 indicates the States where more than one-fourth of the rural population is poor.

From the Table 2.3, it is seen that the percentage terms, Orissa has the dubious distinction of having the highest percentage (47.15) of its population living below the poverty line. It is followed by Bihar which has 42.60 per cent of its population categorised as poor. In third place is Madhya Pradesh with 37.43 per cent followed by Sikkim (36.55%) and Tripura (34.44%).

In terms of actual population of the poor it is Uttar Pradesh which tops the list with about 5.3 crore people in the State living below the poverty line. Bihar with approximately 4.3 crore of the country's poor occupies the second followed by Madhya Pradesh (3 crore), Maharashtra (2.2 crore), West Bengal (2.1 crore), Orissa (1.7 crore) and Andhra Pradesh (1.2 crore), Jammu and Kashmir has a small number of poor people estimated at 3.46 lakhs. Himachal Pradesh has nearly 5.12 lakh poor people.

Table 2.4 : States having more than one-fourth of rural population below the poverty line (1999-2000)

	State	Percentage of poor in the population
1.	Orissa	47.15
2.	Bihar	42.60
3.	Meghalaya	37.87
4.	Madhya Pradesh	37.43
5.	Sikkim	36.55
6.	Assam	36.09
7.	Tripura	34.44
8.	Arunachal Pradesh	33.47
9.	Nagaland	32.47
10.	Uttar Pradesh	31.15
11.	West Bengal	27.02
12.	Maharashtra	25.02

Source : Report published in the *Times of India*, Dt. February 23, 2001, page 9.

2.6 HANDICAPS OF THE RURAL POOR

Handicaps of the rural poor have been pointed out in the book, The Rural Poor (1985) as follows[4] :

"Because of the adverse circumstances, in which they live and work, the rural poor rarely have the opportunity to improve their lot in life. For example, they frequently have insufficient access to water, modern agricultural inputs and credit among others. They also face many disincentives in increasing their level of production because tenancy arrangements are structured to favour landlords or money lenders who normally receive the greater share of any production increases". There are other handicaps that burden the poor. Chief among them is the fact that they are frequently excluded from the development process. While the poor may seem to have the same rights as any one else in their society such equality and opportunity exist in theory only. The poor lack social status and they normally do not have the power or opportunity to participate in designing projects or development programmes that would help them to break out of the cycle of poverty. They are not usually assisted by the Government staff because they are socially excluded from the rural institutions that command the services[4].

2.7 RURAL INSTITUTES AND THE RURAL POOR

This Expert Group based on 10 case studies from seven countries in the ESCAP region concluded that in most cases rural institutions in practice served the interest of only the more wealthy and powerful groups in rural society, even though they were intended to serve a wider target group including small farmers, tenant farmers and the landless. Their activity was often restricted because of the need for collateral loan or aid to farmers and the landlords. The report also stated that the agricultural extension services most frequently served the surplus farmers; access to institutional form of credit was often restricted to big farmers because of the need for collateral to the landless class farmer's associations and co-operatives became a vehicle for furthering interest of wealthier farmers; marketing services were so organized that the marketing needs of the rural poor remained unserved, leaving them at the mercy of middle men; Agrarian reform legislation often remained ineffective because vested interests frustrated its intention; and the rural poor could not participate effectively in village institutions and in village government because the same influential people controlled these institutions for their own benefit[4]. This situation has not changed even now.

2.8 CATEGORIES OF RURAL POVERTY AND POSSIBLE MEANS TO ALLEVIATE THEM

According to a Commonwealth Consultation on Rural Poverty Alleviation held in Colombo, Sri Lanka from 5-9, October 1992, three categories of rural poverty have been identified as follows[11].

(1) Transitory Poverty

This is caused more likely by natural or man made disasters, or through the transitional phases of structural adjustment. This category might also include those vulnerable groups who teeter on the edge of poverty, since they are the potential addition to the poor with the appropriate response probably comprising disaster preparedness, mitigation and emergency, relief measures etc.

(2) Attributional Poverty

This results from problems such as diseases, mental and physical disability, malnutrition, age or position in the household (viz., women and children).

(3) Chronic Poverty

This is caused by general lack of access to adequate resources and opportunities by disadvantaged groups in the society.

Measures to alleviate each category of poverty situation

(1) Transitory Poverty

For example, in targetting the transitory poor, the establishment of early warning systems as proposed in the consultation recommendations could involve national governments, donors and technical assistance agencies, besides incorporating disaster prevention, preparedness, mitigation and rehabilitation into national planning and programmes. From a policy and programmes, perspective, NGOs would most certainly be involved, with Government ensuring that the necessary pre-conditions were satisfied for their full participation. And the poor themselves should not be seen simply as beneficiaries in the aid process but rather as partners, respecting their human dignity and explicitly involving them in decision making, programme development and implementation.

(2) Attributional Poverty

To address attributional poverty similarly would require the co-operative efforts of government information collection agencies, perhaps with external technical and financial assistance where needed. The poor themselves and particularly women must be involved — a process which necessarily would require social and physical infrastructures to be built, probably with government and outside assistance together with the help of NGOs.

(3) Chronic Poverty

The international community has a wide role to play also in terms of financial and technical assistance; technology transfer, exchange of experience; strategic planning; infrastructure development involving the use of food aid; education and training, resources development and the relief of developing country indebtedness.

REFERENCES

1. Report published in the *Hindu Business Line*, dated Nov. 14, 2000, page 2 under the caption "Government admits poverty reduction not enough".

2. Report published in the *Economic Times* Chennai edition dated 15th

November 2000, pp. 3, under the title "Poverty the key word as Wolfensohn makes rounds".

3. United Nations : Department of Public Information, 1995, Platform for Action : Beijing Declaration, page 38.

4. United Nations : Economic and Social Commission for Asia and Pacific (ESCAP), Bangkok, 1985, *The Rural Poor*, page 2-3.

5. FAO : Regional Office for Asia and Pacific, 1993 : Farm Management Notes for Asia and Far East. Reg. Issue, 17.

6. IARI Extension Division, New Delhi : Proceedings of the National Conference and Workshop on Small Farmers, held at New Delhi 1984-85.

7. World Bank, 1975, "*Rural Development*" - A sector policy papers. World Bank, Washington DC, USA.

8. Planning Commission, Government of India : Information furnished from time to time.

9. Government of India, Information released in Feb. 2001, which was reported by *Times of India* on 23-2-2001, page 1 & 9.

10. *Economic and Political Weekly*, 1993 Aug., 21, Table 8.

11. Common Wealth Secretariat, London 1993, Action to reduce poverty, proposals for needful instructions developed by a Commonwealth Consultation on Rural Poverty Alleviation, Colombo, Sri Lanka 5-9, October, 1992. Food production and Rural Development Division, Commonwealth Secretariat quoted by Joseph Mullen "Introduction - poverty rediscovered" in Joseph Mullen (Edt.) Rural Poverty Alleviation, Aveberry, USA, Hongkong, Sydney, 1995.

3

CAUSES OF RURAL POVERTY AND PROBLEMS FACED IN POVERTY ALLEVIATION

There are several important causes responsible for rural poverty. Similarly, there are various factors which have created problems and hence come in the way of effective poverty alleviation. Both these topics have been combined and included in this chapter under the common heading "Causes of Rural Poverty and Problems faced in Poverty Alleviation".

3.1 POOR ASSETS/RESOURCES

Most frequently the rural poor own little, if any, land resources. In the case of completely landless people, they have to depend on either share cropping, or tenancy or labour employment or self employment by developing subsidiary enterprises, for which assets have to be made available to them by providing loans. A few important factors related to these aspects are described here.

Decreasing size of land holdings

A majority of farmers in India's villages own small size holdings below two hectares. The generalized statement in this connection is that 75 per cent of farmers own only 25 per cent of the total land. The size of farm holdings instead of increasing in size year by year as has happened in other developed countries due to the development process, has, however, been dwindling in India. The tables 3.1 and 3.2 show the same.

Table 3.1 : Average size of holding in hectares own by different Categories of farmers (1960-61 to 1990-91)

Categories of farmers	Area per operating holding		
	1960-61	1990-91	Per cent change 1990-91 over 1960-61
Marginal	0.44	0.40	– 9.3
Small	1.47	1.44	– 2.0
Semi-medium	2.84	2.76	– 3.0
Medium	6.10	5.90	– 3.3
Large	17.48	17.33	– 0.9
All groups	2.69	1.57	– 41.6

Source : Data furnished by Centre for Monitoring Indian Economy (CMIE) (1995)[1]

Table 3.2 : Categories of farmers, their percentage to total number of farmers and percentage area operated

Categories of Farmers	Percentage to total No. of farmers		Percentage of total land holdings	
	1960-61	1990-91	1960-61	1990-91
Marginal	40.7	59.0	6.7	14.9
Small	22.3	19.0	12.2	17.3
Semi-medium	18.9	13.2	20.0	23.2
Medium	13.4	7.2	30.4	27.2
Large	4.7	1.6	30.7	17.4
Total	100.0	100.0	100.0	100.0

Source : Data furnished by Centre for Monitoring Indian Economy (CMIE) (1995)[1]

Tables 3.1 and 3.2 indicate that the number of marginal and small farmers which was 63 per cent in 1960-61 has increased to 78 per cent in 1990-91. The average size of holding was 0.44 hectares for marginal farmers and 1.47 hectares for small farmers in 1960-61. This size has decreased further to 0.40 hectare and 1.44 hectares in 1990-91 respectively. While this is so, the percentage of area cultivated by these two categories has increased namely from 6.7 per cent land owned by marginal farmers in 1960-61 to 14.9 per cent in 1990-91. For small farmers the total area cultivated has increased from 12.2 per cent to 17.3 per cent during this period[1].

These statistics indicate that there is no improvement in the land size owned by these two categories of marginal and small farmers inspite of land reforms.

Poor development of land resources

Land belonging to rural poor comprises mostly of dryland. These lands are highly eroded in a majority of cases. These small lands are further segmented into very small patches. Unless land improvement is taken up and consolidation of holdings is achieved, it is very difficult to increase the productivity of these lands[2].

Problems in distributing surplus land to landless poor people

Unless the rural poor are assisted by distributing surplus land available in the country by imposing ceiling on agricultural land, it is difficult to expect them to own land resources. One of the important objectives of land reforms introduced from the beginning of the plan era was to fix ceiling on agricultural land and to take over the surplus land from the land owners who may have more land than the ceiling fixed, so that such surplus land could be distributed to the landless. Inspite of completing Eighth Five Year Plan, there has not been adequate progress in this regard. The Eighth Plan document explains this situation as follows:

> "On the question of land ceilings, the two aspects needing urgent attention are: (a) Detection of surplus land, hitherto not available because of recourse to evasive methods like *benami* transfers, partition, fraud, collusion with official machinery etc. and (b) ensuring that, the allottees retain possession and there is severe penalty for dispossession. The lacuna in the laws will have to be removed so as to help resolve both these issues. Suitable creative options need to be built into the law, so that once the land is declared surplus, unless malafide is established against the official machinery concerned, the land would vest in the Government and it would be open to the Courts to award only compensation to the landlord[3]".

Non-distribution of available cultivable waste land to the rural poor

The percentage of cultivable waste land which can be brought under cultivation in India is very large. In 1991-92 the extent of cultivable waste land was 15.1 million ha. as compared to the cultivated land of 141 million ha. Since the beginning of the Plan, till the end of 1981, only 1.8 million ha.of cultivable land was distributed to the rural landless. Lack of availability of such cultivable waste land for speedy distribution to rural poor continues to remain as one of the important factors affecting rural poverty[4].

Lack of facilities in developing underground water resources to rural poor

Major portion of the land owned by small farmers is under rainfed farming. It should be possible to remove poverty of this section of rural people if potential well irrigation resources are tapped where possible, to help these poor people. So far adequate attention is not given to this vital method, except in a very limited way through the two projects namely; the Ganga Kalyan Project and Million Well Scheme. During the Eighth Plan, out of 1500 crore budget provided for total irrigation, only 22 crore were earmarked for digging 4,000 tube wells under the Ganga Kalyan Project and similarly the Million Well Scheme was not implemented in many areas.

Improper use of water resources under canal irrigation rendering the irrigated land into saline and alkaline condition

It is estimated by the Administrative Staff College of India, Hyderabad that around 100 lakh hectares of canal irrigated land has become water logged and therefore not fit for cultivation. Another 25 lakh hectares is threatened with salinity. Roughly, 68.8 per cent of irrigated land is in danger of becoming saline or alkaline[5]. Approximately, 25 per cent of such problem area under canal irrigation is owned by small farmers. Thus, with canal irrigation, atleast 30-40 lakh hectares of irrigated land, owned by small farmers, have been rendered unproductive. These lands would not be improved unless government meets the full cost of reclamation, which may be recovered later in easy instalments. So far no government scheme to fully finance such lands are available. Thus even irrigated land have not been able to help small farmers to get out of poverty line[5].

Difficulty in providing adequate assets under IRDP for the Rural Poor

Although IRDP is aimed at providing assistance to the rural poor in obtaining assets for assisting in developing self-employment projects, in reality there have been lot of problems in obtaining productive adequate assets by the rural poor. The Eighth Plan document has indicated this problem by stating as follows[3]:

> "Under the IRDP, those living below the defined poverty line in the rural areas are identified and given assistance for acquisition of productive assets of proper scales for self-employment, which in turn, should generate enough income to enable the beneficiaries to rise above the poverty line. It may be partly due to their low levels of initial investments. On the other hand, it is also difficult to expect banks to raise the per capita loan assistance to beneficiaries given the excessive overdues pending[3]".

This difficulty on the part of rural poor in getting adequate assets has also been pointed out in the report of High Powered Committee on Agricultural Policies and Programmes appointed by the Government of India in 1990, which states as follows[4] :

> "In brief it can be said that it is lack of knowledge, financial, organization support, which come in the way of eradication of poverty through adoption of supplementary enterprises by the rural poor. Substantive loans are needed for Animal Husbandry and long term ones for onward raising. Also infrastructure support in the form of research, extension, input supplies and marketing will have t(be provided".

3.2 LOW AGRICULTURAL PRODUCTION

Under this subhead, there are two factors which are important in influencing rural poverty in India.

Low agricultural production in the country

No country in the world has been able to eradicate rural poverty unless agricultural production of the country has improved. The only exceptions are the oil producing countries of the Gulf. UNCTAD[6] (1997) has recently stated that, in most Less Developed Countries (LDCs) the area in which reforms are lacking to have their greatest impact is agriculture. Agriculture is the single most important sector in LDCs economies in terms of its contribution to adequate employment and income. Increased production in agriculture is essential if living standards of a majority of the poor, who live in rural areas, are to be raised and if food security is to be enhanced. "India's agricultural production, even considering the maximum of 199.4 million tonnes of foodgrains in 1996-97, is one of the lowest in the world. The High Powered Committee on Agricultural Policies and Programmes appointed by the Government of India in 1990[4], in its report states : "When a factory or industry produces considerably less than its rated capacity, it is said to be sick and all measures are taken to bring it back to health. But the fact that Indian agriculture has been sick for a long time producing much less than its potential or capacity" has not been even noted by our policy makers, leaves alone taking any steps to bring it back to health and achieve its full potential.[4]

Low agricultural production of the rural poor

If agricultural production of the country is not satisfactory, the agricultural development of the rural poor is still more unsatisfactory. The rural poor cannot improve their agricultural production due to the following reasons:

(a) Improved production either in agriculture or related subsidiary enterprises requires the use of additional inputs like improved seeds, fertilizers, manures and chemicals, cattle feed, hire of implements and storage facilities etc. There are also risks and uncertainties in using these inputs both due to several factors and price fluctuations and due to insect-pests and diseases. Expecially, in drylands the risk situations are frequent. Hence, unless the government policies guarantee safety nets like insurance, price guarantee etc., it will be rather difficult for the rural poor to use inputs.[7]

(b) Rural poor also have poor access to services provided by the Government and non-government institutions like credit, training, supplies, services etc. Special efforts are required to provide assistance to the rural poor to have access to these services which has not been given proper attention so far.

(c) Rural poor are generally not reached by the agencies to educate them regarding development. They are also not properly motivated and involved actively during the planning and implementing of programmes meant for them. This has been a great handicap for their agricultural development.

(d) Most of the existing modern technology is not sustainable one, for the rural poor. Special efforts are needed to develop sustainable technology for improving rural poor. What is needed is to find out more ways to enhance the resource of technology by substituting non monetory or inexpensive inputs, replacing high cost inputs and also methods of minimizing yield fluctuations caused by weather aberrations and pest epidemics. Absence of such sustaining technology is an important cause for low production levels by the rural poor.

3.3 POOR EMPLOYMENT OPPORTUNITIES IN RURAL AREAS

Poor labour absorption in agriculture

In a country like India where almost 70 per cent of the rural poor depend on agriculture, more employment to the under-employed and unemployed rural poor have to be provided in agricultural and related fields. However, experiences of the last eight Five Year Plans reveal poor absorption of labour in agriculture, which is one of the important reasons for perpetuation of rural poverty.

Less progress in the development of non-foodgrain agriculture

The rural poor require intensity of farming through non foodgrain agricultural production"[7]. At present the government policies are not conducive for this. (a) There should be clearcut policies covering research emphasis to reduce yield uncertainties of labour intensive enterprises through greater pest resistance and controlled tolerance to weather fluctuations. (b) Improved credit facilities to meet the high risk conditions of such enterprises. (c) To improve marketing and processing facilities during these price fluctuations and risks.

At present only a small beginning is made regarding this requirement in promoting dairy enterprise and oil seed cultivation and that too in limited areas. However, much more efforts are needed to remove this cause influencing poverty.

Poor progress in establishing small scale industries in rural areas

Growth of small scale industries complements vigorous agricultural development policy by providing employment in rural areas. However, at present vigorous programmes for the development of small scale industries in rural areas are not being taken up. This has come in the way of poverty alleviation.

Low wages of agricultural labourers

Poverty is more widespread than employment. It cannot be said that all rural poors who have been provided with employment have come above poverty line. Full employment will not be a complete solution to poverty unless it is accompanied by higher earnings. Real wage rates of agricultural commodities are generally lower than those of Minimum Wage Act. Unless, these real labour wages are brought to the level mentioned in the Minimum Wages Act, the problem of poverty cannot be alleviated.[4] Government projects of providing rural employment do not provide adequate employment. The National Rural Employment Projects namely; Jawahar Rojgar Yojana has hardly provided adequate employment to the rural poor. The Eighth Plan document says about the JRY as follows[3].

"The survey shows that on an average, about 15 days of employment was generated per person in 1991 at an average wage rate of Rs. 25. This would yield a supplementary income per person of about Rs. 300 to 400 per annum. This is rather meagre in the context of poverty line of Rs. 6,400 during Seventh Plan which has been revised upwards for the Eighth Plan to Rs. 11,000.

Inability of modern agricultural technology to provide more employment

In general the very technologies which are so essential to provide the food, to back wages goods payments provide only a small proportions of increased income directly to labour through increased employment. Mellor (1975)[7] has quoted the results from his survey under 14 diverse situations in India wherein only 5 to 15 per cent of increased income came from new technologies represented by payment for increased labour.

No satisfactory progress in providing increased employment through village and household industries

The age old village and household industries are important sources of providing additional employment to unemployed and under-employed rural poor. Right from the Gandhian era, emphasis has been laid on developing this sector. Unfortunately there is no satisfactory progress in this area. The Eighth Plan document states: "Employment in the cottage and household industry has experienced relative decline due to shrinking markets on account of competition from modern products and often due to lack of technological upgradation to meet the new demands[3]". Earlier, the Seventh Plan had also identified important problems faced by this village industries sector which were listed as[3]—

1. Technological obsolescence,
2. Inadequate and irregular supply of raw materials,
3. Lack of organized market channels,
4. Imperfect knowledge of market conditions,
5. Unorganized nature of operations,
6. Inadequate availability of credit,
7. Constraints of infrastructure facilities, and
8. Deficient management and technical skills.

Difficulties in implementing self-employment projects by the Government

After the IRDP programme was launched, two important projects for promoting self-employment were the TRYSEM and DWCRA. Although lot of money was spent on these schemes, the results obtained are not up to the mark and employment promotion has not been satisfactory. The progress of TRYSEM is indicated in the following Table 3.3.

Table 3.3 : Achievements of TRYSEM 1980 to 1991

Period	No. of persons trained	No. of persons employed	No. of persons on wages	Total employed	Percentage of the youth
1980-85 VI Plan	10,14,695	4,78,396	1,02,097	5,80,483	57.2
1985-90 VII Plan	9,97,960	4,54,036	1,31,096	5,95,132	59.6
1990-91	2,36,177	1,23,785	41,493	1,65,278	70.0
1991-92	1,51,925	51,560	17,457	69,017	45.4
Total	22,48,832	10,66,217	2,74,686	13,40,903	58.8

Source : Rural development report (employment) NIRD (1994)[8].

According to this data, only 58.88 per cent of persons trained have been benefited including self-employed and wage employed. While the percentage of people self employed is less than 50 per cent of the persons trained[8], the details of employment generation through DWCRA, in respect of rural women, are not yet available. However, the progress achieved is not very satisfactory and the important reason for this is that the programme is yet not integrated properly with the IRDP'. The difficulties experienced in implementing TRYSEM schemes have been pointed out as (1) The programme is not provided for an integrated system of supply of raw materials and marketing of products through government sponsored agencies or corporations. (2) The programmes are not adjusted in a way that will enable them to get employed in village industries and artisan pursuit after necessary training instead of expecting them to set up industries, business and service ventures on their own[9].

3.4 INADEQUATE INFRASTRUCTURE

Rural Poverty and Immobility are Associated

One of the important factors related to poverty is said to be immobility from one area to the other. It is, therefore, no wonder that countries like India with low standard of living are also countries with poor roads and transports.

Inadequate Market Facilities

Lack of proper roads to most of the villages has also created a related problem in the marketing of agricultural produce from rural areas specially for the rural poor. They are forced to engage in distress sale at the time of harvest.

Poor Education Facilities

People's education is an important aspect of any poverty alleviation programme. Inspite of 50 years of independence, the country has not been able to provide better educational facilities in villages. As on 1991, only 52.2 per cent people are literate in India. The percentage of people having primary education is much less. In spite of the constitutional provision for providing free education to all people, the progress is not satisfactory. Unless top priority is given to education, poverty alleviation will not be satisfactory.

Nobel Laureate Amartya Sen (1998)[10] has stated that India and Pakistan had neglected education, health care and land reforms is truly regrettable ways and when they opened their economies suddenly there were a lot of people who were not in a position to compete in a global world. He has further added that if a country had globalization at the highest possible speed and pays no attention to lack of social opportunities, illiteracy and lack of health care it will be creating problems for itself.[10]

Slow Progress in providing Minimum Needs

Providing potable drinking water and arranging sanitary environmental conditions and medical facilities, arranging for pucca houses for stay and making available cheap food are supposed to be the most important minimum needs necessary for rural people. The progress achieved on this front cannot be said to be satisfactory. The Eighth Plan document[3] states that the progress in respect of these areas can be said to be quantitatively better but not qualitatively and points out[16] that "(1) In the case of rural health, there is an extensive network of primary health centres and subcentres, but these have not been operationalized in terms of adequate staff or medicines. (2) Similarly in the rural water supply programme, the coverage of villages is not enough by itself. It is necessary to ensure, that 40 litres of potable water per capita per day is available on sustained basis and to ensure its quality upgradation by making it free from salinity and chemical and bacteriological contamination"[3].

3.5 INCREASE IN POPULATION

India is already facing the problem of rural poverty for many years. With this situation, the problem is likely to get worse if the population expands at an unprecedented rate while limitations continue to be imposed by available resources, technology and institutions and organisations. This is what has been happening in

India. Inspite of the assertion made in the Second Five Year Plan that the rate of economic development also depends on the rate of growth of population, India's population is growing unabated. The population of India which was 361 million in 1951 and it has exceeded 1 billion in 2001[11] and will soon have the highest population in the world overtaking China. The rural population which was 289 million in 1951, has now reached 628 million mark. Due to this population explosion, there has been a frightening rate of increase in the number of small farms and their proportions in the total ownership holdings. These small farmers, most of whom are marginal along with agricultural labourers, constitute such a large proportion of agricultural labour force and it will be difficult to find out employment for these persons. The increase in population would result in a very serious problem in our planned effort to alleviate rural poverty and unemployment. The country which has reached self-sufficiency in foodgrain by the end of Third Five Year Plan is again posed to face the serious problem of food shortage in another five years, if the same rate of increase of population continues.

3.6 LOW OPPORTUNITIES FOR ACCESS TO SERVICES

The World Bank publication 'POVERTY[12]' states that "In general the poor have less access to publicly provided goods and infrastructure than do other groups. On the whole, governments fail to reach the rural poor". For example, the Grameena Banks primarily meant for the rural poor have not been providing adequate loans to the rural poor. The Taluk Agricultural Marketing Co-operative Societies have failed to market the produce of the rural poor at profitable rates. A new theory has been developed which states that unless the rural poor get special help they will not be able to get access to services of various institutions. So far the efforts made in this direction have not been satisfactory. The governments have not even been thinking seriously about the need for such kinds of services required by the rural poor. Poverty alleviation programmes will continue to suffer till the rural poor get organised assistance of what is known "as farm management services" to get access to the various services of the rural institutes.[13]

3.7 DISADVANTAGES DUE TO THE ECONOMIES OF SCALE

The production of the rural poor is in small quantities and hence unless organised efforts are made to pool the production of the rural poor to get the advantage of the economies of the scale, the income of the rural poor is bound to be at a low level. Reliance the only remedy through co-operative societies has not assisted the rural poor. A new thinking on new ways of organising informal group efforts should be made to assist the rural poor to get the advantages of economies of scale which are being denied to them.

3.8 LACK OF BOLD GOVERNMENT POLICIES TO PROTECT THE RURAL POOR

Government's Failure to provide Safety Nets to the Rural Poor to overcome Risk Situations

The rural poor will not be able to use new technology even if they are aware of them unless the government is willing to provide safety nets to cover risk and uncertainty for the use of additional inputs to be purchased[7]. The dry farming areas present challenging situation in this regard and unless government provides limited insurance to cover the risk of cost of new inputs to be used, we cannot expect the rural poor to adopt new technologies to increase their production[2].

Anti-Poor Government Policies Still Dominate in India

If the government continues to follow Anti-poor policies, it will be difficult to expect the poor to increase their production of agriculture and related enterprises. A National Consultative Discussion Session held in New Delhi in October 1996 has pointed out a couple of such anti-poor government policies[14] as for example : (1) The poor 'Koya' tribals in Orissa are now prevented to use the forest produce to prepare brooms while the paper industry gets bamboo at subsidized rates. (2) Women of Banaskantha of Gujarat who survive on gathering gum from Babool trees have become illegal collectors because license is now required for gum collection. (3) 'Korchis' in Shimoga district of Karnataka have now been prevented from using bamboos for preparing bamboo baskets.

Inadequate Public Distribution System

Inspite of years of work with the Public Distribution System, it has not been possible to help the rural poor with cheap supply of food-grains under the Public Distribution System (PDS). The most required coarse grains for the rural poor are not supplied through the PDS[15]. The quantity of rice now being given at special low price for the rural poor is only 20 kg/ family /month, which is not adequate to meet the needs of the rural poor families.

3.9 LACK OF PARTICIPATORY APPROACH

Non-involvement of the Rural Poor in Poverty Alleviation Programmes

One of the essential requirements for poverty alleviation is the active involvement of the rural poor. Experience so far has indicated that rural poor are kept out of such endeavour. Research/development studies reported by the USAID have pointed out that one of the important factors for the success of rural development programme to alleviate rural poverty is the active involvement of the poor both at the planning and implementing stages (USAID Research Paper, 1975)[15]. The worldwide consultative discussions held at Delhi in 1996 has also highlighted this aspect by pointing out that "it is not so much lack of resources that has inhibited poverty eradication as actual blinkers and a mistaken belief that the poor cannot know what is best for them. Speaker after speaker coming from different sections of the representatives, including planning authorities, conceded this basic flaw in our approach in development plans till now. The discussions therefore sought to highlight the empowerment of the community as a strategy with specific reference to three key areas — Water resource, health and education.[14]

Poors do not have access to information on their entitlements in the Poverty Alleviation Programme

No concerted efforts are made to inform the poor through mass media about their entitlements in the poverty alleviation programmes. As a result, much of the money meant for them is going to those who are well above the poverty line.[14]

Inadequate participation of the three basic village institutes in the Rural Development Programme of Poverty Alleviation

The Three Basic Institutes set up by the Government at the village level are : (1) The village panchayat; (2) The village co-operative, and (3) The village school

At present none of these are actively involved in organising and implementing of the poverty alleviation programmes. So long as this lacuna is not filled, the rural poverty alleviation programmes are bound to suffer.

3.10 PROBLEMS RELATED TO PROGRAMME PLANNING AND IMPLEMENTATION

Absence of Local Planning

Local planning is a must for implementing rural development programmes for alleviation of rural poverty. It is desirable both because rural development cuts across all sectors and because rural programmes need to be framed to meet regional conditions.[17] In the consultative discussions held at Delhi in 1996, Dr. Alaga, the then Planning Minister, himself pointed out that although under the 74th Constitution amendment district planning machinery was required to be set up nationwide, this has not been done.

Divided responsibilities in implementing poverty alleviation programmes. Rural development programmes are not implemented by one agency at the local level. There are many government departments which are required to implement these programmes. However, since there is no clear cut understanding of responsibilities by the relevant organisations, difficulties crop up in getting the co-ordination at the operating level. The Zilla Parishads which are to shoulder the major burden of organising these programmes have no technical staff under their control. Progress of rural development has been hindered by the indecisions as to the appropriate agencies, which should be entrusted with responsibilities of formulating area development plans.[9]

Lack of Co-ordination at the Operating Levels

Rural development work requires responsibilities of various kinds like education, providing finance, making available inputs and services, providing insurance etc. Since many different organisations are involved in implementing these different activities, it becomes necessary that close coordination should take place at the operational level among these various agencies which has not been observed in most places.[17]

Poor and Inadequate Allocation of Resources

The problems under this sub-head can be listed as follows :

1. Allocation for education not adequate
2. Budget given for infrastructure is diverted for other activities in many cases.
3. Very little budget is earmarked for village and small scale industries as compared to big industries.
4. Budget for agriculture not adequate and agricultural research is not given priority.
5. Money given for developing assets not adequate for the purpose.
6. No provision is made to give finance for running expenses for the projects started by the rural poor.
7. No adequate provision is made for providing insurance support especially to small farmers in dry farming areas.
8. Money earmarked for market infrastructure is not adequate.

Unsatisfactory Accountability and lack of Transparency in Government Dealings

The late Prime Minister, Mrs. Indira Gandhi herself had observed that huge sums of money were being frittered away and the masses particularly the weaker sections had not benefited[9]. In a national consultative discussions held at New Delhi in 1996, a number of cases of unsatisfactory accounting and lack of transparency in government dealings were pointed out in implementing rural development programmes.[14] It was agreed that a new system of making available all government records to the public should be recommended to minimise such problems.

3.11 PURSUING WRONG THEORIES OF ECONOMIC GROWTH

For many years, economic theories, which depicted growth as a function of increase in capital stock dominated which wrongly believed in the automatic trickle down effect to alleviate rural poverty once the GNP of the country improves. The concept of growth with equity was not thought of and target oriented development was unknown. Although the target oriented approach has been accepted since India's Fourth Five Year Plan and has covered the entire country in the Sixth Five Year Plan, it is not progressing as expected. United Nations Conference on Trade and Development (UNCTAD) has recently warned (1997) that increased global competition does not automatically bring faster growth and development nor do growth and development automatically bring about reduction in inequality[6]. The annual survey for Asia and Pacific region brought out by ESCAP in 1997[18] has recommended that high economic growth would not have rapid trickle down effect on poor and India particularly need to have more target oriented poverty alleviation programmes. It noted that India provided a massive budget for poverty alleviation but it was not effective enough as targetting of such programmes needed to be sharpened further.

3.12 LACK OF APPROPRIATE STRATEGIES

An appropriate programme of rural development should develop a strategy embracing a wide range and mix of activities including products to raise agricultural output, to improve health and education, to expand communications and to improve housing. Many of the programmes intended to raise rural incomes must centre on agricultural development and rural industries. The implementation of such strategy requires trained manpower and efficient institutions which is still to be attained in India.[16]

3.13 POOR ATTENTION TO DELINEATE WORKING OBJECTIVES FOR RURAL DEVELOPMENT PROGRAMME — OBJECTIVES TO ENABLE EFFICIENT IMPLEMENTATION OF THE PROGRAMME

One of the main deficiencies in the area of programme objectives is that at the operational level very poor attention is paid to develop appropriate working objectives specifying important programme areas which will enable to take the required action to reach the programme objectives. Excepting the statement of broad objectives which are included in the planned document, no efforts are made to spell out the details of programme areas needed for each local region.[17]

3.14 NEGLECT OF EMPOWERMENT PROGRAMME OF RURAL POOR WOMEN

Women's economic production is particularly critical to millions of Indian households which live below the poverty line. Although Rural Development has been started as early as 1964 during the Fourth Five Year Plan and expanded to cover the entire country in 1984 during the Sixth Five Year Plan, no adequate attention has been paid to the programme of empowerment of rural poor women. Women's empowerment through basic education, primary health care, family planning services and access for means of production is a pre-condition of breaking the poverty cycle (Khalija Haq, 1995)[19]. The only national programme to assist the empowerment of rural women was started in 1983 under the DWCRA programme with the World Bank assistance which had an element of subsidy built into the programme. At the way it is being implemented, it is estimated to take atleast 75 years to reach all villages of the country which is no solution to the important problem of women's empowerment.

3.15 POOR DEVELOPMENT OF RURAL GROWTH CENTRES

It is not possible to equip all the villages in India with modern facilities. The only practical way to resolve these difficulties is to indicate regional planning by upgrading the large villages to Growth Centres, preferably one for every 300 sq. kms, that is within the walking distance of all villages which would meet the needs of village communities, cold storages, processing units, input depots, repair shops, research and information centres, banks, on the other hand provide all essential services like good schools, hospitals and means of communication to educated in government services and others who may be interested in establishing agricultural based industries and effective marketing arrangements.[4]

A pilot project on starting of these centres was initiated in the Fifth Five Year Plan, but since then this idea has been forgotten by planners for reasons not known. Infrastructure services in rural areas which are essential to eradicate rural poverty cannot be improved without setting up Rural Growth Centres.

REFERENCES

1. Centre for monitoring Indian economy, New Delhi, 1995, Data furnished on 19th Sept. 1995.
2. Subramaniam, C., 1982, Position paper presented to the seminar on Indian Agriculture held on June 21-22, 1982 at Tamil Nadu Agricultural University, Coimbatore, Published by Rajaji International Centre for Public Affairs, New Delhi.

3. Government of India, Planning Commission : Eighth Plan Document, 1992.

4. Report of High Powered Committee, appointed by Government of India on Agricultural Policies and Programs. Mimeograph Report, 1990.

5. Vasanth Desai, 1994, Rural Development. Himalaya Publishers, Bombay.

6. UNCTAD Report, 1997, Published in *Deccan Herald*, September 27, 1997.

7. Mellor John, W., 1975, "The Impact of new Agricultural Technology on employment and Income distribution - concepts and policy", occasional paper No. 81, Employment and Income Distribution Project, Dept. of Agril. Economics Cornell University, USA.

8. Padmanabhan, M. and Swaminathan, M.C., 1994, Rural development report : Rural employment, NIRD, Hyderabad.

9. Dantwala, M.L. and Barmeda, J.N., 1991, "Rural Development – Approaches and Issues in Dantwala, M.L. (Editor). *Indian Agricultural Development since Independence*, II Edn. Oxford and IBH Publishing Company Pvt. Ltd., Bombay, 1991.

10. Amartya Sen, 1998, Address at the first press conference on 15th October, 1998 after getting the Nobel Prize, published in *Economic Times* on 16th October, 1998.

11. Census Report, 1991, Government of India, New Delhi.

12. World Bank, 1990, Poverty, World Development Report, Washington D.C.

13. Coombs, P.H. and Ahmed, M., 1974, *Attacking Rural Poverty* - Report for the World Bank prepared by the International Council for Educational Development, Baltimore and London, John Hopkins Univ. Press.

14. Sakunthala Narsimhan, 1996, "The failure of poverty eradication" a review report on the national consultation of rural development held at Delhi in October, 1996, published in *Deccan Herald*, dated 10-11-96

15. Morss, E.R. Hatch, J.K., Mickelwait, D.R and Sweet, C.F., 1975, Strategies for Small Farmers Development : An empirical study of rural development projects, Executive summary, development alternatives, Inc., Jefferson Place, Washington D.C., USA, May, 1975. Mimeo Publication.

16. World Bank, 1975, *Rural Development, op.cit.*

17. Kamta Prasad, 1985, "Planning for poverty alleviation". Agricol Publishing Academy, New Delhi, pp. 160-165.

18. UN Economic Annual Survey for Asia and Pecific brought out by ESCAP Reported in *Deccan Herald* on April 17, 1997.

19. Khalija Haq, 1995, "Poverty has a woman's face". *Our Planet*, 7(2) : 15-17.

4

RURAL POVERTY RELATED SITUATIONAL FACTS

An attempt is made in this chapter to present some of the recently reported situational data related to rural poverty with a hope that the data would provide the necessary support for identifying important programme areas to be included in the inventory to be developed as mentioned in the last chapter. Further this information will serve as a broad evaluation of the Rural Poverty Alleviation Programmes conducted in the country. The various aspects of the data will also answer the question of whether rural poverty alleviation programmes conducted so far in the country have succeeded or not in eradicating rural poverty.

4.1 THE BENEFICIARIES

Programme Benefits Grabbed by Non-Eligible Persons

A two-day Consultancy Discussion was initiated by U.N. at Delhi on October 17 and 18, 1996, on the eve of the World Poverty Eradication Day, which fell on 17-10-1996. Participants were an interesting mix of bureaucrats, planners, politicians, NGOs, academics and activists along with representatives of U.N. Bodies like the UNDP, WHO, the European Union, World Bank Units and the Planning Commission. In this discussion, it was pointed out by economist N.C. Jain, who has been associated with the Planning Commission, that even under our poverty alleviation programmes like the IRDP, much of the money was going to those well above the poverty line — because the poor, who deserve assistance, do not even have access to information on what their entitlements are.[1]

Complicated procedure to get enrolled as a beneficiary. "In working of SFDAs in Rajasthan, it was observed that in the course of getting identified as a beneficiary, the farmer has to contact the Patwari, VLW or VEW and the Manager of CSS at village level (but not necessarily in the same village)", BDO at Block level and the manager of the PIDB at the district level. In addition, he may have to contact the CCB and the local Commercial Banks to secure no due certificate. This is ordinarily a time and money consuming procedure.[2]

High Percentage of Ineligible Beneficiaries

Out of 210 beneficiaries studied, 26.7 per cent did not belong to the eligibility criteria of below poverty line income levels. Details reported for different programme areas were as under.[3]

Table 4.1 : Percentage of ineligible beneficiaries

	Area	Total No. of beneficiaries studied	No. of persons really non-eligible	Per cent not eligible
1.	Land development	32	11	33.4
2.	Milch cattle	40	12	30.0
3.	Fisheries	34	7	20.5
4.	Tailoring	33	8	24.2
5.	Farm based industries	38	3	7.5
6.	Handloom	33	15	45.4
	Total	210	56	26.7

Source : Abdul Kareem, Ph.D. Thesis (1995)[3].

Non-Eligible Beneficiaries

In a nation-wide research study entrusted by Government of India to 27 independent research institutes of the country, 16,616 beneficiaries under IRDP of the VII plan were involved. Out of them over 11 per cent were not really eligible to be selected since they were not poor as per norms prescribed.[4]

Beneficiaries are Unaware of their Entitlements

"Numerous field evaluation reports have revealed that even after years of operation, the beneficiaries are unaware of their entitlement— subsidies, concessional rates of interest etc. under the scheme. Taking advantage of this ignorance, brokers and middlemen pocket the benefits. The practice of cuts and commissions is further facilitated by lack of motivation and commitment on the part of officers of the implementing agencies.[5]

4.2 USE OF EXISTING RESOURCES

Large Proportion of Cultivable Land rendered Unproductive

Of the total geographical area, reported of approximately 305 million hectares, an estimated 175 million hectares have been rendered unproductive as per following details.[6]

1. Eighty-seven million hectares of cultivated lands are seriously affected by soil erosion, water logging and salinity.
2. Forty-eight million hectares of forest lands have practically no tree cover.
3. Forty million hectares of cultivable waste lands are currently unproductive but rather capable of production.

India has large area of Marginal Lands which are not used economically

The 1990 report of the High Powered Committee appointed by the Government of India on Agricultural Policies and Programmes has made the following observations on this problem.

"According to land-use classification of 1986-87, out of the total reporting area in India of 304.97 million hectares, an area of

140.15 million hectares was under cultivation, leaving a balance of 164.82 million hectares. Out of this, 66.73 million hectares are under non-agricultural use and 20.29 million hectares are barren and unculturable land leaving 57.05 million hectares which may be called as marginal land. If we also take into account that out of 66.73 million hectares classified as under forest, no more than 30 million hectares are actually under good forest with crown cover of over 40 per cent, there is an additional 36.73 million hectares of almost denuded land which needs to be developed. Thus, the total marginal land adds upto 93.78 million hectares — only a little less than one-third of our reporting area. This, though currently not being put to any economic use, can contribute substantially to the national income. The technological advances made in India and abroad make it possible to put every bit of the marginal land to economic use."[7]

This situation had not improved even during the nineties as revealed by the statistics reported by the centre for Monitoring Indian Economy (CMIE) in September, 1995.[8]

India has large area of Wasted Land which we call as Wasteland

Out of 329 million hectares of our arable lands nearly 175 million hectares are degraded or waste lands. However they are not waste but wasted lands. With application of new science and technology, it is possible to make these lands productive and also millions of our masses productive[7] as reported by Mohan Dharia, Ex-chairman of Government appointed High Level Policy Committee for the Development of Waste lands in India.[9]

Siltation of big reservoirs is taking place at a much higher rate than was envisaged at the time they were built

"Due to extensive denudation and soil erosion, the siltation of big reservoirs, which represent our most valuable and irreplaceable potential for irrigation and power, is taking place at much higher rates than envisaged at the time they were built. It is clearly necessary, in long range interest of such projects that special attention be given to treatment of catchment areas[7].

Vast Percentage of Potential Minor Irrigation not tapped

The ultimate irrigation potential of India is now estimated at 178 million hectares of which 83 million hectares are by major and medium irrigation and 95 million hectares under small irrigation projects including ground water, surface-irrigation. The potential reached and utilisation action by the end of 1995-96 are as follows.

Table 4.2 : Irrigation potential created and utilized

(in million hectares)

Sl. No.	Particulars	Major and medium irrigation	Minor irrigation	Total
1.	Potential possible	83.00	95.00	178.00
2.	Potential created	33.01	56.43	89.44
3.	Potential remaining	49.99	38.57	88.56

Source: 1. Economic Survey 1996-97 G.O.I.[10]
2. Report of High Powered Committee on Agricultural Policies and Programmes, G.O.I., 1990[7]

Land Reforms continue to be a problem

Land reforms were considered as very important since Independence and have been restated uniformly in the successive Five Year Plans. The VII Plan enunciated land reforms to be an intrinsic part of anti-poverty strategy. In spite of this policy the tenets of land reforms remain a problem so far. These are : (1) Abolition of intermediary, (2) Security of tenure for tenants, (3) Redistribution of land by imposing ceiling on holdings, (4) Consolidation of holdings, (5) Updating land records.[11]

Landless are still to receive land from the Cultivable Wasteland Scheme

It was expected that if the large extent of available extra cultivable wasteland could be distributed to landless, the rural poor would get benefit by becoming owners of at least a small piece of land. However, there is a very tardy progress in this direction. Out of 41 million hectares of cultivable wasteland, only 1.8 million hectares have been distributed till 1990.[7]

Making Limited Assets available to Rural Poor has not assisted them to come above Poverty Line

The Eighth Plan document has stated that funds allotted under IRDP are not adequate to help the rural poor to cross the poverty line. The document says "A system of concurrent evaluation of IRDP programme was also introduced under which data were collected by independent research institution for the entire country on a sample basis. The findings suggest that the IRDP was quite successful in terms of providing incremental income to poor families. However the number of households able to cross the poverty line was relatively small.[11]

4.3 AGRICULTURAL PRODUCTION

India's agriculture is sick: According to a Government Appointed High Powered Committee report, Indian agriculture has been sick for a long time producing much less than its potential capacity. All that has been attempted in the past was to achieve self-sufficiency in foodgrains and that too at the subsistence level of consumption.[7]

Our Per Hectare Yields in most of the crops are rather low compared to other important countries

India tops the list in cultivated area of most of the crops grown. However, when we compare the per hectare production, we find India at the bottom rung of the ladder. The following examples illustrate this.[12]

Table 4.3 : Ranking of pulses and cereals based on area and production

	Name of the crop	Area in Thousand hectare	Rank among the world countries	Production kg per hectare	Rank among the world countries
1.	Rice (paddy)	42034	1	2817	7
2.	Wheat	24431	3	2420	8
3.	Sorghum	12800	1	977	5
4.	Pulses	23971	1	607	11
5.	Groundnut (shells)	8500	1	988	6
6.	Potato	1000	5	15000	4
7.	Sugarcane	3578	1	77178	4
8.	Seed cotton	7670	1	898	10

Source : FAO Agriculture Production Year Book, 1994.[12]

Even food production may be a matter of grave concern in the years to come

The economic survey 1996-97 published by the Government of India, states as follows.

"Looking at the first seven years of this decade (1990-97), the annual rate of growth of foodgrains was only 1.7 per cent which is lower than the current population growth rate. If this trend continues it could become a matter of grave concern".[10]

Table 4.4 : Annual growth in foodgrains production

Year	Rice	Wheat	Pulses	Foodgrains
Combined growth rate*				
1967-68 to 1995-96	2.90	4.72	0.93	2.67
1980-81 to 1995-96	3.35	3.62	1.21	2.86
1990-91 to 1996-97	1 .52	3.62	1.0 7	1.70

*Triennium in 1981-82 equal to 100.

Source : Economic Survey, G.O.I., 1996-97.[10]

Inadequate attention to small farm management

"Inadequate attention to small farm management has increased production cost and risk. Agricultural scientists must find more ways to enhance the resource neutrality of technology by substituting non-monetary or inexpensive inputs for high cost inputs and minimising yield fluctuations caused by weather aberrations and pest epidemics.[13]

Even Watershed Development Programmes have not assisted small farmers to adopt technology

The adoption level of new technology continues to be low by the small farmers even in watershed development projects due to the following reasons :

1. Small and fragmented holdings restricted the scope for planning effective soil and moisture conservation measures on a catchment basis.
2. Developing new waterways over a number of independent holdings is bogged by social interruption.
3. New bunds/vegetative hedges on contour as inter-bund conservation measures are not readily accepted by most of the farmers citing operational inconveniences.
4. Inaccessibility to improved inputs results in resorting to local varieties with traditional practices by majority of the weaker sections.
5. Construction of water harvesting structures for small holdings is not feasible because of wastage of land, low catchment area and high cost of lifting water for irrigation.
6. Landless people of the watershed may not care much for this development activity unless they have a stake in it.[14]

Agricultural production of small farmers is very low and their marketable surplus negligible

Roughly, 18 per cent of the cultivating households constituting medium and large farmers, accounts for 61.2 per cent of the operated area and generates over half of the agricultural output and account for over two-thirds of the aggregate marketable surplus. There is enough evidence from the recent micro level studies to suggest that this inequality in the distribution of marketed surplus has been accentuated since 1960-61 because of the introduction of the new technology and its greater adoption by large farmers who have better access to resources.[15]

Small farmer's agriculture neglected by the Government

While 3/4th of the cultivated area in India is unirrigated and half of it will remain unirrigated for all times almost all scientific effort has been concentrated on irrigated agriculture leaving the bulk of the farming community to fend for itself.[16]

Small farmers not benefited by the Green Revolution

Although the new farm technology is primarily scale neutral, it is not resource neutral. So atleast in the initial stages due to better access to credit, seeds, fertilizer, extension and other inputs, the bigger farmers were able to reap greater benefits as compared to the relatively small farmers.[17]

4.4 SUBSIDIARY ENTERPRISES

Subsidiary enterprises programme not yet successful

In helping the beneficiaries to cross the poverty line only 14.87 per cent of the beneficiaries who started subsidiary enterprises could cross the poverty line which was a clear indication of failure of the programme.[18]

Entrepreneurship of beneficiaries not considered

The routine target group approach put all the rural poor in one category without ascertaining about their potential credibility or other capacity to run the enterprise independently.

Suitability of the projects to the local area not examined

Evaluation reports, of the scheme for self employment to educate unemployed youths (SEEUY) prepared in the Economic Research Department of the State Bank of India, prominently mention too much importance is attached to target orientation. The report also draws attention to other drawbacks such as irrelevance of activities to the area concerned, absence of assessment of demand for goods produced and services undertaken by the beneficiaries, lack of infrastructure facilities like water supply, power, raw materials, marketing channels etc.[19]

Majority of beneficiaries are not trained under TRYSEM

The VIII Plan document states as follows :

"On the other hand a sizable proportion of IRDP beneficiaries, who needed training, would not receive it. In fact only 6 to 7 per cent of IRDP beneficiaries were trained under TRYSEM.[11]

Financial and Organisation support for starting Enterprises is not available

As observed by the High Powered Committee in 1990 "it is the lack of knowledge, financial and organisational support which come in the way of eradication of poverty through adoption of supplementary enterprises by the rural poor. Substantial loans are needed for animal husbandry and long term ones for orchard raising. Institutional credit will have to be tailored according to the need of the enterprise. Also infrastructural support in the form of research, extension, input supplies, processing and marketing will have to be provided".[9]

Poultry projects have not helped the rural poor

The estimated value of poultry production has gone up to 10,000 million rupees in 1985, compared to only 650 million rupees in 1961. However, it is pertinent to note that a substantial development of

Poultry industry at present is centred around big cities and towns where a large number of community poultry farms have been established by rich people. The rural communities have received very little benefit from the development of Poultry.[21]

The success of income generating projects depends upon the level of entrepreneurship behaviour developed by the rural poor

A research study[22] has revealed that rural poor who were higher in entrepreneurship ability are active participants in agricultural development projects as compared to those having low entrepreneurial behaviour. This comparative picture for eight different projects is as given below.

Table 4.5 : Entrepreneurial behaviour of participant and non-participants in development programmes.

Project	Mean entrepreneurial behaviour index	
	Participant rural poor	Non-participant rural poor
1. Participation in general	52.90	41.51
2. Animal husbandry programmes in general	48.50	37.17
3. Dairy enterprise	50.60	39.69
4. Sheep and goat enterprise	41.49	31.55
5. Bullock purchase	53.95	39.38
6. Demonstration programme	55.57	41.51
7. Crop loan programme	62.19	42.13
8. Irrigation project	54.20	44.19

Source : Nandapurkar (1980).[22]

In the dairy projects, funds provided are not sufficient for purchase of quality animals

A number of research projects have revealed that funds provided for Dairy projects for the rural poor are not sufficient for purchase of quality animals and as a result due to poor milk yield the purchases have not become viable[23, 24].

No provision made to provide operating capital for managing the projects

The common deficiency of all the projects is that, except for providing some assistance for the purchase of assets, no provision is made to make available operating capital, which deficiency has come in the way of effective implementation of the projects.[23,24]

Handicaps of household enterprise

"As to the economic viability of the household enterprises, it should be noted that such enterprises are already in existence on a wide scale in the developed as well as the less developed regions. In fact, they are a major source of employment and income for the poor in rural areas—next only to land. But they suffer from various handicaps in regard to the supply of raw materials, access to credit, facilities for marketing etc. As a result, there is considerable exploitation of these households by the middle-men. Public intervention to provide the necessary services to these already existing enterprises would contribute to a substantial increase in their incomes. Governments sponsored programmes for the poor, such as dairy and poultry, no account for only a small proportion of the total market for such products, now sometimes even less than one per cent."[20]

4.5 GENERATION OF RURAL EMPLOYMENT

Absorption of labour in agriculture not kept pace with the development

The Government appointed High Powered Committee of 1990 observes that "there are also positive indications, that absorption of human labour in agriculture has not kept pace with the increase in population. According to the Economic Advisory Council report the employment growth had not kept pace with the growth in labour force in spite of GDP growth exceeding five per cent. This is so mainly because employment growth in agriculture has declined sharply from 2.32 per cent per annum during 1972-73 to 1977-78 to only 0.65 per cent during 1982-83 to 1987-88. The conclusion is reinforced by two other indications; (1) Intensity of cultivation is almost stagnant in spite of expansion in irrigational facilities, (2) Secondly most of the gains in production can be attributed to a single factor, namely; application of larger doses of fertilizer for crop production.[7]

Employment in cottage and village industries has declined

Employment in the cottage and in the household industries has experienced a relative decline, due to shrinking markets on account of competition of modern products and often due to lack of technological upgradation to meet demands according to VIII Plan document, 1992[11].

High employment per unit of capital has not been vindicated with the so-called small industries

The VIII Plan document states that the assumption that small capital requirement employs high employment per unit of capital has not always been found valid.[11]

Rural employment is not always associated with high income

The VIII Plan document states that the incidence of poverty is much higher than that of unemployment. An overwhelming majority of the poor are thus those not apparently unemployed but are engaged for a major part of their time in some activity albeit at very low levels of productivity and earnings.[11]

The rate of increasing rural labour force will create a baffling problem by 2001

"The rural component of rural labour force in India in 1981 was estimated at 230 millions. By 2001 India's population is estimated to be 1,000 million and the labour force will increase to about 430 to 435 million of which the rural component will be 303 millions— an increase of 73 millions in 20 years from 1981 to 2001. How and where we shall accommodate this vast increase in the labour force of rural India is a baffling problem."[25]

Agricultural involution is seen in India

Many newly developed countries of the world have shown decline in the share to agriculture in the gross national products as well as in their share of labour force. In India, however has shown near constancy in the share of agricultural workers. This process is known as agricultural involution.[25] Table 4.6 gives details of this phenomenon.

Table 4.6 : Distribution of total work force

Categories	Distribution of total work force census report	
	1951	1981
Agricultural labourers	21.8	26.3
Non-agricultural labourers	28.0	31.6
Cultivators	50.2	42.1

Labour intensity per hectare is low in India as compared to countries like Japan and other South Asian countries

In Japan there are 1,231 agricultural workers per 1000 hectares of arable land as against the Indian average of 978 in 1982. The corresponding numbers in China, South Korea and Thailand are 2729, 2551 and 859 respectively.[25]

Only 5 to 15 per cent of increased income from new technologies go to increased labour payment

There is great variability among new agricultural technologies in the proportion of added output paid to labour, but in general, the very technologies so essential to provide the food to back wages, goods payments provide only a small proportion of the increased income directly to labour through increased employment. From a survey of 14 diverse situations in India, approximately only 5 to 15 per cent of increased income from new technology was represented by payment for increased labour.[26]

Agricultural workers get far less labour wages as compared to urban workers

The approach in payment of labour wages in rural areas has been that the wages must be the minimum wages which exist in the area. Often these minimum levels are even lower than the minimum wages provided under the minimum wages legislation. Hence agricultural workers get far less labour wages as compared to urban workers.[25]

4.6 PROMOTING SMALL INDUSTRIES IN THE RURAL AREAS

So-called small industries developed have not provided more employment for the rural unemployed

"It has, however, been observed that the policy for the promotion of small scale industry has not been very effective in serving the employment objective; the assumption that small capital necessarily implies high employment per unit of capital has not always been found valid.[11]

Small scale industrial policy has not benefited real small units

Due to the cumbersome procedures and non-existence of the promotional and services network in small towns and villages the concessions and assistance have only reached the not so small sectors.[11]

A large contribution of the small and unorganised sector industries is likely to raise the employment elasticity and employment growth in the manufacturing sector

The small industry sector currently contributes about one half of value added and four-fifths of the total employment in manufacturing. If these schemes of manufacturing can be made to grow at 10 per cent per annum with the organised groups of about 5 per cent, the overall employment growth in the manufacturing sector will be above 4 per cent as against 2 per cent.[11]

Large number of small scale industries are sick

The number of sick small scale industries units from 1993 to 1995 were as follows.[10]

March 1993	March 1994	March 1995
2,38,176	2,56,416	2,66,815

Ref: Economic Survey, 1996-97, p. 135.[10]

Apparent causes of such large number of sick industries in the small scale industries sector has been identified by Singh (1994) which can be stated as follows:

1. Government officials, banks and other financial institutions are more concerned with financing SSI units mercilessly and indiscriminately to achieve their targets of exposure of loans either under pressure or with over enthusiasm without evaluating viability of projects submitted for sanctioning of loans.
2. Most of SSI units suffer from the problem of lack of experience of managerial ability as well as problem of lack of use of latest technology in the process of production.
3. The entrepreneurs of such units generally face the constraints in availing economies of scale and full utilization of capacity

on account of low level of production and poor availability of marketable production.

4. There are allied problems like erratic supply of power, high labour turnover, industrial unrest caused by strikes and lockout, paucity of working capital, insufficient execution of financial and promotional schemes by the several schemes undertakings.
5. The sick units are a drain of misuse of resources.
6. Due to low level of production and ever increasing inputs for such units, the entrepreneurs are not competent to fend off challenges of the world market.

Approach of small industries is more towards employment and not towards more earnings by the wage earners

The approach to rural industries perceived so far has been characterised primarily by a concern for employment. The level of earning of those employments has not been considered.[16]

Government support to small scale industries like Khadi and village industries has been found to be inadequate

The report of the working group of Khadi and village industries[20] has pointed out the inadequacy of government support to rural industries. The report says, "Although, there have been several policy announcements, according important place to KVI, in concrete terms, the policy support made available to KVI sector has been in the shape of concessional finance, small extent of subsidisation and limited fiscal concessions. This policy support is quite inadequate, since the benefit conferred on the organised large and non-sector almost neutralise the benefits provided to KVI.[27]

4.7 RURAL WORKS PROGRAMME

The Jawahar Rojgar Yojana (JRY) has provided job only for 15 days in a year

The programme evaluation organisation conducted a survey on JRY and the results were as follows. On the average about 15 days employment was generated per person in 1990-91, at an average wage rate of Rs. 20 to 25. This would yield a supplemental income per person of about Rs. 300 to 400 per annum. This is rather meagre in the context of the poverty line of Rs. 6,400 during the VII Plan, which has gone up in the VII and VIII Plans.[11]

Assets created in JRY are not maintained well

In a nationwide study conducted by the Programme Evaluation Organisation of the Government of India, in 1991-92, the following findings were reported :

1. Some of the Village Panchayats did not utilise the funds.
2. Although a majority of the beneficiaries described the assets created by the scheme as useful, adequate attention was not given to maintenance of assets.[28]

Rural works programme are treated as only a temporary relief sub-strategy

Experience with the implementation of rural works programme has highlighted some operational problems as well as some basic policy issues. Operationally the programmes have faltered, because of leakages on account of corruption and administrative delays and inefficiency at local level. They have seldom succeeded in creating durable assets because of restrictions on the material components in such projects and because of poor technical formulations, in spite of indirect indications of unutilized under-employment labour, mobilisation of labour for such employment has been quite inadequate. The programmes have in general been operated as relief-cum-subsidy programmes, rather than as programmes for increasing the productivity potential of the community. The rural work approach of employment planning can only be done by a sub-strategy of temporary relief.[25]

Rural works should be used as a strategy to raise the level of wages in local areas

Full employment will not be a solution for rural poverty unless it is accompanied by higher earnings. This has implications for policy with regard to the wages to be paid in rural works. So far the approach has been that the wages must be minimum wages which exist in the area. Often these minimum levels are even lower than the minimum wage legislation; Rural works can be made into a conscientious strategy for raising the level of wages in rural areas. A fear that this will have an adverse effect on employment seems unfounded.[7]

JRY must guarantee at least 90 to 100 days of employment for persons as under the Maharashtra employment guarantee programme

Under the JRY any additional allocation must be linked to certain backward districts/blocks with an element of guarantee of at least 90-100 days of employment per person as under the Maharashtra Employment Guarantee Programme. Only then it will provide the safety nets for the poor unemployed who will find it difficult to subsist in lean seasons.[7]

Six important problems observed in implementing JRY programmes

A research[24] study has identified the following six important problems in implementing the programmes :

1. Release of resources to Nyaya Panchayats were delayed, thus delaying the implementation of the programme itself.
2. JRY wage rates were low as compared to local prevailing wage rates.
3. Non-availability of workers and materials during certain seasons caused delay in completing works.
4. Foodgrain distribution to the workers as part of their wages is

difficult due to irregular supply, lack of storage facilities, low quality etc.

5. Lack of coordination between different agencies involved in implementing the schemes.
6. Work given on contract basis, though it was not permitted.

4.8 INFRASTRUCTURAL FACILITIES

Overall infrastructural development

India stands last in the list of 53 countries surveyed for the quality of overall infrastructure in 1998.

This survey was conducted by World Bank for the global competitiveness report of the World Economic Forum. According to the World Bank president, the recent data on the incidence of poverty in India indicates that more than 52 per cent of the country's population lives on less than one dollar a day. More than 180 million people are denied access to safe water and less than fifty per cent of the villages in the country have access to electricity. Moreover 45 per cent of the people do not have the use of a pucca road.[29]

Even after 53 years of independence the provision of basic services in rural areas remains very unsatisfactory

According to the statement made by the Union Finance Minister in his budget speech of 2000, 40 per cent of our villages are without proper roads; 1.8 lakh villages do not have a primary school within 1 km; 4.5 lakh villages have drinking water problems; some estimates indicate a shortage of 140 lakh rural dwelling units; rural health infrastructure suffers from large deficiencies.[30]

Health

Health status in rural India is much worse compared with urban India

According to Health Indicators the health status in rural India is much worse as compared to urban areas as could be seen from Table 4.7.[31]

Table 4.7 : Health indicators of rural and urban areas

(Per 1000)

Indicators	Year	Level	
		Rural	Urban
1. Infant mortality rate	1987	104	61
2. 0-4 age specific mortality rate	1987	39.7	18.2
3. Crude death rate	1987	12.0	7.4
4. Life expectancy at birth (years)	1981-85	53.7	62.8

Ref: Vital Statistical Division, Office of the Research Council of India.[31]

Hospitals and curative health services are concentrated in Urban areas as compared to rural areas

Over the years, efforts are being made to create infrastructure facilities to provide hospitals for curative health services in rural areas also. However, the results indicate that these facilities are more concentrated in urban areas as compared to rural areas.[31] Table 4.8 gives the details.

Table 4.8 : Hospitals and dispensaries as on 1-1-1980

	Rural	Urban	Total
Hospitals	3099	6732	9831
Hospital beds	103069	492820	595889
Dispensaries	13209	14206	27415

Ref: Health Information India, G.O.I., 1988.[32]

Adequate staff or medicines not available to Primary Health Centres/Sub-centres

In the case of rural health, there is an extensive network of primary Health Centres and sub-centres, but these have not been operationalised in terms of adequate staff or medicine.[10]

Mobidity is still persisting with the rural poor

The nutrition and health situation with the rural poor can be described as follows[33]

1. A large percentage of households did not consume adequate amount of calories and proteins due to poverty, ignorance and various other socio-economic factors.
2. Almost two-thirds of children suffer from mild and moderate degrees of malnutrition.
3. The incidence of Vitamin-A deficiency and Iron deficiency is high.
4. Poor environmental sanitation, poor personal and food hygienes and lack of safe water lead to infections in large sections of the rural poor.
5. Incidence of morbidity is quite high among women.

Due to these causes the health situation in rural areas is most crucial, frequent illness and untimely death is still the lot of the average rural poor, with some sections of the rural poor, morbidity has increased rather than decreased.

Rural Housing

A majority of rural poor have not got Pucca houses

A majority of rural families have not got pucca houses especially the rural poor as per the following figures.[33]

Table 4.9 : Types of residential housing in rural and urban areas

				Percentage forms		
Type of structures	Year	Pucca	Semi-Pucca	Serviceable kutcha	Unserviceable kutcha	Total
Rural	1981	23	43.5	23.4	10.1	100
Urban	1981	65.2	24.2	6.7	3.9	100

Ref: Rural Social Services, Indira Gandhi National Open University School on Continuing Education, Aug. 1992).[33]

Drinking Water Supply

Eighty two per cent of rural population was covered by Drinking water supply by March 1996

The progress achieved in providing drinking water supply to villages is furnished in Table 4.10.[10]

Table 4.10 : Coverage of drinking water supply

Area	Percentage coverage with drinking water supply as on 31st March		
	1985	1990	1996
Rural	56.3	73.9	82.0
Urban	72.9	83.8	85.0

Ref: Economic Survey, G.O.I., 1996-97, p. 193.[10]

Coverage of villages with mere water supply is not guaranteed for safe drinking water

Similarly under rural water supply programme, the coverage of villages is not enough by itself. It is necessary to ensure that 40 litres of potable water per capita per day is available on sustained basis ensuring its quality upgradation by making it free from salinity and chemical and bacteriological contamination.[11]

In 1985-86 about 23000 villages i.e., 39 per cent of our villages were the problem areas regarding safe drinking water

The following details are given regarding problem areas.[34]

Table 4.11 : Problem areas of safe drinking water.

	Major problem	Number of villages
1.	Finding resources	154300
2.	Biological contamination	43600
3.	Chemical contamination	29100

Only 26.5 per cent of rural households had access to safe drinking water in 1981

As per 1981 census[35] only 26.5 per cent of rural households had access to safe drinking water. There were considerable differences between the States as indicated below :

Table 4.12 : India's selected States having safe drinking water

Selected states	Percentage of rural households having safe drinking water
Punjab	81.80
West Bengal	65.78
Haryana	42.94
Orissa	9.47
Madhya Pradesh	8.09
Kerala	6.26
Total	26.05

Ref: Household Literacy, Drinking Water and Toilet facilities – Occasional paper No. 1, 1989 – Census of India, 1989.[35]

Village Population covered by Sanitation

Only 4.64 per cent rural population was covered by sanitary facilities in 1996

Even with the quick coverage of rural population with sanitary facilities the percentage coverage was only 4.64 by 1996 as shown in Table 4.13.[7&8]

Table 4.13 : Sanitary facilities coverage in rural and urban areas

Area	Percentage coverage as on 31st March		
	1985	1990	1996
Rural	0.7	2.4	4.64
Urban	28.4	45.9	50.00

Ref: Economic Survey, G.O.I., 1996-97, p. 93.[10]

Education

Literacy

Rural literacy rates lag behind the urban literacy rates : Rural areas are lagging behind as compared to urban areas in the literacy rates.[35]

In rural India the number of illiterate persons is more than literate persons : The total number of literate and illiterate persons in the rural India over a period of years is given in Table 4.14[37] :

Table 4.14 : Literacy rates by sex, India, Rural and Urban areas

Year	Rural			Urban			India
	Male	Female	Total	Male	Female	Total	
1961	34.21	10.00	22.37	66.01	39.74	54.10	28.30
1971	39.75	15.49	27.97	69.91	48.81	60.24	34.50
1981	46.73	30.66	34.04	73.92	54.40	64.85	43.60
1991	Not available			Not available			52.20

Ref: Census Data 1991, GOI New Delhi.[35]

In 1981, 38.48 per cent of rural households did not have a single literate member : According to census report, literacy has been defined as ability to read and write in any language. The 1981 census revealed that 38.48 per cent of rural households did not have a single literate person in the family. In some States almost half of the households did not have a single literate member[36].

There are more number of illiterates in the country than the literates in the country as given in Table 4.15.

Table 4.15 : Yearwise literacy level

Year	Illiterates	Literates
1961	228.045	65.717
1981	259.280	100.681
1991	291.679	215.317

Ref: Census Report 1991, GOI, New Delhi.[36]

Education of Children

Ninety per cent of primary schools and 83.30 per cent of upper primary schools in India were in rural areas in 1986

The existence of different kinds of schools in the rural areas as in 1986 are given in Table 4.16.[37]

Table 4.16 : Number and kinds of schools in rural areas

	Number in thousands		
Kinds of schools	Number in all areas	Number in rural areas	Percentage in rural areas
Primary school	529	476	90.00
Upper primary school	139	116	83.30
Secondary school	52	39	75.00

(Ref : 5th Indian Education Survey, 1986).[37]

The school drop-outs comprise of almost 50 per cent of enrolment

The percentage of drop-outs in school education is very high. The following figures indicate this phenomenon for both rural and urban areas combined[38].

Table 4.17 : Drop-outs in schools

Classes	Drop-out percentage
1 – 5	47.60
1 – 8	64.40
1 – 10	77.60

Ref : Rural development programme – RDD2 – unit-3 Education, Published by Indira Gandhi National Open University School of Continuing Education, 1992, p. 52.[38]

Less than 50 per cent of rural students attend schools

According to 1981 census only 40 per cent of rural children of 6-9 years and 44.2 per cent in age group 10-14 years attend schools.[34]

In rural areas most of the primary schools are within habitat while most of the upper primary schools are away from habitat

The percentage of schools in rural areas within habitat and away from habitat are given below[34]:

Table 4.18 : Percentage of rural schools and distance from habitat

	Distance	Percentage of Primary Schools	Percentage of Upper Primary Schools
1.	Within habitat	80.31	36.98
2.	Up to 1 km	14.36	17.83
3.	1.1 to 3 km	3.97	17.63
4.	2.1 to 3 km	-	12.63
5.	3.1 to 4 km	1.43	6.07
6.	4.1 to 5 km	-	3.82
7.	5.1 km and above	-	4.72
	Total	100.00	100.00

Ref: Report of Indira Gandhi National Open University published in 1992.[34]

Thirty-two million children in India have not seen school

According to a World Bank study reported in 1997[36], despite increase in enrolment rate for Primary education in the Plan era, about 32 million tiny tots in India have not seen school.[39]

Enrolment of Primary Education

The enrolment in Primary education in India has increased from 85 million in 1987 to 100 million in 1993. In spite of this, there is a problem to reach full enrolment of the 6-10 years age group which has been made as a challenge in all States of India.[35]

In 1981, 38.48 per cent of rural households did not have a single literate member : According to census report, literacy has been defined as ability to read and write in any language. The 1981 census revealed that 38.48 per cent of rural households did not have a single literate person in the family. In some States almost half of the households did not have a single literate member.[37]

Majority of the rural students are drop-outs and do not complete their education : Eighty per cent of the students are drop-outs by the time they reach the 5th class. Fifty per cent of the students pass SSLC and out of them only 10 per cent of students continue higher studies.

Note : No separate figures are reported for rural areas. However it is expected to be higher than the aggregate figures reported here.

Most of the primary schools are either single teacher or two-teacher schools : The teacher has to take all school classes in the same room as most of the schools are either single teacher or two-teacher schools. Table 4.19 describes this situation.[37]

Forty-one per cent of rural schools have not got pucca buildings: According to Fourth Education Survey of 1978[39] the following information pertinent to the condition of the rural school building is available as shown in Table 4.20.

Table 4.19 : Percentage of schools having number of teachers

	No. of teachers per school	Percentage of schools
1.	No teacher	0.50
2.	One teacher	22.96
3.	Two teachers	32.38
4.	Three teachers	15.18
5.	Four teachers	8.91
6.	Five or more teachers	15.00

Ref : The Fifth All India Education Survey, 1986.[37]

Note : Although separate figures are not available for rural areas, it is estimated that the situation will be more adverse in the rural schools.

Table 4.20 : Percentage of schools having pucca building and kutcha space

Type of building	Percentage of schools
Pucca or semi pucca	59.00
Open space/thatched huts/tents/kutcha buildings	41.00

Ref: GOI, New Delhi, Fourth Education Survey, 1978.[39]

In 1999, even after a decade of the launching of "Operation Black Board" Project, primary schools in the country are not fully equipped as far as basic infrastructure is concerned

A sub-committee set up by the standing committee on human resource development conducted field visits to various schools for assessing the progress of "operation black board". In its report of 1999, it is said that the school which the committee visited were lacking in basic facilities.[40] By and large, school buildings were there and in some cases extensions were also being carried on. But these were not adequate for the needs of the school children. Drinking water and toilet facilities were also inadequate. In some of the schools which the committee visited, the students were being made to sit on bare floors. The committee also observed that in a majority of primary schools 2 or 3 classes were being held in one room under the supervision of only one teacher.[40]

Most of villages are 2 to 5 kms away from most of the basic amenities

Table 4.21 : Basic Amenities in Villages (Percentage of villages having a particular amenity located within a specified distance by States.[41]

Facility	All India	Minimum	Maximum
A. Within 2 Kms			
1. Metalled road	45.80	22.20 Meghalaya	98.30 Kerala
2. Bus stop	40.30	17.30 Nagaland	98.00 Kerala
3. Post Office	53.20	18.60 Meghalaya	99.70 Kerala

Contd.

Table 4.21 (Contd.)

Facility	All India	Minimum	Maximum
4. Primary school	90.10	81.30 Rajasthan	99.70 Kerala
5. Middle school	43.80	39.40 Nagaland	98.60 Kerala
6. High school	20.90	20.20 Gujarat	96.70 Kerala
7. Dispensary	24.60	8.70 Meghalaya	90.60 Kerala
8. Health care	12.00	5.60 Rajasthan	46.70 Kerala
9. Daily market	14.80	7.40 Maharashtra	56.10 Kerala
10. *Hat*	26.80	13.40 Gujarat	51.80 Kerala
11. F.P. Shop for Grocery	35.10	10.20 Nagaland	98.80 Kerala
B. Within 5 kms			
12. Railway station	18.30	— Sikkim	33.20 Punjab
13. Hospital	35.50	9.10 Meghalaya	78.40 Kerala
14. Fertilizer depot	43.90	6.80 Nagaland	93.20 Kerala
15. Seeds store	40.30	6.50 Nagaland	64.90 Kerala
16. Agri. Pump Repair	18.80	2.90 Meghalaya	64.90 Kerala
17. Storage and Warehousing	20.70	3.30 Sikkim	65.50 Nagaland
18. Veterinary dispensary	45.20	17.20 Rajasthan	81.50 Kerala
19. Credit cooperative	60.80	7.20 Nagaland	95.90 Kerala
20. Bank	39.90	6.90 Nagaland	96.10 Kerala
C. General			
21. Electrical	33.40	4.70 Meghalaya	99.80 Haryana
22. Drinking water within Village	92.60	75.30 Sikkim	99.40 Punjab

Ref: Economic and Political Weekly 6-4-1985.[41]

4.9 ORGANIZATION

There is no proper agency to administer rural development

Progress of rural development has been hindered by the indecisions as to the appropriate agency that should be entrusted with responsibility of formulating area development plans.[5]

There is lack of coordination among different organizations

Most poverty alleviation programmes were agency driven and unresponsive to the real needs of the poor and lacked coordination among the multiple agencies which led to duplication; frictions and unutilized synergies.[42]

Inter-departmental coordination meetings often have resulted in inter-departmental bickerings

Coordination is usually done through inter-departmental coordination meetings under the leadership of district collector. But this hardly measures up to an effective coordination. Some of these coordination meetings tend to become a routine affair. Sometimes these are as inconvenient interference with the autonomy of departments and hence result in inter-departmental bickerings.[16]

There is too much centralised planning in rural development programmes

Even with regard to projects and programmes which are suited for local level planning, it is revealing to find that quite a few of them are centrally sponsored and partly or wholly financed by the centre. This applies particularly to projects meant for weaker sections.[5]

4.10 PROVIDING SAFETY NETS TO RURAL POOR

Little or no progress has been made in the crop insurance sector in relation to rural poor

There is no system of even limited crop insurance to cover cost of additional inputs for rainfed crops in dry areas which are prone to aberrant weather conditions resulting in risk and uncertain situations.[43]

Wages for agricultural labourers are not related to the rising cost of living from year to year

This has resulted in making the rural poor families continue to be below the poverty line inspite of employment.[7]

Anti-poor policies are still prevalent in many areas in the country

In the consultation workshop held on 17 and 18, October 1996 at New Delhi, which was sponsored by the U.N. bodies, examples of many anti-poor policies were cited and such wrong policies still exist in many States of India.[1]

Small farmers frequently choose lower income but more stable crop combinations

This is because the small farmer often has difficulty in obtaining capital necessary to application of high yielding farm technology; but even more important, he faces serious problems of risk and uncertainty aversion which makes him reluctant to borrow or innovate even when other conditions are favourable.[26]

Public Distribution System

Coarse grains needed by the rural poor are not supplied in adequate quantities by the PDS

The interest of the rural poor are not adequately served by the PDS, though the system is working since many years. The commodity composition of the PDS leaves much to be desired. On the one hand, coarse grains, which dominate the consumption habit of the rural poor in India and whose prices have tended to rise faster and with a good crop also declined faster than the prices of superior cereals are given less importance.[44]

All items are not stocked by the fair price shops

Due to inadequate funds, the fair price shops do not stock all the items every time. As a result, the rural poor suffer the most, since they are required to purchase all their items every week or fortnight.[44]

Off take of PDS commodities is more in urban areas as compared to rural areas

According to a study, urban areas which account for only 20 per cent of population receive 68 per cent of the off-take of foodgrains from PDS, while the remaining 32 per cent has to be supplied to the 80 per cent of the rural population which cannot satisfy their requirements.[45]

4.11 PEOPLE'S PARTICIPATION

Officials' mindset discouraging people's involvement in the rural development programmes

In the National Consultation Discussion, initiated by the United Nations which was held on 17 and 18, October 1996, in New Delhi, a point was raised again and again that it is not money that is primarily the bottleneck in poverty alleviation, but the mindset of the officials who fail to involve people, and their corruption.[1]

Local data useful for planning not available

Data specially useful for the IRDP and NREP such as comprehensive data on the incidence of poverty at the block level are not readily available. A Junior Statistical Supervisor attached to the block office is concerned primarily with the collection of basic data. He is not associated with the collection and completion of specialised data related to poverty alleviation programmes such as the IRDP and NREP.[16]

District planning not implemented

Although under the 74th Amendment in the Constitution, District Planning Machinery was required to be set up nationwide this has been not done.[1]

4.12 GENDER AND POVERTY

There is close relationship between gender and poverty. Women's labour force participation and their relative contribution to total family income are higher in households with lower economic status. The poorer the family, the more it depends on the earnings of its female members. In very poor households, women's capacities to work, their health, knowledge and skills are often crucial for family survival.[46]

Women's economic productivity is particularly critical to 60' million Indian households which live below the poverty line

Women may be the main or only earners in these households. Over 35 per cent of households below the poverty line are headed by women. Hence, there is a need for greater attention to the creation of employment activities for poor women, and to efforts to increase the productivity of women workers, particularly those in the primary sector.[46]

Comparatively few rural poor women have access to utilise health services which contribute to the continuing high morbidity among women.

During adolescence and early adulthood, rural poor women are involved in domestic labour, economic work and reproduction. Nutritional deprivation in the face of these energy demanding tasks and the high risk of exposure to disease in the environmental conditions in which the poor live, result in high morbidity among women.[46]

Poor women particularly in rural areas are unable to secure institutional credit and capital to undertake and sustain productive self-employment

Due to this, although women constitute over one-third of the total labour force in India and half the agricultural labour force, their production is limited. Thirty per cent of rural women workers are classified as unskilled. If women are more visible in work such as agricultural labour or construction, it is more an indication of the poverty of their families than of the significant shift in cultural perceptions.[46]

REFERENCES

1. Narasimhan, Sakuntala (1996), *The Failure of Poverty Eradication, op.cit.*
2. Bhatty, I.Z. and Kulawant Madan (1982), *Delivery System in Support of Small Farmers in the context of Rural Development Centre on Integrated Rural Development for Asia and Pacific*, Comilla, Bangladesh, May 1982, pp. 82-83.
3. Kareem, Abdul (1994), "Integrated Rural Development Programme in Kerala— An impact analysis". Unpublished Ph.D. Thesis, Dept. of Agril. Extension, UAS, Bangalore.
4. Gaur, K.D. (1992), "Effectiveness of the Integrated Rural Development Programme (IRDP) in eradication of poverty in India" in K.D. Gaur (Editor). *Dynamics of Rural Development*, Mittal Publishers, New Delhi, 1992.
5. Dantawala, M.L. and Barmeda, J.N. (1991), "Rural Development — Approaches and Issues". *op. cit.*
6. Sawant, S.D. (1991), "Irrigation and Water Use" in M.L. Dantwala (Editor), *Indian Agricultural Development since Independence, op.cit.* pp. 93-107.
7. Report of High Powered Committee on Agricultural Policies and Programmes, Govt. of India (1990), *op. cit.*
8. Centre for Monitoring Indian Economy (CMIE), 1995, India's Agricultural Sector a compendium of statistics.
9. Dharia, Mohan (1999), Freedom from Hunger — Agrarian Challenges, *The Hindu* paper, April 8, 1999.
10. Government of India, Economic Survey 1996-97, New Delhi.
11. Government of India (1992), VIII Plan Document, New Delhi.
12. FAO (1994), Agriculture Production Year Book.

13. Swaminathan, M.S. (1983), "Agricultural Progress — Key to 3rd World Prosperity — 3rd World Lecture 1983. 3rd World Foundation Monograph—71, 3rd World Foundation, London.

14. Krishnappa, A.M. *et al.* (1996), "Watershed Development in Karnataka"—Agricultural College, Hebbal, Bangalore' Golden Jubilee 1946-1996, Alumni Association, UAS, Bangalore.

15. Subba Rao, K. (1991), "Agricultural Marketing" in M.L. Dantwala (Editor) Indian Agril. Development since Independence, *op. cit.* p. 279.

16. Kamta Prasad (1985), "Planning for Poverty Alleviation". Agricol Publishing Academy, New Delhi, pp. 160-165.

17. Siddu, B.S. and Singh, A.J. (1991), "Technological Change in Agriculture" in M.L. Dantwala (Editor), *Indian Agricultural Development since Independence, op. cit.* p. 129.

18. Government of India, 1995, 95th Report of the Public Accounts Committee of the Loka Sabha. Extract quoted by *Deccan Harrald* paper on 26-4-1995, Bangalore.

19. State Bank af India (1989), Evaluation of Seetu Scheme State Bank of India. *Monthly Review*, Vol. 28 No. 5, May 1982, pp. 255-275.

20. Desai, Vasant (1991), *Fundamentals of Rural Development — A system approach.* Himalaya Publishing House, Mumbai 1994.

21. Jain, T. (1991), "Poultry" in M.L. Dantwala (Editor), *Indian Agricultural Development since Independence, op. cit.* pp. 171-187.

22. Nandapurkar, C.C. (1980), "A scale for Entrepreneurial behaviour of small farmers". Unpublished Ph.D. Thesis, Dept. of Agril. Extension, University of Agricultural Sciences, Bangalore.

23. Hirevenkanagoudar, L.V. (1983), A Scientific Investigation of Impact of Dairy Development Programme of KDDC among small farmers, marginal farmers and agricultural labourers, Bangalore district, Karnataka, Unpublished Ph.D. Thesis, University of Agricultural Sciences, Bangalore, Dept. of Agricultural Extension.

24. Sripathi, K.P. (1994), Let industrialization be focussed on JRY : A case study of D.K. district, *Kurukshetra*, 42(5) : 11-14.

25. Ahuja, Kanta (1991), "Agricultural Labour and Rural Employment" in Dantwala (Editor), *Indian Agricultural Development since Independence, op. cit.*, pp. 367-398.

26. Mellor John, W. (1975), "The Impact of New Agricultural Technology on Employment and Income Distribution —Constraints and Policy". *op. cit.*

27. Government of India, Planning Commission, New Delhi (1983), Draft Report of the Working Group on KVI.

28. Government of India (1994), Planning Commission, Report of the Project Evaluation Organization.

29. World Bank (1998), Global Competitiveness Report of the World Economic Forum released on June 18, 1999 and reported in *Deccan Herald* Paper on June 19, 1999.
30. Detailed Budget Speech of Union Finance Minister. Printed in *Economic Times* of 1st March 2000.
31. Office of the Registrar General, Government of India, "Vital Statistical Division Report".
32. Government of India (1988), Central Bureau of Health Intelligence, Ministry of Health and Family Welfare, Health Information, India.
33. Government of India (1991), Report of the Study Group of ICSSR and ICMR — "Health to All".
34. Indira Gandhi National Open University (IGNOU), School of Continuing Education, Rural Social Services, August 1992.
35. Government of India (1989), Registrar General and Census Commissioner, India, "Household Literacy, Drinking Water and Toilet Facilities"— Occasional Paper No. 1.
36. World Bank Study Report (1997), Quoted by *Deccan Herald* Paper dated April 28, 1997.
37. Government of India, New Delhi, 5th Education Survey (1986).
38. Indira Gandhi National Open University (IGNOU), School of Continuing Education Development Programme — RDD-2 Unit-3 Education, p. 52.
39. Government of India, New Delhi (1978), 4th Education Survey.
40. Government of India, Report of the Sub-committee set up by the Standing Committee on the Human Resource Development published on June 18, 1999 quoted by *Deccan Herald* dated June 19, 1999.
41. *Economic and Political Weekly* 6-4-1985.
42. UN Economic and Social Commission for Asia and the Pacific, Annual survey, released on April 16th, 1997, Published by *Deccan Herald*, April 17, 1997.
43. Subramaniam, C. (1982), Seminar on Indian Agriculture — Theme paper presented at the seminar on Indian Agriculture: June 21-22, 1982 at Tamil Nadu Agricultural University, Coimbatore, *op.cit.*
44. Elizabeth Oughton (1995), Targetting Foodgrains to the Rural Poor — A micro level study in India in Joseph Mullen (Ed.) , *Rural Poverty Alleviation*, Avebury, USA.
45. World Bank, Washington, D.C. (1991), Gender and Poverty in India — A World Bank country study.
46. Singh, B.N.P. (1994), India's rural development through industrialization in A.S. Bhalla and A.K.N. Reddy (eds.). *The Technical Transformation of Rural India*, Intermediate Technology Pub., ILO, London.

5

SOME RESULTS OF THE RURAL POVERTY ALLEVIATION EFFORTS

Rural poverty alleviation has been and will continue to be at the centre of Indian economic planning. Keeping this in view, various high cost programmes are in operation for alleviating rural poverty from the beginning of the plan era in 1950 and especially after the introduction of the targetted approach meant specifically for the betterment of rural poor with the beginning of the Fourth Five Year Plan and particularly after the coverage of the entire country with IRDP since the Sixth Five Year Plan. An objective assessment of the programme is, therefore, necessary to find out whether the programmes are making satisfactory progress in the required direction of poverty alleviation. However, such assessment is not an easy task since there are various components of the programme which are also complex in nature. A sincere attempt is made in this chapter to find out objective information on this subject with a hope that the outcome of results will assist in suggesting some useful guidelines for improving the future programme of poverty alleviation. The methodology used for this difficult task has been to utilize the published literature and results of research and evaluation studies and the findings of several government appointed committees and expert groups and also the opinions expressed by the experts through books, newspaper articles, seminars and workshops. In view of this enormous task only a few important aspects of the programme have been taken up.

5.1 REDUCING THE NUMBER OF RURAL POOR

The number of poor people has to be determined by fixing the line of poverty and measuring the number of people falling below this poverty line. The method followed in India is based on finding out a national minimum expenditure for every household of five persons so as to provide a minimum nutritional diet in terms of 2400 calories intake as well as to allow for a modest expenditure on items other than food except on education and health which were expected to be provided cost free by the State. The Planning Commission set up a distinguished working group in 1962 to find out the poverty line and this working group advocated a national minimum expenditure for every rural household at the rate of Rs. 100 per month or Rs. 20 per capita per month in terms of 1960-61 prices. Since then, the Planning Commission has been estimating the number of rural people, calculating the percentage of the rural poor periodically considering the price rise from time to time. Table 5.1 gives the percentage of rural poor people from 1970-71 onwards based on this method as earlier estimated by the Planning Commission.

Table 5.1 : Percentage of rural poor from 1970-71

Year	Per cent of rural poor
1972-73	54.10
1977-78	51.20
1987-88	33.40

Ref: Economic and Political Weekly, August 21, 1993[1]

Till 1996-97, the Planning Commission continued to publish estimated percentage of rural poor periodically and claimed that the poverty alleviation measures are producing required results and the percentage of poor people is being reduced year by year. However, there was difference of opinion in the country regarding estimates made by the Planning Commission. In 1990, a High Powered Committee[2] appointed by the Government of India on Agricultural Policies and Programmes, in their report (page 9) commented on poverty situation as follows :

> "The claim that the incidence of poverty has been substantially reduced does not carry conviction as different indicators point out in the opposite direction. The per capita consumption of the two most essential needs of poor, namely, foodgrains and cloth, has not increased as is clear from Table 5.4 and Table 5.5. The annual per capita availability of foodgrains is still substantially short of the minimum recommended by nutrition experts. Likewise, annual average per capita availability of cloth has declined as compared to the sixties. The number of unemployed registered at Employment Exchanges has also been increasing rapidly. The number of marginal land holdings has multiplied one and a half times faster than the growth in population".[2]

The Planning Commission in view of this controversy regarding the number of rural poor existing in the country appointed another expert committee chaired by late Dr. Lakadawala to review the estimates of rural poverty keeping in view the price index rise from time to time. This expert committee submitted its report in 1993. For some time, a controversy went on between the expert committee and Planning Commission regarding the recommendations made by the expert committee. The revised percentage of people below the poverty line, as estimated by this expert committee, is indicated below.[3]

Table 5.2 : Percentage of people below the poverty line according to Lakadawala Committee

Year	Per cent of rural poor below poverty line
1970-71	57.30
1983-84	49.00
1984-85	44.90
1987-88	39.10
1989-90	33.70
1990-91	35.00
1992-93	41.70
1993-94	36.50

Ref : Social Dimensions and Post-reforms Growth, p. 196.[3]

Economic Survey for the year 1998-99[4] has published the percentage of population below the poverty line probably based on Lakadawala Committee report as follows.[4]

Table 5.3 : Revised poverty ratio estimated, 1998-99

Year	Poverty ratio/rural sector
1973-74	56.40
1977-78	53.10
1983-84	45.70
1987-88	39.10
1993-94	37.30

Ref. : Economic Survey 1998-99, Table 10.6, pp. 146.[4]

In February 2001, the Planning Commission approved poverty estimates made by the National Sample Survey Organisation (NSSO) which, reported that the percentage of poor people in the country was 26.1 per cent of the total population during 1999-2000 (27.9% in rural areas and 23.62 per cent in urban areas). In absolute terms 26.02 crores of people have been officially identified as poor.

Poverty estimates indicate a drift in poverty percentage which was earlier estimated in 1993-94, when national average was 36 per cent of poverty, with rural poverty at 36.37 and urban poverty at 36.04 per cent. Published in *Times of India*, February 23, 2001 (11).[5]

After releasing the figures of poverty estimates on 22nd February 2001, the Planning Commission deputy chairman said that there is a ten per cent decrease now seen in the poverty estimates. However, it fell short of the targetted 16 per cent in the Ninth Five Year Plan. Even the mid-term appraisal of the plan released by the Planning Commission in October 2000 had noted "Recent estimates suggested that the projection on reduction of proportion and number of people below the poverty line made in the Ninth Plan have not been realized in the first-two years (1997-99) of the plan period.[5]

The percentage of the country's population below the poverty line has only declined from 56 per cent in 1973 to 39 per cent in

1987, 35 per cent in 1994 and 27 per cent in 1999. Poverty has declined but not at the targetted pace to reach 16.5 per cent in 2001 to 2002. The Planning Commission has further said that the percentage of poor in India is much higher than five per cent level for China.[6]

To sum up, it can be said that, there has been a very slow growth in the rural poverty reduction index, particularly when compared to the progress achieved in selected Asian countries as indicated below :

Table 5.4 : Comparative poverty percentages in selected Asian countries

Country	Poverty ratio		
	1975	1995	1999-2000
India	54.90	36.00	27.09
China	59.50	22.20	
Indonesia	64.30	11.40	
Korea	23.00	5.00	
Malaysia	17.40	4.30	
Philippines	35.70	25.50	
Thailand	8.10	0.90	

Ref. 1.: Economic Survey 1998-99, Table 10.7, pp. 146.[4]
2.: Times of India, February 23, 2001, pp. 1 and 9.

5.2 HELPING BENEFICIARIES TO COME ABOVE THE POVERTY LINE

In any rural development poverty alleviation programme, it is necessary that the target group is not only reached as assigned but the beneficiaries should also be actually helped to cross the poverty line. There should be what is known as sustainable growth. The Government of India's presumption that all beneficiaries reached must have crossed over the poverty line is primarily based on the budget amount spent on the programme and the number of beneficiaries reported to have been reached by the development administration.

Many of the evaluation reports of the Planning Commission provide this kind of information only. For example, the evaluation report of the VII Plan as quoted by Dantwala and Barmeda (199, pp. 436)[7] reads, thus : "During the first four years of the VII Plan, 134.17 lakh families were assisted under the programme, against the target of 131.28 lakh families. An expenditure of Rs. 2272.70 crores was incurred and financial institutions provided Rs. 3862.82 crores as loans". It is also necessary to know how much money has reached the really deserving poor people, whether with the help of this money, the beneficiaries have really increased their assets as well and have come out of the poverty line. Many non-official evaluation and expert opinions have indicated their findings on these aspects.

Dantwala and Barmeda (1991, pp. 436) state: "A recent survey on the progress made in the implementation of programme in selected blocks has revealed a number of irregularities in carrying out the programme. It was found that the well-to-do and the influential sections of the rural population were trying to appropriate the benefits of the programme. Thus, it vitiated the identification process with the result that less than 25 per cent of those who benefited belong to the lowest income level (upto Rs. 1500). Further, DRDAs seem to be more concerned about achieving targets than fulfilling the needs of the poor. Banks also did not adhere to the liberalised security norms and insisted on additional security for loans advanced".[7]

The Government's claims that because the beneficiaries have received government assistance they must have crossed the poverty line, has also not been accepted by the government's own Public Accounts Committee of Lok Sabha[8]. This committee in its 95th report, which was presented to the Lok Sabha on 25-4-95 states : "The fact that only 14.87 per cent of beneficiaries of IRDP had been able to cross the existing poverty line of Rs. 11,000 per annum for a family of five persons was a growing indication of the failure of the programme in achieving its objectives". This Lok Sabha Committee has also identified some major areas of concern under IRDP which need immediate attention. These are (1) Low per capita investment, (2) Non-preparation of Five Year perspective and annual plan, (3) Failure to conduct household surveys for identification of prospective beneficiaries, (4) Coverage of ineligible families, (5) Diversion of funds meant for IRDP to other programmes and (6) Lack of proper monitoring and evaluating in IRDP. This committee report concludes : "Despite the government's acceptance of objectives and the extensive organisation apparatus built to translate them to reality, the IRDP has not achieved the desired results".[8]

Another *Deccan Herald* report dated July 20, 1995 states that the Planning Commission itself in its mid term appraisal of the VIII Plan had sharply indicated the centre for negative efforts of the economic reforms and criticised the policy pursued by the Government saying that they have reached an increased level of unemployment and poverty in the country. *Deccan Herald* report also states that the meeting in this regard has been postponed by the Government.[9]

The Government appointed High Powered Committee on Agricultural Policies and Programmes (1990), in its report[2] (pp.13) has commented, as follows: "Thus, the previous Planning Commission had admitted in its Mid-term Appraisal Report of the Seventh Five Year Plan (1985-90) that only 12 per cent of beneficiary families with an annual income of less than Rs. 3500, could cross the poverty line of Rs. 6400 in 1985-86. The claims of poverty alleviation programmes have ignored the fact, that side by side with these programmes, the process of poverty aggravation is also going on, due to fragmentation of holdings and declining real income per worker in agriculture sector. Owing to these two trends, millions above the poverty level are being pulled down below year after year".[2]

Many research studies have also indicated that a majority of the beneficiaries have not crossed over the poverty line. Some of the results of these studies are indicated below :

(1) A nationwide study, entrusted by the Government of India to 27 independent research institutions of the country, by using the data collected by the concurrent evaluation teams of the programme evaluation committee, evolved a sample of 16616

beneficiaries of the IRDP. Fifty per cent of the beneficiaries in this sample had also received the second dose of financial assistance during the VII plan as per new instructions. This research finding reveal that "eleven per cent of the beneficiaries were actually not eligible to be selected as beneficiaries as per norms, since, they were not poor as prescribed. Of the remaining 89 per cent of sample farmers, only 5 per cent could cross the poverty line.[10]

(2) According to concurrent evaluation on IRDP (Sept. 1992-93) only 15.96 per cent of the beneficiaries were observed to have crossed the poverty line of Rs. 11000/year/family.[11]

(3) Research results obtained from another 21 studies are tabulated in the Table 5.5 :

Table 5.5 : Percentage of IRDP beneficiaries crossing the poverty line as per different studies

Percentage of Beneficiaries crossing poverty line	No. of research Studies Reporting	Authors of research studies
More than 75	1	Esakky (1990)[12]
50 - 75	5	Hirevenkangowder (1983)[13]; Malyadri (1985)[14]; Balishter Singh (1984)[15]; Dhillon *et al.* (1985)[16]; Sarawagi *et al.* (1986)[17]
40-50	1	Jain (1986)[18]
30-40	3	Kareem (1994)[19]; Rathi and Sharada (1992)[20]; Kadian and Kaushik (1993)[21]
20 - 30	4	Devilakshmi (1985)[22]; Harikumar (1985)[23]; Aziz (1986)[24]; Pratap Reddy and Buchanan (1992)[25].
Less than 20	5	Rath (1985)[26]; Chandra Kavate (1985)[27]; State Planning Board Kerala (1984)[28]; Vasant Desai (1991)[29]; Ghosh (1991)[30].
Nil	2	Kutty Krishnan (1984)[31]; Tiwari and Kanwar (1983)[32].

From Table 5.5 it is revealed that in a majority of these research studies i.e., 14 out of 21, the percentage of beneficiaries, who were able to cross the poverty line, was not more than 40 per cent.

From the foregoing information it will be seen that a majority of the beneficiaries who have received assistance have not been benefited to cross the poverty line.

5.3 AGRICULTURAL DEVELOPMENT

The Government of India has been stating that agricultural production in the country is making steady progress. The major point in support of this viewpoint is that the country has made substantial increase in food production since 1951 and has stopped the import of foodgrains. It is true that large foodgrain imports are not being made in recent years. The point in question is whether mere increase in foodgrain production is an adequate evidence for satisfactory increase in agricultural production of the country. There are several factors which need to be considered to determine the nature of agricultural production of the country. Some of these can be listed as follows: (1) Has per hectare increase in food production kept pace with increase in population? (2) Whether per capita availability of foodgrains of different kinds has also increased to benefit the people ? (3) What is the rate of growth of agricultural index?; (4) What is the performance of agricultural production of important agricultural crops in relation to the potential possible based on demonstration results of yields in farmers' fields?, (5) How agricultural production of India compares with that of other important countries of the world?

Relevant information on the above mentioned items has been collected and furnished in the following paragraphs.

Food production and per capita availability

Observation : Although food production has increased progressively over the years, we have not yet reached the minimum per capita availability requirement of 181 kg except in one year i.e., 1991.

Table 5.6 : Increase in food production vis-a-vis increase in population growth

Year	Population (in mln)	Food production (mln. tonnes)	Per capita availability (kg/year)
1951	361.1	51.99	144.1
1961	439.2	82.02	171.1
1971	548.2	108.42	171.1
1981	683.3	129.59	166.0
1991	846.3	176.39	186.2
1998		199.32	175.0

Ref : 1. Agri-Statistics at a Glance, Govt. of India, 1998[33] Tables 1.1, 2.2 and 8.2 pages 1, 10 and 87)

Note : The minimum requirement of foodgrains availability in kg per capita per year as recommended by nutrition experts is 181 kg.

Recently the United Nations Population Fund (UNPFA)[34] has warned India in its report released on 19-10-1999 regarding India's food situation stating that India's food security is in danger due to its growing population and unsustainable agriculture. This study further reports as follows "Although the aggregate production of cereals has increased by about three times in 45 years (1951-1996), protein by 1.5 times, foodgrains by 3.5 times, oil seeds by more than four times, the increase in per capita availability has been much less about 27 per cent increase in foodgrains, 35 per cent in cereals and about two times for edible oils. On the other hand, the per capita availability of protein in 1996 had dropped to only half of what it was in 1951".[34]

Growth Rate of Food Production

Observation : Looking to the first seven years of this decade (1990-91 to 1996-97), the annual rate of growth of foodgrains was only 1.70 per cent which is less than the corresponding previous growth. If this trend continues, it could be a matter of grave concern.

Table 5.7 : Annual Growth Rate of Foodgrain production

Period	Annual Growth Rate
1967-68 to 1995-96	2.67
1980-81 to 1995-96	2.86
1990-91 to 1996-97	1.70

Ref: Economic Survey, Govt. of India 1996-97.[35]

Coarse Grain Production

Table 5.8 : Coarse grain production and per capita availability

Year	Production (in million tons)	Per capita Availability (kg/year)
1951	15.38	40.0
1961	23.74	43.6
1971	30.55	44.3
1981	29.02	32.8
1991	32.70	29.2
1997	34.27	27.7

Ref: Agri-Statistics At A Glance, Govt. of India, 1998.

Table 8.2 page 87, Table 2.5A page 16).[33]

Observation : The per capita availability of coarse grains in India has actually decreased from 40 kg/year in 1951 to 27.3 kg/year in 1997. That means that rural poor whose staple foodgrains are coarse grains are facing a hard time due to shortage of per capita availability of coarse grains.

Production of Pulses over the Years and Per Capita Availability

Observation : The per capita availability of pulses in the country has considerably decreased as compared to 1951. A stage has come when the country is now thinking of importing pulses from other countries. In 1997-98, 9.97 lakh tonnes of pulses were imported at a cost of 1184 crores of rupees.[36]

Table 5.9 : Production of pulses

Year	Production (in million tons)	Per capita Availability (kg/year)
1951	8.41	22.1
1961	12.70	25.2
1971	11.82	18.7
1981	10.63	13.7
1991	14.26	15.2
1997	14.46	14.0

Ref: Agri-statistics At A Glance, Govt. of India, 1998[33], Table 2.9, page 24 and Table 8.2, page 87.

Agricultural Index : The 1998-99 economic survey published by the Government of India[36] furnishes the following table regarding the index of agricultural production.

Table 5.10 : Index of agricultural production for 46 selected crops (Base-triennium 1981-82 = 100)

Year	Index	Per cent change
1994-95	165.2	5.0
1995-96	160.7	–2.7
1996-97	175.4	9.7
1997-98 (p)	164.9	–6.0
1998-99 (p)	171.3	3.9

Ref: Economic Survey, Govt. of India, 1998-99[36], p. 115.

Observation : The growth of agricultural production is not uniform in the 90s. In some years there has been negative growth.

Performance of agricultural production in relation to potential available

A study by Druv Srivastava and T. Haque[37] gave the following information regarding the performance of agriculture in relation to the potential available.

Table 5.11: State-wise unrealized potential of Indian Agriculture (million rupees at 1970-71 prices)

	Actual gross returns at prevailing level of adoption of new techniques in 1978-79 (million rupees)	Return possible with adoption of recommended level of technology in 1978-79 (million rupees)
Total for all the states of India	164695	473409

Observation : Actual return of the country is only 35 per cent of the returns possible (or the potential)

(Unutilized potential) = 473409 — 16469 million rupees
= 308714 million rupees
= Half the national income (approximately).

Comparison of Indian Agricultural Production with other important countries of the world

Besides, not realizing the full potential of our agriculture, the performance of most agricultural crops in India as compared to other important countries of the world is lower than the world and Asian averages as is evident from the following information summarised from the FAO Agriculture Production Year Book 1994.[38]

SUMMARISED INFORMATION ON INDIA'S AGRICULTURAL PRODUCTION COMPARED WITH OTHER COUNTRIES IN THE WORLD (1994)

(1) Rice (Paddy)

India is number one in the area of rice grown in the world with its share of 42.03 million hectares out of the world area of 146.45 million ha. As far as the production per hectare, it takes the 7th rank out of eleven important countries growing rice. The Indian average per hectare yield is only 2817 kg as compared to the world average of 2651 kg per hectare and the Asian average of 3731 kg/ha. Japan's yield is 6770 kg/ha while China grows 5869 kg/ha.

(2) **Wheat**

India's rank is number three in the area of wheat cultivation in the world next only to China and USA which are number one and two respectively. India's wheat area is 24.43 million ha as against the world area of 215.7 million ha. In terms of yield per hectare, India takes the eighth rank with an average production of 2420 kg/ha as against the world average of 2,501 kg/ha. U.K. produces the highest yield in the world with 7,178 kg/ha, followed by Germany which produces 6706 kg/ha.

(3) **Maize**

India is the fifth largest country growing maize in the world with an area of 6 million hectares compared to the world area of 131.52 million ha. The yield per hectare production in India is only 1750 kg/ha and is placed ninth in the rank. The world average production of maize is 4330 kg/ha and that of Asia is 3664 kg/ha. China produces 5,633 kg/ha while USA tops the list with 8697 kg/ha.

(4) **Sorghum**

India is the largest sorghum growing country in the world with an area of 12.80 million ha compared to the world area of 43.72 million ha. India's rank in the per hectare production is however number five in the world with an average yield of 977 kg/ha as against the world average of 1,394 kg/ha and Asian average of 1,214 kg/ha. In USA the average yield is 4,585 kg/ha and China's production is at the rate of 3,707 kg/ha while the yield in Mexico is 2,934 kg/ha.

(5) **Pulses**

India's share in the world area of 69.27 million ha is 23.97 million ha. The yield per hectare in India in pulses is 607 kg/ha compared with the world average of 847 kg/ha and the Asian average of 773 kg/ha. Ukrain produces three times the yield of India with 2,417 kg/ha. Russian average yield is 1500 kg/ha, while that of Canada is 1712 kg/ha.

(6) **Soybean**

India grows 3.9 million ha of soybean out of world area of 62.65 million ha. India produces only 835 kg/ha of soybean as against world average of 2182 kg/ha and the Asian average of 1348 kg/ha. Italy is number one in production for unit area with an yield of 3606 kg/ha followed by USA (2815 kg/ha) and Canada (2712 kg/ha). India does not find a place in the first 10 ranks according to production.

(7) **Groundnut in shell**

Area of groundnut crop in India is 8.5 million ha which is approximately 1/3 of the world area of 21.78 million hectares. The world average of groundnut production is 1,308 kg/ha and Asian average is 1,479 kg/ha as compared to India's production which is only 988 kg/ha and India is placed sixth in the rank out of 10 important countries growing groundnut. The countries taking the first five ranks in the production per unit area are (1) USA (2995 kg/ha), (2) China (2688 kg/ha), (3) Indonesia (1770 kg/ha), (4) Nigeria (1145 kg/ha) and (5) Vietnam (1100 kg/ha).

(8) **Safflower**

Out of the world area of 1.16 million hectares in safflower, India occupies the first rank with 0.9 million hectare. The average yield of safflower in India is however only 478 kg/ha and has the last place among the six important countries growing safflower. The highest yield is obtained by USA with 2097 kg/ha followed by China with an average production of 1905 kg/ha and Mexico producing 1190 kg/ha.

(9) **Cotton with seed**

The world area of cotton is 31.1 million hectares with an average production of 1712 kg per hectare. Asia contributes 16.8 million hectares with an average production of 1584 kg per hectare. India grows cotton on an area of 7.7 million hectares and is ranked No. 1 in the areas grown out of 12 important cotton growing countries of the world. However, in the production per unit area, India takes only the eleventh rank with an average production of 898 kg per hectare. The first six countries in the ranking of production per unit area almost produce three times the yield produced in India. These countries in the order of their ranks are (1) Turkey (2796 kg/ha), (2) Egypt (2780 kg/ha), (3) Greece (2736 kg/ha), (4) Uzbekistan (2559 kg/ha), (5) China (2523 kg/ha) and (6) USA (2086 kg/ha).

(10) **Millets**

The world area of millets is 37.7 million hectares out of which Asia contributes 17.7 million hectares. India tops the eight important millet growing countries of the world in area cultivated with an area of 14.7 million hectares. In production per unit area however, the Indian average of 708 kg per hectare is below the Asian average of 804 kg per hectare. It is slightly above the world average of 689 kg per hectare. Although India is placed at No. 3 in the rank of production per unit area, with 708 kg/ha, the per hectare yield is less than half of the yield obtained in China, which is 1667 kg/ha. Even Nigeria's average production is 300 kg more per hectare than India's average production per unit area.

(11) **Sugarcane**

India's area under sugarcane is 3.6 million hectares out of the world area of 17.6 million hectares and the Asian area of 7.8 million hectares. India ranks No. 2 in the area cultivated as compared to 13 important sugarcane growing countries of the world. However, when yield per unit area is considered, India with per hectare yield of 64,561 kg, ranks No. 8. The top 5 countries in the higher production range are : (1) Columbia (90,625 kg/ha), (2) Australia (90,582 kg/ha), (3) Mexico (78,297 kg/ha), (4) Indonesia (77,778 kg/ha) and (5) USA (76,251 kg per ha). The world average of sugarcane production per hectare is 61,108 kg and Asian average is 58.592 kg per hectare.

To sum up the position of India's agricultural development, some opinions based on empirical reviews of eminent economists and government appointed committees are presented below :

1. According to Rao and Deshpande (1991, pp. 85) "Agricultural growth is still modest in its rate and has little capability to insulate production from the vagaries of rainfall".[39]
2. A report of the High Powered Committee[2] appointed by the Government of India on Agricultural Policies and Programmes (1990, page18) states : "Indian agriculture has been producing much less than its potential or capacity and this fact has not been recognized by the policy makers, leave alone taking any steps to bring it back to health and achieve the full potential. All that has been attempted in the past has been just to attain self sufficiency in foodgrains and that too at the subsistence level of consumption. A country that has all the potential of emerging as No. 1 agricultural power in the world has been aiming only at survival and in achieving even this modest goal, it has failed as is evident from the fact that during the last 38 years (1950-51 to 1988-89), India has imported foodgrains in as many as 31 years and attained subsistence level of foodgrain consumption in only four years".[2]
3. An official reappraisal of the agricultural sector made in 1995[40] has expressed concern over the fact that despite series of good monsoons, production of farm products has grown at a meagre rate of 2.2 per cent per year. The picture that emerges is one of contrasts. While food stocks are exceptionally large, production has grown only modestly and has been virtually stagnant for the five years since 1990. In fact, foodgrain production has remained around the level of 171 million tonnes achieved in 1989-90, even dropping to 158 million tonnes in

1991-92. The appraisal concludes that Indian agriculture has to grow by atleast 3 per cent annually if gross domestic product is to increase to the level of 5.6 per cent a year. The fact is that the rate of investment in agriculture has declined in recent years.

4. A review by Sidhu and Singh (1991, page 132)[41] states that "Although India has made significant progress in technical development in the field of agriculture, the productivity of land and labour still remained low in terms of world standards". The technological breakthrough in terms of green revolution has helped only to maintain and not to improve per capita availability of foodgrains (175 kg/year) due to the rapid growth of population".
5. Dantwala (1991, page 9)[42] in his review states as follows : "Reverting to the equity aspect of agricultural development there is no gainsaying the fact that the process of development has had little impact on reduction of poverty, inequality and unemployment".

In view of the above given information we may conclude that Indian agriculture has developed to some extent as compared to 1950, but not in a satisfactory way to have its effect on improving the total agricultural economy. Thus, there is a need for more development of agriculture.

5.4 ALLOTMENT OF GOVERNMENT WASTE LANDS TO THE POOR

In India a large per cent of uncultivated land is available under the class culturable waste. The extent of these lands was 22.9 million hectares in 1950. In 1991 the extent of this land continues to be 15.1 million hectares (Ref. CMIE data).[43] This means that although a special programme called waste land development scheme was started in the VII Five Year Plan, the progress achieved in distributing these lands to the rural poor, is far from satisfactory and still a large portion of such land remains undistributed. The High Powered Committee appointed by the Government of India on Agricultural

Policies and Programmes (1990, page 60)[2], have stated as follows regarding non-utilization of culturable land.[2] "In their approach paper to the Seventh Five Year Plan, the Planning Commission have said that country's land stock can be increased by bringing 17 million hectares of culturable waste land and 20 million hectares of old and current fallows, totalling 37 million hectares, under cultivation. Since this observation was made, there has been a further addition to fallow land and the total now exceeds 41 million hectares. This area was 29.5 per cent of the net sown area in 1986-87. The cultivable land which we have left uncultivated exceeds the total area of arable land and land under permanent crops of four countries namely, Pakistan, Bangladesh, Nepal and Japan. This area also exceeds the total area of land held by large land holders in the country. The total land distributed to landless under land ceiling laws till the end of 1989 was only 1.8 million hectares which has been allotted to 4.5 million families each getting on an average not more than 0.4 hectare. While land redistribution has failed to reduce the incidence of poverty, it has effectively stopped addition to the net area sown".

5.5 ASSET BUILDING AND CAPITAL FORMATION

5.5a Distributing to the Rural Poor Surplus Land obtained by Enforcing Land Reforms to Provide them Assets

This programme has been implemented with the help of land reform measures since independence and even a little earlier. Ceiling laws have been introduced and the surplus land obtained has been distributed over the years but what has been the outcome of these measures?

The programme implemented in respect of land reforms has been summarized as follows by Dantwala (1991, page 60).[44]

> "Efforts have often been made, as pointed out earlier, to strengthen the land base of marginal farmers. According to the information provided in the Seventh Five Year Plan, only 7.2 million acres had been declared as surplus land through

the application of ceiling laws. Of these, 5.2 million acres have been acquired and 4.4 million acres have been distributed (Government of India, 1985, page 62).[45] Latest data (March, 1988) hardly show any improvement in performance. An intriguing aspect of the problem is that though a sum of Rs. 30 crores was provided for the period 1980 to 1985, under a central scheme and an equal amount was to be provided as a matching outlay by the States for enabling the assignees of surplus land to put it to profitable use, the actual utilisation of funds has however, been very low, largely because the States have not been providing their matching share (Government of India, 1985, page 62).[45] The Plan admits that the full potential of land distribution has not been realised both in respect of covering the entire surplus land that may be available and taking possession and distribution of that already identified".

This author further states :

"Imposition of ceiling and redistribution is advocated on the ground that in the absence of an egalitarian asset distribution, particularly land ownership, which determines political equations, the root cause of poverty and exploitation will not be eliminated. As such, poverty alleviation programmes will not be effective and may even be perverted to the advantage of the non-poor".[44]

The above information indicates that there is no improvement in the land size owned by these categories of marginal and small farmers inspite of land reforms.

5.5b **The Rural Asset Status**

One of the important indicators of alleviating rural poverty is the net savings — rural income ratio and the improvement of the rural asset structure. The Union Finance Minister himself has stated in his 1995 budget speech[46] that inadequacy of public investment in agriculture is today a matter of great concern. Majumdar and

Menon (1991, page 233)[47] have reported that the performance of rural sector in the area of savings was poor in the three decades starting from 1960. Regarding financial asset structure, the proportion of national income channelled for investment in agriculture has not shown any spectacular improvement in the past three decades. According to these authors, it is only the latest IRDP, started in the VI Plan, which has some prospects of improving the savings and capital formation in the rural areas by its specific programmes to strengthen a capital base of the poor by providing required assets to specific target groups and to improve the availability of credit, input, training programmes and other services with a view to boosting the productivity of the existing stock of assets held by the poor. They further state that the outcome of these programmes are still not known clearly but it is hoped that if the programmes are implemented imaginatively these programmes could create a better environment for rural savings and capital formation.

Some of the indicators however have been made available on these aspects in recent years. According to High Powered Committee on Agricultural Policies and Programmes of Government of India[2] (1990, p. 27), the gross capital formation in the farm sector during the period 1980-81 to 1987-88 was only 10.2 per cent of the value added by agriculture. This committee further points out, thus : "A more crucial symptom which should immediately engage the attention of planners is how to raise capital formation of farm sector atleast to the level of 21.2 per cent of the value added by it. If this target is not achieved, rest of the planning will be of no significant use to 3/4 of our population living in villages. There are further indications of some of the research studies on this topic.

1. In a detailed systematic study of the IRDP programme in Anantapura district of Andhra Pradesh, it was revealed that although the IRDP may have a positive contribution in the CADA Block (Irrigated Area) in the DPAP Block (Dry Area) the programme did not contribute significantly (Y. Eswaraprasad, R. Ramanna and Lalith Achotha, 1991).[48]
2. In a research study reported by Pandey and Panday (1991),[49] it was found out that the increase of asset was only 21 per

cent due to IRDP in case of beneficiaries.

3. A micro level study indicated that 69 per cent of the beneficiaries diverted the funds for unproductive purpose and hence the asset formation was not seen (Balishter and Singh, 1984).[15]
4. Subbarayudu *et al.* (1991)[50] reported that "There is no improvement in the income even after receiving the animal. Moreover, almost all the categories of beneficiaries have incurred heavy losses.[55]
5. In a study by Satish Verma and Singh (1991)[51] it was reported that only 23 out of 60 beneficiaries could be contacted to evaluate the programmes, since no trace could be made about the others. All the 23 contacted[56] reported failure, 7 others told that they are not earning any more than before. Only the remaining 12 were earning a little more than before. Twenty two of these 23 beneficiaries were facing problems in getting working capital for their enterprises.
6. An Evaluation Report prepared by the Planning Commission indicated that the singular focus of IRDP has been on improving targets in terms of financial allocation and number of persons to be covered and not on job creation and income generation through sustained asset formation (Dantwala, 1991).[7]
7. A Ph.D. research by Hirevenkanagoudar[13] (1983) has revealed that out of 200 beneficiaries studied, 90 per cent felt that the money provided was not sufficient to purchase quality animals, which is necessary to create a good asset. Seventy five per cent of them could not repay the loans. Fifty four per cent beneficiaries, who wanted operating capital to make the assets really productive, were helpless.
8. Kareem in his Ph.D. study (1994)[19] reported that out of 210 beneficiaries studied 95, that is 45.22 per cent, did not increase their assets. Another 71 did not use it for the purpose to create assets. Twenty four of the remaining 140 could not generate any assets. Of the 35 beneficiaries who developed dairy enterprise, 17 were provided loan for purchasing only one cow/buffalo and 18 for purchasing 2 cows/buffaloes.

9. Gaur in his study[10] with 16,186 beneficiaries reported that in 23 per cent cases, the assets provided were not available and were either disposed of as defective and not functioning.

The above information indicates that there is vast scope for improving the asset building work with rural poor, under IRDP and suitable steps should be taken to avoid a large amount of wastage of public money.

5.5c **Improvement of assets through consolidation of holdings**

As discussed earlier, small farmers land holdings are becoming smaller with each decade and the number of small farmers is also on the increase. Along with this, there is also the problem of land consolidation. A number of small farmers fields are in separate pieces making the cultivation in such fragmented pieces of land difficult. Even after 50 years of planned development, consolidation of holdings has not been completed and not caught the imagination of the governments, inspite of a successful work carried out in Punjab and Haryana. In the absence of consolidation, the land assets of the poor farmers are not likely to be developed.

5.5d **Land development and assets building — Watershed development programme**

The percentage of rainfed area in the country is quite high. Nearly 60 per cent of the cultivated area in India comes under rainfed agriculture and dryland farming. Almost all the land in this area is eroded and concerted efforts have not been made to solve this problem so far in spite of the soil conservation programme in operation in the country from the time even before independence. Although wide publicity has been now given to the recently started high cost programme of National Watershed Development, the problem has not been effectively tackled. In very few of these Watershed Development Programmes, land has been really developed satisfactorily by following a combination of graded bunds, levelling between the two bunds and construction of effective waterways. The Senior Author of the present book was a member of a National Committee to evaluate the working of National Watershed Development Schemes in the country during 1987-88 and had an opportunity to visit 27 National Watershed programmes in different States of the country. During his visit he had to see, to his dismay, that only in four out of 27 watershed programmes, the work was up to the mark. The most pathetic site was the visit to a watershed adopted by one of the premier dry farming institute of the country, where the bunds were mostly put up on old system without levelling the land and developing the waterways. As a result, within two years of the construction of these bunds at a huge cost, most of the bunds were found breached with heavy rains and aggravated the problems of soil erosion which these projects were meant to control.

5.6 GENERATING MORE RURAL EMPLOYMENT

5.6a **Employment in general**

The Government of India claims that more employment is created by its several measures undertaken through the planned programmes in IRDP. Its main argument is that the growth is taking place satisfactorily and this has resulted in more employment. The Union Finance Minister[52] in his 1995 Budget speech stated : "Growth has created new jobs for our people. In 1991-92, total employment grew by only about three million. In each of the two years thereafter, employment increased twice as fast, with about six million new jobs added each year. The increase is expected to be even higher in 1994-95. The Drawing Room Cassandras, who predicted massive unemployment as a consequence of the reforms have been conclusively proved wrong". Another reason given for an optimistic view is that the guaranteed manpower employment programmes in rural areas have been strengthened which has ensured increased employment in rural areas. The above mentioned optimistic view is however not supported by statistics and empirical evidences. On the other hand, the evaluation reports of labour absorption in rural areas are not that encouraging.

The estimates for unemployed persons seeking employment is expected to increase from 303 million in 1981 to 476 million by 2001 (Kanta Ahuja, 1991),[53] p. 54. The rural labour force alone is expected to increase by over 100 million from 242 million to 342 million during this period (Sundaram[54], 1984). The High Powered Committee on Policies and Programme (page 24) points out as follows : According to Economic Advisory Council report, employment growth has not kept pace with growth in labour force in spite of G.D.P. growth exceeding 5 per cent.[2] There has been a deceleration in rural employment growth, the annual growth declining steadily from 2.82 per cent during 1972-73 and 1977-78 to 2.22 per cent during 1977-78 and 1983, further to 1.55 per cent during 1983 and 1987-88 (Rural Development report, NIRD, 1994[55]). Another, point is that the number of people enrolled in employment exchange has swollen up in recent years. It is reported that the Planning Commission in its mid-term appraisal of the Eighth Plan is understood to have expressed concern over the adverse impact of the reforms started in 1991. The poverty level has increased, but needs and opportunities have shrunk from planned targets.[2] Assessing the performance of the economy in the first three years of the Plan period, it is reported to have said that an employment generation during the period 1992-93 has fallen short of the targets envisaged in the Plan. Indeed, the level of unemployment should have gone up from the estimated 17 million at the beginning of the Plan to 18.9 million at the end of 1994-95. If the employment targets of the Plan are to be achieved, expansion needs to reach 3.64 per cent a year on average in the remaining two years. Achieving the near full employment by 2002 requires that the employment grows at a rate of 3.1 per cent a year and economy rises by at least 7 per cent (*Deccan Herald*, July 20, 1995).[56]

There is also a growing skepticism regarding government policies of the present. To provide employment to rural poor through *ad hoc* programmes like "Jawahar Rojgar Yojana" which the government has so much emphasized as a solution to the difficult task of providing rural employment. The question arises as to whether *ad hoc* supplementary schemes can solve the problems of employment and poverty. In fact the solutions of these problems of poverty and unemployment have to be found within the framework of the Development Plan itself (G.V.K. Rao, 1979).[57]

The Integrated Rural Development Programme has been the principal plank of the poverty alleviation strategy since 1981. Evaluation of this programme has raised the question of whether asset distribution or direct employment generation was the more appropriate strategy for poverty alleviation. In this context, it was felt that both strategies should complement each other. The mix of the two would also vary from area to area. Experience with implementation of rural works programme has highlighted some operational problems as well as some basic policy issues.

"Operationally, the programmes have faltered due to the cause of leakage, on account of corruption and administrative failure and inefficiency at local level. They have seldom succeeded in creating durable assets because of old material component in such projects and because of poor technical formulation. In spite of indirect indications of unutilized, underemployed labour, mobilization of labour for such employment has been quite inadequate. The programmes have, in general, operated as relief-cum-subsidy programmes rather than as programmes for increasing the productive potential of the community. Their implementation has clearly shown that the rural force is not a lumped mass of under employed workers, who would come forward to work as soon as unskilled work opportunities are created for them. The basic issues in employment policy, therefore, relate to how best to incorporate the development of employment objectives in local level plans" (Kanta Ahuja, 1991).[53]

The rural work approach of employment planning can only be a sub-strategy of temporary relief as Dantwala (1978)[58] has so aptly remarked. "The Public Works approach to unemployment would make sense if it is so organised that there will be progressively less and less reliance on it".[58]

In any case since poverty is far more widespread than employment it follows that full employment will not be a solution for rural poverty unless it is accompanied by higher earnings (Kanta Ahuja, 1991).[53]

The Rural Development Report on rural employment prepared by the NIRD (1994)[55] summarizes the rural employment problem as follows : "A singular failure in the development efforts during the last few decades of many a country, including India, has been the inability to provide adequate employment opportunities to their growing populations. Unemployment remains the most troublesome problem for them, with serious implication for social order. The slow down in employment growth has been more marked in the rural sector from 2.52 per cent per annum in the early seventies to a low of 0.95 per cent during mid eighties".

In view of the above, it could be said that the problem of rural unemployment is still a gigantic one and needs very careful attention through well conceived Plan programmes and their effective implementation.

5.6b **Labour Absorption in Indian Agriculture**

It was expected that the agricultural sector should accommodate for absorption of additional labour force created in the rural areas since the possibilities of absorbing the increased labour force in non-agricultural sector, like non-farming employment and rural industries, was limited. However, this was not achieved and it is the farm sector which had experienced the worst deceleration in employment growth. "The annual rate of employment growth in agriculture and allied sectors in the rural areas declined sharply from 1.96 per cent during 1972-73 and 1977-78 to 0.39 per cent during 1983 and 1987-88 as compared to a decline from 2.52 per cent to 0.95 per cent for the rural sector as a whole" (Rural Development Report — Rural Employment NIRD, 1994, p. 88).[55]

It has been pointed out time and again that unemployment in the developing countries like India is mostly in the rural areas. Statistics also reveal that the rural labour population is on the increase year by year with the increase in population. The only possibility is to provide more employment opportunities in the agricultural sector, since the expansion of industries and other services in rural areas are not adequate to absorb this growth of rural unemployment and under-employment.

An assumption, that a higher agricultural production in rural areas will by itself provide the required increased labour requirements, still prevails even in scientific circles. This is not true. On the contrary, the so called Green Revolution, which has increased the agricultural production in several pockets of rural circles, has produced inequality and has not created the required amount of employment opportunities. Green Revolution however, is only the first step in this process. In cases of widespread adoption of new agricultural technology the small proportions of creating employment opportunities may still present a significant increase in employment and incomes for the poor. It should be noted that expanding consumer expenditure for demand elastic agricultural commodities will be accompanied by commensurately large or larger increased demand for non-agricultural consumer goods which also have elastic demand and have a potential for substantial labour absorptive capacity. Thus, the large increases in productivity in foodgrain production are required to provide both the most basic wages, goods to back up increased employment and a portion of the increased income to purchase non foodgrain agricultural commodities (Mellor, 1975, p. 20).[59] The most important action taken up by the national government through the planned programme has been to provide funds for employing rural people in labour activities like road building, land development, construction of irrigation structures etc. mostly in government land. These programmes started by the end of the Fourth Five Year Plan are known by various names such as (1) Rural Works/ Manpower Programmes, (2) Crash Scheme for Rural Employment, (3) Pilot Intensive Rural Employment Programme, (4) Food for Work Programme, (5) National Rural Employment Programme, (6) Rural Landless Employment Guarantee Programmes.

The latest in the series are 'Jawahar Rojgar Yojana' (JRY) launched in 1989. The employment assurance scheme started in 1993 and (2) Some of the old programmes have also been merged in JRY. However, many inadequacies have been observed in relation to these programmes in providing increased employment. Despite progress achieved in spending huge amounts in implementing these programmes, widespread unemployment still persists. The magnitude of the problem of employment can be guaged from the forecast that the total labour force that is seeking unemployment is expected to increase from 303.3 million in 1981 to 476 million by the year 2001. As for rural labour force, the same is estimated to increase by 100 million from 242 million to 342 million in the same period (Sundaram, 1984).[54]

Magnitude of the problems

The magnitude of the task of employment planning can be judged from the following information furnished in the report of Kanta Ahuja (1991)[53] which reads as follows:

> "The pressure on employment has led to a stupendous marginalisation of operational holdings. The Agricultural Census Data (1984) indicates that the percentage of marginal holdings to the total is not less than 65. While the holdings are getting marginalised, the ranks of landless labourers are swelling. The number of agricultural labour households has increased by half million a year. In 1981, the number of rural male workers according to the Golden Registers, show an increase of 12 million in 10 years. The 32nd round NSS (1983) has estimated the total number of rural male workers at 140 million and female workers at 60 million. According to 38th round of NSS the magnitude of unemployment in rural areas was 18 million. An important aspect of rural employment policy is the place such policy can occupy in the overall poverty alleviation strategies. A close relationship between unemployment and poverty has been observed in a large number of empirical studies".

Labour and Rural Employment

The historical experience of the now developed countries has led to the hypothesis that development results in a decline in the share of agriculture in the gross national product as well as in its share in labour force. An inbringing factor of the Indian situation is the near constancy in the share of workers dependent on agriculture. This process described as 'Agricultural Involution' has occurred in a few other countries also facing similar demographic pressures (Kanta Ahuja, p. 367).[53] The following statistics indicate the strength, distribution and total work force — census wise :

Table 5.12 : Agriculture Involution in India

Category	Sex	1951	1961	1971	1981
	Male	51.9	51.0	46.2	43.7
Cultivators	Female	46.0	55.3	30.6	37.6
	Persons	50.2	52.3	43.1	42.1
Agricultural	Male	16.5	13.7	21.2	19.8
labourers	Female	31.8	24.6	50.3	44.8
	Persons	22.8	17.2	27.0	26.3
Non-	Male	37.6	35.3	32.5	36.5
Agricultural	Female	19.4	20.1	19.2	17.7
workers	Persons	28.0	30.5	29.9	32.6

Ref: Kanta Ahuja, Table 4, p. 373.[54]

The rural work approach of employment planning can only be a substrategy of temporary relief. The public works approach to employment would make sense if it is so organised that there will be progressively less and less reliance on it (Dantwala, 1978).[58]

It could be said that employment growth in agriculture has declined sharply from 2.32 per annum during 1972-73 and 1977-78 to only 0.65 per cent during 1982-83 and 1987-88. This conclusion is reinforced by two other indicators; firstly the intensity of cultivation is almost stagnant inspite of expansion in irrigation facilities; and secondly, most of the gains in production can be contributed to a single factor, namely application of a large dose of fertilizers for crop production (High Powered Committee on Agricultural Policies and Programmes, Government of India, 1990, p. 24).[2]

5.7 DEVELOPING RURAL INDUSTRIES TO PROVIDE ADDITIONAL EMPLOYMENT

Among the objectives of developing the village and small industries have been the generation of employment opportunities on a decentralised and dispersed basis and the upgradation of the existing levels of skills of artisans and quality of products (Rural Development Report — Rural Employment NIRD, 1994, p. 82).[55]

The Government of India has stated in the VIII Plan document[60] that the employment policy through establishment of small industries in India has not succeeded so far. This report further states : "Promotion of small scale industries has not been very effective in serving the employment objectives". It is not directly related to employment in so far as the eligibility for preferential treatment in terms of incentives and other assistance is related to fixed capital investment. The assumption that small capital necessarily implies larger employment per unit of capital has not always been found valid. Thus, while the criteria of capital size may be necessary for other socio-economic objectives, it is felt that employment criteria should be superimposed on it. In fact, some studies point out that in the absence of such criteria, many small industries have tended to become unnecessarily capital intensive. To the extent such a tendency is observed, it suggests the need to examine the relative factor prices and changes in them over time, so as to check the tendency towards avoidable capital intensification.

Employment in the cottage and household industries has experienced a relative decline due to shrinking markets on account of competition from modern projects and often due to lack of technological upgradation to meet the new demands.

There has been technological unemployment, caused in traditional industries by the growth of an intermediate sector between the traditional unorganized sector and the modern organized sector. An example of this is the power-loom sector which has caused technological unemployment in the traditional handloom sector. Efforts to strengthen the organizational base of the traditional industries by the formation of cooperative societies of artisans in order to provide economies of scale to small entrepreneurs and improve their bargaining power have also not succeeded. Most of the industrial and weavers cooperative societies are sick or dormant.

The successive population censuses show that the employment in household industries is declining, such declines being more pronounced in traditional industries like processing of cereals, pulses, gur and khandsari, edible oil, wool and silk spinning and curing and tanning of hides and skins. There is also evidence that the decline is much sharper in family employment (Rural Development Report—

Rural Employment NIRD, 1994, p. 83-84).[55]

The non-traditional industries coming up in rural areas are both agriculture related as well as those which have no connection with it. Examples are, agro-based and food processing industries, textile based industries and those producing construction materials like bricks, tiles etc. These are relatively better organized than the traditional household industries and the activities are generally pursued as main occupation. Although their locations may not be strictly rural, in the sense that they are tending to get located in smaller towns, they provide employment to rural workers. Detailed information are not available in respect of these sub-sectors of the non-agricultural sector as are available for the manufacturing. However, the sectors have recorded higher employment growth. Transport, trade and services have done well in the recent years apart from construction.

To sum up it could be said that the objectives of increasing employment through small scale and village industries have not been realized adequately.

5.8 SPECIAL PROGRAMMES FOR SELF-EMPLOYMENT IN RURAL AREAS

There were three major sectors under the self-employment programme undertaken as part of attacking rural poverty under the IRDP. These are (1) Self-employment under regular IRDP programme by providing assistance for various projects like Dairy, Poultry, Sheep rearing, Piggery etc. (2) TRYSEM programme and (3) DWCRA programme for women. Since 1999, a new holistic self employment programme namely Swarna Jayanthi Grama Swarozgar Yojana (SGSY) has been in operation, with this original programme namely IRDP, DWCRA, TRYSEM, SITRA, GRY, MWS, ceased to be in operation.

5.8a **Self Employment under IRDP**

Under this programme rural poor families are identified and selected for project work by providing 25 per cent money required as subsidy and the remaining 75 per cent to be provided as loan from financing agencies like Banks. The target was too poor. Forty million families below the poverty line, from 1980-81 to 1991-92 with a total investment of subsidies and credits amounting to Rs. 6,543 crores and Rs. 10,743.04 crores respectively (Figures furnished by Planning Commission as quoted in the Rural Development Report — Rural Employment NIRD, 1994).[55]

A recent study on the overall impact of this programme on poverty reduction, estimates that the programme to assist self-employment through various projects has helped only about 9.34 per cent of the poor families who are beneficiaries of this gigantic programme to help the rural poor to cross the poverty line in the decade 1980-1990, which achievement is positive, but is small (MCRL, 1991) and also quoted by Rural Development Report — Rural Employment, NIRD, 1994).

The above results therefore indicate that nearly 91 per cent of the beneficiary families reached who were provided assistance have not been benefited. This is a colossal waste of huge amounts of public funds which need to be avoided in future work of IRDP.

5.8b **Self Help Employment Under TRYSEM**

Training of Rural Youth for Self-employment : This programme was introduced along with the IRDP programme. This was a direct attempt to bring rural unemployed youth under self employment by imparting skills in various traditional as well as vocations in the area of services, trade and manufacturing activities. Under this programme 30-40 rural youths of poor families are selected in each block based on their needs, and finance is provided for training in the area concerned. Training is given in approved training institutes like Industries Training Institutes, Khadi and Gramodyog and Handicrafts Training centres, other vocational institutions of government as well as non-governmental institutions. Financial support is provided to the trainees, trainers as well as training institutions.

Number of persons trained and the number of persons self-employed giving the percentage of effectiveness of the programme are given in Table 5.13.

Table 5.13 : Achievement of the TRYSEM programme 1980 to 1991

Period	No. of Persons Trained	No. of persons Self-Employed	On Wages	Total employed	Percentage of success
1980-92	22,48,832	10,66,257	2,74,686	13,40,903	58.80

Reference : Rural Development Report Rural Employment, NIRD, 1994[55].

Observation : Though TRYSEM is a component of IRDP, it remains a loose anchor for the programme and therefore would not be made more effective for generating self-employment.

Some research studies conducted on TRYSEM scheme have revealed the following results :

(1) A study by Malik *et al.* (1986)[61] indicated that the trainees selected for TRYSEM expressed lack of guidance in identification of the trades, difficulty in getting financial help, inability to compete with the existing trades and non-availability of supply of raw materials required and no follow-up guidance and no help in establishing linkages with marketing channels etc. and as a result they are not able to start their self-employment projects.

2) Myladri (1986)[14] reported that selection of TRYSEM beneficiaries was not properly done. There were only a few training institutes to serve the beneficiaries, there was inadequate supply of raw materials to TRYSEM trainees to start their industry, and also lack of contact with marketing agencies or help in marketing. As a result the programme could not succeed enabling TRYSEM Trainees to start their industries.

(3) A study by Ramadasa Reddy (1987)[62] indicated lack of capital for trainees, no risk covering help, poor coordination which deterred the trainees to take to industries.

(4) Shripathi (1989)[63] reported that the duration of training and

the nature of training of TRYSEM were not to the satisfaction of the trainees to enable them to take up industries. He also reported that, only 20 per cent of the TRYSEM trainees were self-employed after completion of their training. A majority of the trainees could not start self-employment schemes due to several problems.

(5) Singh (1989)[64] identified the problems of TRYSEM like; (i) No proper selection of vocation for the benefit of trainees, (ii) Non availability of raw material and (iii) No linkage help to support marketing of the products and lack of follow-up technical aid to start their industries.

(6) Shivalinge Gowda (1994)[65] reported that only 10 per cent of the TRYSEM trainees could start industries to help them cross the poverty line. Only four out of 40 TRYSEM trainees studied were able to cross the poverty line.

(7) Vallabha Reddy (1985)[66] reported that only 39 out of 108 TRYSEM beneficiaries were able to start their schemes after training and 63 were only wage earners.

In sum, it could be stated that the TRYSEM scheme has not been generating self-employment for the trainees, so as to help them come above the poverty line as was expected by the scheme objective. Lot of money spent on this scheme has not been adequately rewarded.

5.8c **DWCRA (Development of Women and Children in Rural Areas)**

This special programme was introduced in 1982. The main idea behind this project was to provide employment and income generating opportunities to the women of targetted group. This programme particularly aimed at assisting women who can take up any economic activity independently and organise them into vocational groups to take part in income generating activities. The target and achievements of this scheme from 1980-1991 are given in Table 5.14 :

Table 5.14 : Target and achievement of DWCRA

Period	Coverage of districts	Number of groups	
		Target	Achievement
1980-81	533	48535	38478

Evaluation : Like TRYSEM scheme, though DWCRA is also another component of IRDP, the two have not been integrated properly resulting in overlapping in some cases and inadequate funding for income generating schemes in many other cases of DWCRA (IRDP report, NIRD, 1994)[55].

5.9 WAGE EMPLOYMENT PROGRAMMES

Wage employment programme as a project to eradicate poverty is conceived mainly to provide additional gainful employment to the unemployed and under-employed. Such employment can also result in the creation of durable assets.

A number of wage employment programmes were designed and implemented during 60s and 70s. The publication, the Rural Development Report — Rural Employment published by NIRD Hyderabad[55] has evaluated these programmes and the following paragraphs provide details of this evaluation.

5.9.1 *Rural Manpower Programme (RMP)* : It started during 1960-61, twenty more during 1968-69. The outlay was estimated at Rs. 150 crores. However, only 20 per cent of this money was provided due to resource crunch. It was estimated that 137 million man-days of employment would be generated in the scheme.

5.9.2 *Crash Scheme for Rural Employment (CSRE)* : The scheme was launched in April 1991 for a period of three years with an annual outlay of Rs. 15 crores. The objective was to provide employment to atleast 1000 persons every year in each of the 350 districts of the country, through labour intensive public works and creation of durable assets.

A sum of Rs. 122.6 crores was spent on this project. Again to the target of 140.7 crores it was estimated that the scheme would generate 316 million man-days of employment as against the target of 315 million man-days. The schemes pertained to road construction, land development and minor irrigation.

The evaluation of this scheme indicated the following :

(i) The benefits in terms of direct employment and asset creation were not found to be too widely scattered.

(ii) Emphasis was only given to road works.

(iii) There was lack of preparedness on the part of the local institutions to implement the projects.

(iv) The floor wages varied between Rs. 150 per day in some States to Rs. 15 per day in other States.

(v) The assets created were found to be non-durable in many cases.

5.9.3 *Pilot Intensive Rural Employment Programme (PIREMP) :* This was started in 1972 for a three-year period in 15 selected CD blocks. The programme generated 18.16 million mandays of employment.

Evaluation : A committee set up in 1974 to review the programme reported that the entire development strategy should be based on labour intensive technologies so that the maximum labour absorption takes place through regular development process, leaving only a small back-log of unemployed for tackling through such employment projects.

5.9.4 *Rural Works Programme (RWP) :* Started during 1970-71, in 54 selected districts of 13 States which were identified as drought prone. The scheme covered 600 lakhs of population and 5.55 sq kms of the area in the country. The object of the scheme was to be achieved through taking up of schemes of long term productive nature in areas prone to recurrent drought and providing employment opportunities to the people in these areas. The programme focussed mainly on the execution of rural works such as medium and minor irrigation, soil conservation and afforestation, road building, drinking water supply and generation of employment opportunities through these rural works.

Evaluation : In the mid-term appraisal of the IV Five Year Plan and also based on the report of the task force for IRDP set up in 1971, the strategy of development under the rural works programme underwent a change after realising that real development of drought prone areas required long term measures and cannot be achieved through such short term projects. Accordingly in 1973 the programme was re-oriented and merged with the long range drought prone area programme.

5.9.5 *Food for Work Programme* : In April 1977, this was taken up as a non-plan scheme with the following objectives :

(i) Generation of additional gainful employment in rural areas.
(ii) Creation of durable community assets and strengthening of the rural infrastructure.
(iii) Utilization of the surplus foodgrains for human resource development.

Evaluation : The following points were brought out : (1) Erratic disbursement of foodgrains or wages, (2) Delays in measurement of rural work, (3) Non-durable nature of the assets created, (4) Inadequate technical supervision, (5) Lack of supervision leading to dilution of technical requirements of the projects, (6) Continuation of the programme on a year to year basis, (7) Lack of attempts on the part of the State governments to prepare shelf of projects and to make adequate financial provision, (8) Only kutcha roads were taken up in the projects which were non-durable.

5.9.6 *National Rural Employment Programme (NREP)* : It was started in October 1980 to replace the then existing food for work programme. From April 1981, NREP became a centrally sponsored plan programme on a 50-50 sharing basis between the Government of India and the State governments. The objectives were : (1) to generate additional gainful employment in rural areas, (2) to create durable and productive community assets, (3) improve the overall quality in rural areas.

This scheme had the following important special features; (i) A shelf of projects and an annual action plan were to be prepared, (ii) Only creation of durable productive community assets can be taken up, (iii) Wages to be paid partly in cash and partly in foodgrains, (iv) Wages to be paid in accordance with the rates fixed under the minimum wages act, (v) 50 per cent of central money was based on the number of rural poor in each State and the balance of 50 per cent on the basis of incidence of rural poverty in each State, (vi) Contractors or middlemen were not permitted to be engaged.

During the VI Five Year Plan a sum of Rs. 1834.25 crores and 20.57 lakh metric tonnes of foodgrains were utilized in the programme. About 1775 million man-days of employment was generated. During the 4 years of the VII Five Year Plan a sum of Rs. 2940 crores was spent to generate 1478 million man-days of employment.

5.9.7 *Rural Landless Employment Guarantee Programme (RLEGP)* : The programme was started in 1983 particularly for providing employment opportunities for the landless during the lean agricultural periods. It was completely a Central Plan Scheme.

REFERENCES

1. *Economic and Political Weekly*, August 21, 1993, pp. 1743-1765.
2. Report of the High Powered Committee appointed by Government of India on Agricultural Policies and Programmes, 1990, *op.cit.*
3. Social Dimensions and post-reform growth in post-reform India emerging trends, pp. 196.
4. Government of India, Economic Survey for the year 1998-99 published by the Ministry of Finance.
5. *Times of India* dated February 23, 2001, pages 1&9.
6. "Government admits poverty reduction not enough", Report in the *Hindu Business Line* of November 14, 2000, p. 2.
7. Dantwala, M.L. and Barmeda, J.N., 1991, "Rural Development Approaches and Issues" in Dantwala (Ed.), *Indian Agricultural Development since independence*, *op. cit.*, p. 436.
8. Government of India, 95th Report of Public Accounts Committee of the Lok Sabha, presented on 25-4-1995, reported by *Deccan Herald* paper on April 26, 1995.
9. Government of India, Planning Commission : Mid term appraisal of the VIII Plan reported by *Deccan Herald* paper dated July 20, 1995, p. 1.
10. Gaur, K.D., 1992, "Effectiveness of the IRDP in eradication of poverty in India" in K.D. Gaur, *Dynamics of Rural Development*, Mittal Publications, New Delhi, 1992, pp. 8-34.
11. Statement by the Honourable Union Minister of State for Planning and Programme Implementation made in Lok Sabha in answering the question on June 3, 1998 and published by *Deccan Herald* paper on June 4, 1998, p. 6.
12. Esakky, S., 1990, "The impact of IRDP on eradication of poverty among weaker sections in Tirunelveli district of Tamil Nadu", Unpublished Ph.D. Thesis, Dept. of Economics, Ayyanad - Janice Ammal College.
13. Hirevenkangouder, L.V., 1983, A scientific investigation of the impact of Dairy development programme of KDDC among small farmers, marginal farmers and agricultural labourers in Bangalore District, Karnataka State. Unpublished, Ph.D. Thesis, Department of Agricultural Extension, University of Agricultural Sciences, Bangalore.
14. Malyadri, P., 1985, Success of IRDP — Myth or Reality, A study : *Kurukshetra*, Vol. **33**(11), pp. 17-20.
15. Balishter and Singh Roshan (1984), Role of lead bank in implementing IRDP in Bichpuri block of Agra district, UP. *Agricultural Situation in India*, Vol . **41**(1).

16. Dhillon, D.S., *et al.* (1985), Monitoring and evaluation of IRDP. *Indian Journal of Extension Education*, Vol. 21 (1&2), pp. 48-52.

17. Sarawgi, A.A., *et al.* (1986), Financing by State Bank of India, Agricultural Development Branch in Patan Block of Jabbalpur District of M.P. under IRDP, *Indian Journal of Agricultural Economics*, Vol. **21**(4), pp. 669.

18. Jain, S.C., 1986, Poverty alleviation programme in India : Some issues of micro-policy. *Indian Journal of Agricultural Economics*, Vol. 41(3), pp. 383-404.

19. Abdul Kareem, K., 1994, Integrated Rural Development Programme in Kerala — An impact analysis, Unpublished Ph.D. Thesis, Department of Agricultural Extension, University of Agricultural Sciences, Bangalore, p. 173.

20. Rathi, V. and Sharada, M.K., 1992, Impact of IRDP on the rural poor, Agricultural Situation in India, Vol. 47(2), pp. 117-119.

21. Kadian, R.S. and Kaushik, C.R., 1993, An impact study of institutional finance under IRDP in Kurukshetra district of Haryana, Ag. Banker, Vol. **16**(1).

22. Devilaxmi, R.R., IRDP and Rural women - the case of panchayats in Kerala, *Indian Journal of Ag. Economics*, Vol. **40**(3), pp. 269-270, 1985.

23. Harikumar, S., IRDP succeeded, *Yojana*, Vol. 28(16), pp. 17-20, 1985.

24. Aziz, A., 1986, IRDP in Karnataka — An evaluation ISEC, Bangalore.

25. Prathap Reddy, K. and Buchanan, K., 1992, Impact of Integrated Rural Development Programme on Rural Poor — A micro study in K.D. Gaur (Ed.) *Dynamics of Rural Development, op. cit.*, pp. 35-49.

26. Rath, N., Loknatha, Garibi Hatao, 1985, Can IRDP do it?, D.R. Shah (Ed), *Alternatives in Rural Development*, Sterling Publishers, New Delhi,

27. Chandra Kavate, M.S., 1985, Tardy implementation of IRDP, *Yojana*, Vol. **29**(19), pp. 13-15,

28. Government of Kerala : State Planning Board : Evaluation Division, Integrated Rural Development Programme : An evaluation study, Trivendrum.

29. Desai, Vasant, 1991, *Rural Development*, Himalaya Publishing House, New Delhi.

30. Ghosh, D.R., 1991, Making IRDP investment efficient, a district study, *Kurukshetra*, Vol. **40**(3), pp. 19-33.

31. Kutti Krishnan, B.C., 1984, A case study of IRDP in Kerala Village, *Indian J. of Ag. Economics*, Vol. **39**(3), pp. 256-259.

32. Tiwari, R.H. and Kanwar, P.C., 1983, IRDP — Can it improve rural income distribution? *Kurukshetra*, Vol. **24** (6), pp. 7.

33. Government of India, Agricultural Statistics At A Glance, 1998-99.

34. United Nations Population Fund Report dated 19-10-1999 published in *Deccan Herald* dated 20-10-1999.

35. Government of India, Economic Survey of India, 1996-97.

36. Government of India, Economic Survey of India 1998-99.

37. Srivastava Druv and T. Haque, 1990, "Technology, Agricultural Growth and Regional Imbalances", IARI, New Delhi

38. FAO : Agriculture Production Year Book, 1994.

39. Rao, V.M. and Deshpande, R.S., 1991, Agricultural production - pace and pattern of growth in M.L.Dantwala (Ed.). *Indian Agricultural Development since Independence, op.cit.*, pp. 75-92, 1991.

40. Official reappraisal of Agricultural Sector made in 1995 as reported in *Deccan Herald* paper, dated April 30, 1995.

41. Sidhu, D.S. and Singh, A.G., 1991, Technological change in Indian Agriculture in M.L. Dantwala (Ed.). *India's Agricultural Development since Independence, op. cit.*, pp. 117-136.

42. Dantwala, M.L., 1991, Strategy of Agricultural Development since Independence in M.L. Dantwala (Ed.), *Indian Agricultural Development since Independence, op. cit.*, pp. 1-16, 1991.

43. Centre for Monitoring Indian Economy Pvt. Ltd., 1995, India's Agricultural Sector — A compendium of statistics.

44. Dantwala, M.L., 1991, Agrarian Structure and Agrarian Relation in India in M.L. Dantwala (Ed.), *India's Agricultural Development since Independence*, 1991, *op. cit.*, pp. 51-71.

45. Government of India, 1985, *VII Five Year Plan*, 1985-90, Vol. 2, Planning Commission, New Delhi.

46. Government of India, 1995, Budget speech of the Union Finance Minister delivered on 16-3-1995 in Parliament at the time of presenting the Union budget of 1995-96 published by *Economic Times*, paper dated 17th March 1995, p. 1.

47. Muzumdar N.H. and Menon, K.A., 1991, Saving and capital formation in Agricultural Sector, A review in M.L. Dantwala (Ed.), *Indian Agricultural Development since Independence, op. cit.*, pp. 207-242.

48. Eshwara Prasad, Y., Ramanna, R. and Lalitha Achotha, 1997, Performance of IRDP in a Drought Prone District of Andhra Pradesh, Pandey and Jalal (Eds.), *Rural Development in India : Issues and Policies*, Vol. II, Anmol Publications, Delhi, pp. 563-583.

49. Pande, G.C. and Pandey, P.C., 1991, Drought Prone Areas and Rural

Development — A review of policy and programme in Pandey and Jalal (Eds.), *Rural Development in India*, Vol. 1, *op. cit.*, pp. 129-148.

50. Subbaraydu, C., Sambashiva Rao, B. and Narayana, E.V., 1991, "Impact of IRDP on income and employment through milch cattle distribution scheme" in Pandey and Jalal (Eds.) *Rural Development in India — Issues and Policies*, Vol. 1, *op. cit.*, pp. 28-29.

51. Verma, Satish, and Rajendra Singh (1991) 'Self employment scheme — An evaluation in Pandey and Jalal (Eds.) *Rural Development in India — Issues and Policies*, *op. cit.*, pp. 43-63.

52. Government of India, 1995, Budget speech of the Union Finance Minister delivered in Parliament on 16-3-1995 at the time of presenting the Union Budget for 1995-96, Budget speech reported by *Economic Times* paper dated 17th March 1995, p. 1.

53. Ahuja, Kanta, 1991, Agricultural labour and Rural employment in M.L. Dantwala (Ed.), *Indian Agricultural Development since Independence*, 2nd Ed. *op. cit.*, pp. 367-398.

54. Sundaram, K., 1984, Registrar General's population projections, 1981-2001. An appraisal and an alternative scenario, *Economic and Political Weekly*, Vol. 19(34), Aug. 25.

55. Padamanabhan, M. and Swaminathan, H.L., 1994, Rural development report — Rural employment, National Insitute of Rural Development, Hyderabad (AP), p. 1.

56. Government of India, 1985, Mid term appraisal of the VIII Plan, 'Unpublished Report Quoted by *Deccan Herald* paper on July 29th, 1995.

57. Rao, G.V.K., 1979, "Employment expansion among agricultural labour and small farm households — An Indian experience", paper presented at the ILO Seminar organised at the University of Agricultural Sciences, Bangalore on Agricultural Labour Employment.

58. Dantwala, M.L., 1978, Some neglected issues in employment, planning, *Economic and Political Weekly*, Vol. 13(6-7), Annl. No.

59. Mellor, John, W., 1975, *The Impact of New Agricultural Technology on Employment and Income Distribution — Concepts and Policy, op. cit.*

60. Government of India, VIII Plan Document, 1992.

61. Malik, R.S., Punia, P.K. and Deeppunia, 1986, Achievements, accelerators and barriers in TRYSEM, *Khadi Gramodyog*, **36**(6).

62. Ramdas Reddy, J., 1987, "TRYSEM in a drought prone area", *Khadi Gramodyog*, **33**(4).

63. Shripathi, K.P., 1989, "Training of rural youth for Self-employment", *Kurukshetra*, **37**(7).

64. Singh, S.K., 1989, "TRYSEM and rural employment generation", *Kurukshetra*, **37**(7).

65. Shivalingegowda, N.S., 1995, An analysis of poverty alleviation programmes in Bangalore Rural District of Karnataka, Unpublished Ph.D. Thesis, Dept. of Ag. Extn., Univ. Agril. Sci., Bangalore.

66. Vallabh Reddy, G.P., 1985, "TRYSEM programme — A study in Madhya Pradesh", *Kurukshetra*, **33**(12).

PART II

PRAGMATIC RURAL DEVELOPMENT FOR RURAL POVERTY ALLEVIATION

6

ATTACKING RURAL POVERTY THROUGH RURAL DEVELOPMENT
Some Basic Concepts

6.1 PREAMBLE

Rural development has always been a challenging task to perform, namely; in the upliftment of rural poor, one is required to fight against the grim situation. According to Mukerji, the principle features of this unfortunate situation include "Poverty of the people and their governments; a very low level of production due largely to the employment of primitive methods of production; lack of resources for investment on development and a very low rate of capital formation; considerable unemployment and more underemployment; physical and cultural isolation of most rural communities that constitute the bulk of the population and their social and community life often in a state of disintegration and decay; a high percentage of illiteracy; and finally the very low capacity of the rural people to take advantage of science and technology because they have not the resources nor the knowledge[1]".

6.2 ORIGIN

The roots of Rural Development ideology can be traced to the value which Indian religion and philosophy attached to the individual development and in the Indian tradition of recognising the village community as the custodian of human values.

Mahatma Gandhi recognised the need for rural development

which he called as village reconstruction. He laid so much importance on rural development that he made it an integral part of his philosophy of improvement of rural areas by calling it as "Grama Sudhara Programme". Gandhiji's ideas emanated during the period when practically no attention was paid by the educated to the development of the rural poor. After Gandhiji gave a call for fighting rural poverty by constructive programme and after "Gurudeva". Tagore endorsed these ideas by initiating rural development work through his famous Sriniketan programme, world-wide thinking gradually took place on this crucial issue of attacking rural poverty through national/ international rural development programmes.

6.3 WORLDWIDE PROGRAMME

On a world-wide basis, rural development work was first initiated as Community Development by the World Bodies in the middle of the 20th Century after the Second World War. This was primarily to face the aftermaths of war torn countries and to help the rural poor in these countries. Community Development was then described as a process, method, programme and movement and Theories of Community Development were also developed. Community Development was thought of (a) as a process of change from the traditional way of living of rural communities to progressive ways of living; (b) as a method, by which people can be assisted to develop through their own capacity and resources; (c) as a programme, for accomplishing certain activities in fields concerning the welfare of rural people, and (d) as a movement for progress with a certain ideological content.

Community Development was primarily guided by the western trained economists including those who belonged to Less Developed Countries (LDCs). The entire process largely depends upon National Planning which emphasised mostly the matter of planning investment to generate growth of national income.

During the development decades of 1950s and 1960s the United Nations gave a lead to this programme and recommended a 5 per cent growth rate of National Income as an important goal to be achieved. This target was almost accomplished by a majority of

LDCs and this increase in growth had been nearly double the rate of growth in the now advanced countries during their days of rapid industrial progress and was also double the rate of growth in developing countries, in the century or so before World War-II. But this high rate of growth of national income did not enjoy development in the sense of wide and deep improvements in welfare for the rural poor.

Benzamin Higgins has remarked as follows :

> "On the contrary, unemployment grew, inflation accelerated, the number of mal-nourished and under-nourished people increased, the number of illiterate people also increased, there were more children out of school than in school, health targets were not attained and inequality of income distribution became worse than ever. It was clear that high rates of growth had not brought clear cut progress towards more effective and more representative government, more respect for civil liberties and more social mobility or equality of opportunity. It eventually became evident that the 'models' offered by Western educated economists or the developed countries themselves seemed less than ideal as even those countries could not sustain their own development indefinitely. Some of these concepts were addressed at the World Conference on Agrarian Reform and Rural Development (WCARRD)—which was convened by FAO in 1979. Since that time there has been a break through from the past. WCARRD marked a turning point in the conceptualisation of strategies and policies to alleviate rural poverty post-WCARRD strategies are based on key integral elements of growth with equity, redistribution of economic and political power and effective people's participation through their own organisations[2&3]."

In the meanwhile, the World Bank[4] had prepared a policy paper on rural development work with the specific idea to attack rural poverty. It involves extending the benefits of development to the poorest among those who seek a livelihood in the rural areas. The group includes small farmers, tenants and the landless.

6.4 REQUIREMENTS FOR SUCCESSFUL RURAL DEVELOPMENT

Since rural development is primarily initiated to alleviate rural poverty, it must be carefully designed and developed to increase production in rural areas as well as increase production per unit. Attacking rural poverty involves a three pronged strategy; viz.,

1. Labour intensive growth in agriculture and allied enterprises and rural industry,
2. Access to improved social services for the rural poor, and
3. Providing safety nets to the poor to protect them from natural calamities and risky technologies.[5]

6.5 TARGETTED GROUP APPROACH

Effective rural development work can be undertaken only by identifying targetted groups among the rural poor for whom special measures to raise production of agriculture and other enterprises along with the income increase can be designed and in whose case the benefits resulting, direct and indirect, can also be identified and measured. The pragmatic process of economic growth to alleviate rural poverty would require emphasis on three aspects: (1) The direct effects of new agricultural technology on employment, (2) The expenditure pattern incident to the increased income, from new agriculture technology, (3) The employment content in producing the goods experiencing increased demand.[5]

6.6 TECHNOLOGY TRANSFER

Transfer of technology therefore becomes an important and rather a central concern of a successful rural development programme for attacking rural poverty. Where technology is available, it is often not made use of because development educational services, support services, like credit and input supply, transport, storage, marketing facilities etc. are not adequate[4]. Research specially oriented to problems of rural poor and local demonstrations on poor farmers fields are also the prerequisites in this context. Through good planning, providing adequate budgets and fixing workable targets are essential factors. These alone are not sufficient to deliver the goods in a rural development programme. Paul Leagans an eminent extensionist pleads; "Rural development in democratic societies is not a matter only of plans and statistics, targets and budgets, technology and method, material aid and professional staff, or agencies and organisations to administer them. Rather, it is an effective use of these mechanisms as educational means for changing the mind and actions of people in such ways that "they help themselves attain economic and social improvements. Hence, the process is one of working with people not for them; of helping people become self-reliant not dependent on others; of making people the central actors in the drama, not stage hands or spectators; in short, helping people by means of education to put useful knowledge to work for them[6].

6.7 PEOPLE'S PARTICIPATION

The important feature of rural development is that it cannot be delivered to a passive group. Where the programmes sought are in the field of agriculture, health, education, public works or any other, the active participation and assistance of the rural poor must be solicited if the expected changes are to be effective, widespread and of a permanent nature. Local organisation's work, especially to promote cooperative efforts by people becomes essential to obtain people's involvement and participation in a rural development activity. It is only by encouraging the rural poor to involve them in the programme of improving themselves, through their own active effort, that we can assist them to develop their capacities and self help, a group way of life in them and enthusiasm in the rural areas. This then makes it as essential with rural development programme to attack rural poverty should not only have the approval but also the active participation of the rural poor located in hundreds of thousands of rural communities.

To achieve this action requires a very carefully designed development programme for educating and enthusing the rural poor.

6.8 SUPPORTIVE GOVERNMENT POLICIES

Active participation by the rural poor in developmental activities should not mean that rural poor can create satisfactory programmes to reduce their poverty by themselves. They are primarily poor with all the deficiencies of the required resources, expertise and protection. It is, therefore, essential that along with their active participation, supportive national policies, assistance and guidance are equally essential. Often, the poorest areas are overlooked by such policies or the subsistence farm is not treated as a system. Research and administration on a local basis to facilitate adoption is required in all these areas.

6.9 ADMINISTERING RURAL DEVELOPMENT PROGRAMME

Equally challenging is the task of organising and planning for effective rural development work. This involves pragmatic regional planning, strong central coordination, effective local level organisations and the equally difficult task of active participation of the rural poor in this entire task of planning and implementation. As pointed by the World Bank few countries have been able to achieve these ideals so far[4].

In bringing about an effective rural development work, coordination at the rural level is very crucial and this can be achieved only by a substantial increase in decentralisation and promoting local control of the programme. People's participation, which is often stated as essential for a sustained rural development work, can be only promoted by encouraging local rather than centralised control[4].

Effective local planning envisages the collection of local statistics on regional basis and its effective use of local surveys and resource inventories forms the most important basis of programme development and implementation[4].

Assisting rural poor to work in groups provides an organised basis for handling many of the requirements for providing access to services for large number of rural poor. Such an arrangement also provides a measure of involvement through participation and enables the rural poor for collective efforts for getting credit, input supplies, delivery of marketable surpluses[4].

It should also be understood that the rural development work has always been a challenging one. The present day challenge is however primarily concerned with eradication of poverty of rural masses and in the difficult task of helping them to come above the poverty line in as short time as possible.

6.10 GLOBALIZATION WITH SAFETY NETS ESSENTIAL

Rural development recognises the true and pivotal place of rural improvement in the total development of a nation. It has deep concern and commitment over the fact that the majority of the rural poor who stay in villages are living in conditions of extreme poverty, ill-health and illiteracy or poorly organised for effective participation in programmes of their own welfare and lack technical knowledge and have no resources except human capital of spending their economic conditions. The aim of rural development is to focus attention on the philosophy that the nation will not really progress no matter how fast is the development may be in the field of industries, transport, railways, shipping etc., unless the rural areas also progress simultaneously with equal speed. Rural development cannot be promoted by the Government which will be active in intervening industry. Since, this approach is counter productive, if the government is inactive in education and health. To compete in the world, land reforms and micro credit are positive factors. Globalisation by itself is no solution to rural development. It is essential to have safety nets for the poor as in the industrialised countries of Western Europe to take care of rural poor when things go wrong for one reason or another[7].

6.11 OPERATIVE OBJECTIVES

The operative objectives of rural development extend beyond any particular sector. They encompass improved productivity, increased employment and thus greater incomes for the masses as well as minimum acceptable standards of food, shelter, education and health as per norms prescribed. Therefore, a national programme of rural development should include the combination or a mix of various activities including projects to raise agricultural production, create increased employment, improve health and education and provide safety nets for the rural poor, develop communication and improve housing.

REFERENCES

1. Mukerji, B., 1961, *Community Development in India*, I Edn. Orient Longmans, Bombay.
2. Higgins, Benjamin, 1977, "Economic Development and Cultural Change Seamless web or Patchwork Quilt", University of Ottawa, in Essays on Economic Development and Cultural Change in Honor of Bert. Hoselitz, Chicago, University of Chicago Press, pp. 99-100.
3. ESCAP 1985, The Rural Poor — Human Capital for Nation Building — A review of the EXCAP/FAO program on social benefits generated by projects Targeting the rural poor, Bangkok, UN.
4. World Bank, Jan, 1975, Rural Development Sector Policy paper.
5. Mellor, John W., 1975, The Impact of New Agricultural Technology on Employment and income distribution concepts and policy—occasional paper No. 81, Employment and Income Distribution Project, Dept. of Ag. Economics, Cornell Univ., USA.
6. Leagans, J. Paul, 1961, Extension Education for Community Development in Extension Education in Community Development, I Edn. Directorate of Extension, Ministry of Food and Agriculture, GOI, New Delhi.
7. Sen, Amartya, 1998, Globalisation without safety nets for poor is absurd". Statement made in his first press conference reported in *Deccan Herald* paper, Oct. 16, 1998.

7

ISSUES TO BE CONSIDERED FOR SUCCESSFUL RURAL DEVELOPMENT

7.1 PREAMBLE

Fom the information furnished earlier on rural development and rural poverty, it should be clear that the job of rural development in attacking rural poverty embraces a mix of activities evolved around what can be called a systems approach or a holistic approach which also necessitates simultaneous action on several issues involved.

Issues of rural development are the view points on some important items of work related to rural development, which may differ from time to time. A pertinent point in this regard is that the issues involved in each country depend on the prevailing constraints at a point of time and must be aimed at removing these constraints so as to support the programmes in that country which again will be dependent on the nature and content of rural development programme designed and operated. The issues also vary according to the political, social and economic circumstances of each country.

Issues involved in any country are also primarily related to the ways in which the present rural development programmes are formulated particularly with respect to provide the needed interactions between the modern and traditional sectors.

According to World Bank (1975), there are three major points involved in considering issues for rural development for attacking rural poverty. "Firstly, the rate of transfer of the poor out of low production agriculture and related enterprises into more rewarding ones has been slow and given their relative size of the modern sector in most developing countries, it will remain slow. Secondly, the mass of people in the rural areas of developing countries, face varying degrees of poverty; their position is likely to get worse if population expands at unprecedented rates, while limitations continue to be imposed by available resources, technology and institutions. Thirdly, rural areas have labour, land and at least some capital, which if mobilised will reduce poverty and improve the quality of life. This implies fuller development of existing resources including the construction of the infrastructure such as roads, irrigation works, introduction of new production technology and the creation of new types of institutions and organisations[1]".

The major plank of attack on rural poverty can be achieved, provided two goals are reached simultaneously. (1) Production in rural areas is increased substantially which includes agriculture, allied enterprises and village industries. (2) Along with these the income level of the rural poor should also be raised simultaneously to bring them above the poverty line[2]. These two goals depend upon the technology breakthrough in agriculture and other enterprises in such a way that more employment is also generated for the rural poor. Besides these basic requirements which are applicable to any part of the world, there are some additional requirements for the development of poor in third world countries like India, where population is large and most of farmers' land holdings are very small. The latter categories are also related to some important considerations which can be grouped under five broad classes, namely; (1) Economic concerns, (2) Equity concerns, (3) Employment concerns, (4) Energy concerns and (5) Ecology concerns[3].

There are also issues which are related to the impact of modern technology on employment generation. The serious problems of developing countries in attacking rural unemployment and under-employment, demand that the modern technologies which bring about labour economy, will have to be concurrently accompanied by measures for creation of alternate means of providing employment in rural areas. In the absence of such steps, considerable hardship can be the only result from such technology breakthrough which may substitute capital and machines for human labour. This will lead to improved requirement for an employment assessment before any technology can be promoted for large scale use[3].

Factors related to technologies causing adverse effect on ecology also need special attention in the implementation of successful rural development programmes. These cover areas like, the soil erosion and loss of plant and genetic resources, vulnerability to insect pests and disease epidemics arising from genetic homogeneity, destruction of soil fertility and soil degradation and pollution caused by the continuing erratic use of fertilizers and chemicals and heavy doses of fertilizers[3].

The issues involved relating to modern technology are, therefore, complex which require integration of various kinds of consideration including ecology, economies to employment generation, energy and generation of social equity in the development of modern technologies and in its promotional efforts.[3]

There are also several other important issues involved other than those related to technologies in implementing this difficult task of attacking rural poverty[2, 3 & 4]. These are :

1. Issues related to planning and implementing rural development programmes.
2. Issues related to participatory development.
3. Issues related to access of public promoted services by the rural poor in obtaining those services.
4. Issues involved in providing safety nets to the rural poor to cover them from the risks involved by natural calamities and other risks.
5. Issues relating to gender and poverty.

A brief description of these issues is briefly given in the following paragraphs.

7.2 GROWTH AND EQUITY

In attacking rural poverty it is not only the extent of increase of G.N.P. of a country *per se* but to what extent the rural poor have got their share in this increase of national income. The specific points involved under this issue are :

(a) To what extent the national plan has considered the development of equity growth related to rural poor with its special programmes along with the other projects meant for increasing the national growth. Both these programmes have to be taken up simultaneously in a unified manner to achieve the result of improving economic growth of the rural poor.

(b) The appropriate strategy should be such that development investment, administration and management are tilted in favour of the rural poor. The poor cannot forever be mere beneficiaries of special programmes; they must become dominant partners in growth.

(c) To make the agrarian structure and the agrarian system more egalitarian apart from redistribution of land, other equally important measures like social control of underground water, consolidation of holdings, land levelling and promoting solidarity of weaker sections should be taken up[9].

7.3 SUSTAINABLE GROWTH

Over the longer period rural welfare cannot be improved continuously unless economic growth in rural areas significantly exceeds the rural population growth. Sustainable growth calls for a development policy that does not compromise the welfare of future generations and it is recently, public policy and international donor programme have largely neglected the issue of sustainability. Instead spurts of growth have been based on external borrowings, inflationary financing, rapid depletion of natural resources and the degradation of ecological systems of such growth cannot be lasting.

When growth depletes, capital gets eventually slowed down.

Capital in this context, includes not only plant machinery and infrastructure but also natural resources such as land, water, minerals and human capital in the form of knowledge, health and social organisation. Thus, to ensure sustainable growth, the future strategy will need emphasis on both sound environmental management and human resources development. Unlike physical capital, human capital grows through use. Moreover the health and education of parents improves the health and education of their children. Properly managed renewable natural resources can last forever. However, there is a pervasive tendency to consume or destroy through over use.

7.4 IDENTIFICATION OF TARGET GROUPS

The World Bank paper (1975) makes a strong plea for specifying target of groups as follows : "A good programme for attacking rural poverty requires that target groups are specified among the rural poor for whom specific measures to raise production and income can be designed and in whose case the resulting flow of benefits, direct and indirect, is both identifiable and potentially measurable. The notion of target groups lies at the root of definition of rural development as a separable and distinct component of general development strategy. It provides that necessary focus on groups of the rural population, in terms of whose well-being policy actions and programmes, can be designed and evaluated. Target groups are best defined in the context of the individual country. However, a basic standard for identifying target groups would be the income necessary to cover minimum nutritional requirements and essential non-food expenses. In addition, an income equal to or less than one-third of the national average would be an appropriate additional criteria to allow for extreme relative poverty in developing countries[1]".

7.5 EMPLOYMENT

Eminent Agricultural Scientist M.S. Swaminathan (1985), raised this issue as follows : Developing countries with large rural population have already serious problems of unemployment and under-employment. This is reflected in the unplanned migration of rural poor to towns and cities seeking opportunities to earn their daily bread. Therefore technologies which reduce labour use will have to be concurrently accompanied by the creation of alternative avenues of employment. Unless job destruction and job creation are concurrent events, considerable human hardship can be the outcome from the adoption of technologies which substitute capital and machines for human labour[3]. In several countries of Asia, undernutrition or calorie inadequacy is the major problem. This in turn tends to be more related to inadequate purchasing power rather than to the lack of an adequate supply of food in the market. Hence, an employment revolution is important for families without assets in the form of land or livestock to derive economic and nutritional benefit from the green revolution. New technologies should hence be subjected to an employment impact analysis before they are recommended for large scale adoption[3]".

7.6 ECONOMICS

The adoption of technology relating to limited capital conditions assumes importance and also government policies on input and output potentials become crucial to sustain the interests of poor people. Under limited capital conditions, poor farmers decisions on technology change and acceptance will always be based upon net return per unit area and not by gross yield per unit area[3].

7.7 DEVELOPMENT OF EXISTING RESOURCES

Present Plan programmes on attacking rural poverty should recognize that rural areas have labour, land and at least some capital which must be mobilized properly so that they could reduce poverty and improve quality of rural areas. This means the need to utilize fuller development of resources existing now and improving the infrastructure development needs of the rural areas[1].

7.8 DECENTRALIZED PLANNING

Programmes for attacking rural poverty have to be developed and planned for each region separately, which necessitates work at decentralized level[1]. Without a firm understanding of the variations in natural endowment, soil and climate, social and cultural milieu, historical legacy and group alignment, decentralized planning will not be pragmatic[4]. Decentralization should include all aspects of local level planning, its formulation, implementation, monitoring etc. For effective and purposeful rural development, "such planning necessitates the collection of statistics on a regional rather than a sectoral basis and the use of regional surveys and resource inventories. Inter-regional allocations of technical and financial resources must be decided in relation to resource endowments, the domestic and foreign funds available, a balance of equity and growth considerations and mutually acceptable arrangements for sharing responsibilities between the central and local authorities[1]".

7.9 STRONG COORDINATION

Programmes for attacking rural poverty cut across different departments and therefore strong coordination is required at various levels. It starts with coordination at the central level which is basic to any successful programme for attacking rural poverty. This is a reflection both of the political nature of many of the decisions that must be made and of the need to coordinate the activities of different sectors or departments organized along sectoral lines. Coordination at local level is a must for successful implementation of all programmes. This is because there is a growing evidence indicating that all multi-sectoral programmes are implemented most effectively when properly coordinated at the operational level[1 & 4].

7.10 LOCAL LEVEL CONTROL

There has to be an effective local level organisation with full responsibility for operating the programme. Community involvement which is essential to sustained development process is greatly facilitated by local level control rather than by the centralised control. This has been the idea behind the establishment of Zilla Parishads or District Councils. A special advantage of this local control is that the problems of the community, as perceived by the local people, are discussed by local officials, and are easily accepted for immediate decision and action[1].

7.11 INVOLVEMENT OF LOCAL LEVEL INSTITUTIONS

Participation of the people in the regional planning and implementation of the programmes to attack rural poverty is essential. To enable this, it is necessary to enlist the involvement of local level institutions functioning in the area, both governmental and non-governmental ones. Promoting new NGO's in the area to assist in this direction will also be helpful.

7.12 ACCESS TO RURAL POOR OF THE SERVICES ALREADY PROVIDED BY THE GOVERNMENT

This is an important area which has direct bearing on the improvement of rural poor. Although the governments have provided various kinds of institutes in rural areas to provide services to rural poor, the rural poor are still out of reach of these various institutes. To enable them to utilise the services from locally established institutes, it is necessary to make available a special help providing management service to rural poor through various means. This then becomes an important issue in implementing programmes for attacking rural poverty[5].

7.13 PARTICIPATORY DEVELOPMENT

This issue is of recent origin. It is based on the recognition that the key to success in any programme for alleviating rural poverty is the rural poor persons themselves and their active participation in these programmes. This implies that given the opportunity and incentives, the rural poor will adopt new technologies which increase yields and also undertake activities that generate extra income and thus provide the means of striking to break the cycle of poverty. This view implies that the rural poor be involved in the anti-poverty programme and be enabled to participate in the decision making process and implementing the decisions. This principle is closely related to the entrepreneurship development and increasing achievement motivation of the rural poor[6].

7.14 PROVIDING SAFETY NETS TO THE RURAL POOR

The rural poor often have difficulty in obtaining capital needed for the use of new technology. But even more important is the fact that they face serious problems of risk and uncertainty, aversion which make them reluctant to borrow or purchase inputs even when other conditions are favourable. Thus the rural poor often choose lower income yielding but more stable crop combinations and technologies. Thus policy to reduce uncertainty and increase farmers' ability to absorb risk are important for improving the incomes of poor rural people. These policies may include orientation of research to reduce risk and uncertainty; providing access to credit on terms which reduce risk and uncertainty as well as development and provision of income stabilisation schemes. The important point for policy is that simply providing access to credit, may not be a sufficient condition for widespread participation of rural poor in adopting income increasing technology[2].

7.15 IMPROVED SOCIAL SERVICES

Regarding this issue, the World Bank Paper (1975) states that "The need for special intervention to raise rural production and income applies also to the provision of social and other services such as health and education. Poverty is reflected in poor nutrition, inadequate shelter and low health standards. These affect not only the quality of life but also the productivity of rural people. In particular, there is a need for nutrition and preventive health programmes, including improved water supplies and sanitation. Better education is an important element and may also provide an opportunity for the rural young to escape from poverty. In order to remedy both quantitative and qualitative educational deficiency, increased use of basic education is considered imperative. Thus special effort is needed to provide appropriate social and economic infrastructure for the rural poor and it is important to integrate these components into an effective programme at attacking rural poverty. Without a concerted effort, rural poverty will remain pervasive.[1]"

7.16 PROVIDING RURAL INFRASTRUCTURE

Rural poverty and immobility are inter related. Lack of proper roads connecting villages and the related problem of lack of market facilities for the proper marketing of agricultural produce from rural areas, are responsible for increasing the rural poverty. In the absence of these facilities rural poor are forced to engage in distress sales at the time of harvest in the village itself. Thus rural poverty is not only due to lack of resources but also due to isolation and when poverty is accompanied by absence of these facilities, road to progress is totally blocked and poverty gets petrified[7].

7.17 GENDER AND POVERTY

Inequalities persist in the social and economic status of rural women and men. Women also play a vital role in the development of rural economy. Women's labour force participation and their relative contribution to total family income are higher in households with lower economic status. The poorer the family, the more it depends on the earnings of its female members. In very poor households women's capacities to work, their health, knowledge and skill are very crucial for family survival. In the rural poor families, which live below poverty line, the women may be the main or only earners. Thirty five per cent of such households below the poverty level are headed by women. Hence, employment opportunities for poor women and efforts to increase the production of women workers, particularly those in the primary sector, requires greater attention[8].

REFERENCES

1. World Bank, 1975, Rural Development—Sector Policy Paper, Washington, D.C., U.S.A., pp. 3-4.
2. Mellor, John, W., 1975, The impact of new agricultural technology on employment and income distribution—concepts and policies, *op. cit.*
3. Swaminathan, M.S., 1985, Achieving rural-urban harmony in agricultural development, Guest lecture series, No. 3, Institute of Rural Management, Anand, Gujarat, pp. 5-8.
4. Dantwala, M.L. and Barmeda, 1991, Rural Development, approaches and issues in Dantwala (Ed.), *Indian Agriculture Development since Independence, op. cit.*, pp. 425-451.
5. Coombs and Ahmed, 1974, *Attacking Rural Poverty, op. cit.*
6. United Nations Economic and Social Commission for Asia and Pacific, 1985, The rural poor — human capital for nation building, Bangkok.
7. Government of India, Report of High Powered Committee on Agricultural Policies and Programmes, 1990, Mimeograph report.
8. The World Bank, *Gender and Poverty in India*, World Bank, New Delhi, 1995.
9. Dantwala, M.L., 1991, Strategies of Agricultural Development since independence in M.L Dantwala (ed), *Indian Agricultural Development since Independence*, Oxford & IBH Pub. Co. Pvt. Ltd.

8

MODELS OF ECONOMIC GROWTH AND THEIR EFFECTS ON RURAL DEVELOPMENT

8.1 THEORIES OF ECONOMIC GROWTH DURING THE COMMUNITY DEVELOPMENT ERA

With the initiation of Community Development idea in the 1950s, theories of economic growth that might promote rural development were also thought of. For over two decades, starting from the 1950s, development planning was in the hands of Western trained economists, including those who were nationals of the less developed countries. They mostly relied on the theory of economic growth depending on increased national income. Much of the then predominant theories of economic growth in low income countries as well as the bulk of the multi-sectoral planning models which had been important in planning were derived from the Harrod-Domar type growth models, developed for analysis of growth in high income countries and from Feldman-Mahalanobis models for auto-archaic growth of the Soviet type.[1] These models depicted growth as the function of increase in capital stock and emphasised allocation of resources to capital goods industries at the expense of consumer goods industries such as agriculture. These theories, pleaded that once there is economic growth in the country, the trickle down effect will automatically start and help in reducing poverty, both urban and rural. In this connection an ESCAP publication comments as follows.

"One might have thought, then that the first development decade would have been regarded as a howling success. Instead it was a miserable failure".[2]

"In part the disappointment and frustration arose from the wide difference in performance masked by the average rate of growth of LDCs as a whole; some of the largest and poorest countries faired worst. But there was still a more disturbing element of the experience of the 1960s. Even countries with quite respectable rates of growth of national income did not enjoy development in the sense of wide and deep improvements in welfare for the masses of the population. While economists did not talk much about such things, it was clear that high rates of growth had not brought clear-cut progress towards more effective and more representative government, more respect for civil liberties and more social mobility or equality of opportunity. In general, the approach of the 1960s assumed that human resources could be upgraded by promoting essential social services that would eventually result in equitable distribution with rising and diversified consumption for all. Most important it assumed that countries could stimulate development through planning i.e., from the top down. One of the most popular ways of accomplishing this at first was through 'community development' based on the assumption that people's resources within communities were homogeneous. The popular approach to development at that time interpreted the concept of 'people's participation to mean that masses would participate as producers, adopting the skills and attitudes found in developed countries; it viewed as premature their attempts at obtaining larger share of per capita income for themselves. Eventually though, the people would become involved in development and thus increase their income through various political activities of the State. It eventually became evident that the model offered by economists of the Western countries themselves seemed less than ideal as even these countries could not sustain their own development indefinitely. Perhaps most importantly, it was recognized that development involved many non-economic factors and that the elimination of poverty involved more than an increase in wealth".

The measures involve the redirection of policies and programmes which would change the distribution of income as well as of economic and political power. This is necessary because the most complex and politically sensitive elements in national development strategies are not technical production questions, which can often be solved with available resources and technology, but questions concerning the distribution of income and the vigorous measures necessary to motivate the rural poor and give them greater command over productive assets and food. This redistribution is required to alleviate rural poverty and eradicate conditions of severe under-nutrition. The policy objectives and strategies include access to land and water, people's participation, integration of women in rural development, access to inputs, markets and services, establishment of non-farm rural activities, education, training and extension.

8.2 NEW THEORIES HIGHLIGHTING TARGET ORIENTED APPROACH

"Finally, it became recognised that poverty has many social and cultural dimensions in addition to economic deprivation. The poor are not different from other fellow villagers primarily because of their low income, but because poverty has become a way of life, a sub-culture, the values of which maintained poverty and propagate it when passed on to the children of the poor. As a result of identifying such poverty, some countries have begun to place more emphasis on community action rather than on employment policies and redistribution of income. Out of this approach has emerged a new emphasis on finding solutions to poverty that are locally based and that involve both economic and social development[2]".

8.3 MELLOR'S SIMULATION MODEL FOR ECONOMIC DEVELOPMENT OF THIRD WORLD COUNTRIES WHERE AGRICULTURE IS DOMINATING

According to Mellor (1975), the capital oriented theories of growth will have merit only in countries where agriculture offers very little opportunity for efficiency in increasing technological change. He comments regarding poor development in economic theories useful for third world countries where agriculture is predominant. According to him, the process of economic growth with a major role for agriculture should have three important areas namely (1) The influence of modern agricultural technology on employment, (2) Pattern of expenditure which is related in increasing income from the modern agricultural technology and (3) The quantum of employment required in producing the goods which will be in demand. He, therefore, suggests a simulated model of economic development for third world countries which are having agriculture as an important industry. His model focusses on change in agriculture as an essential factor for higher employment strategy of economic growth. This is because the key role to be played by the new agricultural technology due to (1) need for higher expenditure on food from increasing incomes of low income people and (2) A prevailing high cost of increased agricultural production till more efficient production technology is made available. He further suggests that in the earlier stages of economic development the new technologies provide only a small proportion of increased income to agricultural labour force through increased employment. In spite of this small increase in labour it helps the poor sections of the country if the agricultural technologies are adopted on a large area. Nevertheless, besides the improvement in agricultural technology additional sources of employment are required not only to create more employment and welfare objectives but also to provide equilibrium between the increased output of agricultural commodities and the increased demand required to maintain remunerative prices for agricultural production. He proposes that the increased employment in non-foodgrain agricultural commodities and non-agricultural sector like infrastructure development and growth of rural industry are required for sustenance of the green revolution and for reducing rural poverty.

Mellor further advocated his economic model for India which concentrates on the development of foodgrains and non-foodgrain agricultural sector and also calculated non-agricultural employment as residual.

In his model, Mellor provides an important place for non-foodgrain agricultural use, development of improved infrastructure like roads and electricity, small scale industry for increase is assured employment in the rural areas, which will be experiencing rapid increase in incomes and consumer demands. This Mellor's model suggests a commitment to technological change in agriculture as the engine of growth, to increased investment in rural infrastructure focussing improving roads and electrification on a massive scale and developing small scale industry in rural areas. Mellor recommends 10 important policies for employment oriented growth as a corollary to his simulation model. These are :

1. Practices and sequencing for agricultural production increase.
2. Fostering the rural poor.
3. Developing small scale industries in rural areas.
4. Potentials and role of integrated rural development.
5. The place of rural public works.
6. Rural development problems and prospects.
7. Price policy related to agriculture.
8. Land reforms and the multiplier effects.
9. Sound welfare programmes in perspective.
10. Rural education.

8.4 INDIA'S PLANNING APPROACHES FOR RURAL DEVELOPMENT

When India started the Planning approach in 1950, it primarily relied on the Mahalanobis model which believed that the greatest good of the greatest number can be achieved only by expanding the role of the public sector by imposing steady control over the importance of production and by concentrating production in large scale industries. This approach also thought that there will be a trickle down effect helping the development of poor classes, once the national economy improves. The Seventh Plan too emphasised growth with social justice.[4] It was realised that a sustainable strategy of poverty alleviation has to be based on increasing the production, employment opportunities in the process of growth itself. This approach is still being continued with some change calling it as liberalised economic planning since the Eighth Plan. Some change which was introduced from the Third Plan was the specific attention to the category of rural poor. It should be separately given through the rural development programme which was taken up throughout the country from the Sixth Plan onwards. However, to the extent the process of growth bypasses some of the population, it is necessary to formulate specific poverty alleviation programmes for generation of a certain minimum level of income for the rural poor.

Indian Planning model, however, did not attach the needed importance to agriculture and village industries, which resulted in poor effects in tackling increasing agricultural production, unemployment, inflation, in revitalising the economy and in stemming the tide of rural urban migration and in relieving the pressure on non-renewable natural resources and environment.[3]

This type of centralised planning was contrary to Gandhiji's idea of decentralisation for the village development. As a result, the Panchayat Raj Development model recommended by Balwant Rai Mehta Committee, which wanted democratic decentralisation,[5] was soft peddled and the local planning idea which wanted people's involvement in the planning was given a goodbye in our Five Year Plans starting with rural development.[6]

The present planning model for alleviating poverty was explained in the Eighth Plan as follows : "the decline in rural poverty is attributable both to the growth factor and to the special employment programmes launched by the Government in order to generate more income in the rural areas."[7] Hence, in its more limited interpretation, rural development has been confined to a direct attack on poverty through special employment programmes, area development programmes and land reforms. In addition, the role of Panchayat Raj institutions and voluntary organisations in the implementation of these programmes has also to be kept in view.

Even in the currently started post VIII Plan period, this rural approach is being continued. The Union Finance Minister in his Statement on the Eighth Plan made this point clear in his budget speech of 1995-96 as follows[8] :

"I shall now deal with some issues of social equity and poverty alleviation. In my first budget speech itself I had emphasised that economic growth and restructuring are not ends in themselves. They are only the means to improving the lives of ordinary citizens. I wish to assure the House that this concern has been central to our strategy from the very beginning. Experience in our own country, as also from all over the world, shows that the surest anti-dote to poverty is rapid and broad based growth. This is precisely what our economic reforms seek to achieve. We also recognise that the fruits of growth will take time to reach some of the poorest and weakest sections of our society. To ensure that they too derive benefits in the short run we have given highest priority to strengthen programmes of rural development, employment generation, primary education, primary health and other key social sector programmes. These programmes coupled with accelerating economic growth over the last three years are beginning to have desirable effects on employment and poverty.[8] The message is clear, that the task of lifting the age old burden of poverty in our society is daunting. But we are on the right track. We must persevere with our two track strategy of accelerating growth, investment and modernization on one track and strengthening anti-poverty programmes on the other. The central plan allocations and the tax proposals in this budget are designed to advance both elements of this strategy".

REFERENCES

1. Mellor John, W., 1975, The Impact of New Agricultural Technology on Employment and Income Distribution : Concepts and Policy, *op. cit.*
2. United Nations Economic and Social Commission for Asia and the Pacific, 1985, The Rural Poor : Human Capital for Nation Building, *op. cit.*
3. Roy Kartik, C. and Tissdell Clement, A. and Rajkumar Sen (Eds.), 1992, *Economic Development and Environment : A Case Study of India.* Oxford University Press, Delhi.

4. Planning Commission, Government of India, 1985, The Seventh Five Year Plan, 1985-1990.

5. India Planning Commission, Government of India : Report of the Team for the study of community projects and National Extension Service, Vols I and II, November, 1957 (popularly known as the Copp Team or the Balwantrai Mehta Team), published by the Government of India, Planning Commission.

6. Roy Kartik, C. and Tissdell Clement. A., 1992, : Gandhi's concept of development and Nehru's central planning, [Roy Kartic C. *et al.* (Eds.), *Economic Development and Environmental, op. cit]*.

7. Planning Commission, Government of India, 1992, The Eighth Five Year Plan, 1992-1997.

8. Government of India, 1995, Union Finance Minister's Budget speech, 1995-96, Reported by *Economic Times* on 17-3-1995.

9

COMMENTS OF NOBEL LAUREATE AMARTYA SEN AND THE GOVERNMENT POLICIES RELATING TO POVERTY ALLEVIATION

9.1 NOBEL LAUREATE AMARTYA SEN'S VIEWS ON ECONOMIC DEVELOPMENT

The following statements briefly explain Nobel Laureate Amartya Sen's views on economic development to benefit the rural poor which he pointed out in his first press conference after the award of Nobel Prize in 1998.[1]

1. Globalisation could be a major force for prosperity, only if it was backed by adequate national policies in a conducive social and economic environment.
2. Countries threatened by globalisation are those where human development is very low.
3. There is no one economic theory to benefit the rural poor. We have to take what is good in each theory and use it profitably to help the poor.
4. Economic development, without providing safety nets to the rural poor, is meaningless. Social safety nets, as in the industrial countries of Western Europe to take care of the people when things go wrong for one reason or another, are required.
5. On India's planning, Dr. Sen said "The government had been active in intervening the industry, which however proved

counter productive, while it was inactive in education and health.

6. If a country had globalisation at the highest possible speed and pays no attention to lack of social opportunity, illiteracy and lack of health care, it was creating problems for itself.
7. To compete in the world, Dr. Sen said, land reforms and micro credit, are positive factors. To make things according to specification, literacy is needed and for raising some capital, micro credit is important.
8. India and Pakistan had neglected education, health care and land reforms in truly regrettable ways. And when they opened their economies suddenly, there were a lot of people who were not in a position to compete in a global world.

9.2 POLICIES OF GOVERNMENT OF INDIA ON RURAL POVERTY ALLEVIATION

Policy statements issued in 1998

While addressing the meeting of the preliminary Consultative Committee attached to the Finance Ministry at New Delhi on December 17, 1998, the Finance Minister, Mr. Yashwant Sinha said "It was necessary to assess the impact of liberalisation and economic reforms on poverty alleviation and employment generation in the country."[2] Continuing his address, he said, "Growth with social justice and alleviation of poverty have been the primary objective of Indian planning since its inception in 1951 and the Government had relied mainly on three approaches for reducing poverty and increasing employment opportunities. These include pursuit of higher economic growth, direct anti-poverty and employment programmes and high priority to government's expenditure on social sectors. However, the experience during the last few years shows that higher economic growth did not significantly reduce poverty and increase employment opportunities." Mr. Sinha said, "although it is difficult to assess the impact of economic reforms and liberalization on poverty alleviation, in the absence of literature, it is noticeable that the desired reduction in poverty has not been achieved so far. According to him the shortfall is attributed to the ineffective implementation of poverty alleviation and employment generation programmes, to the duplication of schemes and the multiplicity of agencies implementing programmes." In many cases he said that the States and the Centre could not complement each other in implementing programmes.

The challenge before us is to make the programmes effective and ensure optimum utilisation of resources so that the targetted beneficiaries, particularly the weaker sections like SC and STs and OBCs, are reached promptly.

A suggestion was made by the committee to create a separate implementing agency especially for poverty alleviation and employment generation programmes which are beneficial to weaker sections of the rural society.

Policy statement issued in 2000

The Union Government has now recognised the need for agricultural development as an essential factor for poverty alleviation. Similarly empowerment of rural women, control of population, improvement in the social structure, education and health are being given more attention. Infrastructure development and microfinancing are being highlighted. Some extracts from the Union Finance Minister's budget speech on 28-2-2000 are reproduced below which explain the latest policy statements.[3]

The Union Finance Minister started by stating "it is my firm belief that sustained and broad based growth of agriculture is essential for alleviating poverty, generating incomes and employment, assuring food security and sustaining a buoyant domestic market for industry and services.

Regarding credit he said "We must take all necessary measures to strengthen the rural economy. Credit flow to agriculture through institutional channels of Commercial Banks. Co-operative Banks and Regional Rural Banks is estimated at about Rs. 41,800 crores this year. It is expected to increase by over 20 per cent to a level of Rs. 57,500 crores in 2000-2001.

On the need for rural infrastructure development, the Minister said "The Rural Infrastructure Development Fund (RIDF) managed by NABARD has emerged as a popular and effective scheme for financing Rural Infrastructure projects. This year, the corpus of RIDF VI will be increased to Rs. 4,500 crores as against last year's provision of Rs 3,500 crores".

On the need for microfinance he said "micro-finance has emerged as an effective tool for alleviating poverty in many countries. In my last budget, I had asked NABARD and SIDBI to cover 50,000 Self-Help Groups to develop micro-enterprises. To give a further boost to this programme a Micro Finance Development Fund will be created in NABARD with a starting contribution of Rs.100 crores from RBI".

Lamenting on the poor infrastructure development over the years, the Finance Minister revealed "even after 52 years of independence, the provision of basic services in rural areas remains very unsatisfactory. Forty per cent of our villages are without proper roads, 1.8 lakh villages do not have a primary school within 1 km; 4.5 lakh villages have drinking water problem; some estimates indicate a shortage of 140 lakh rural dwelling units; rural health infrastructure suffers from large deficiencies. These large gaps in basic services in rural areas are not acceptable and Government is committed to removing them rapidly".

Commenting on primary education, he said "Universalization of elementary education is one of our key objectives. A new Department of Elementary Education and Literacy has already been created under the Ministry of Human Resources Development to give a new thrust and focus in these efforts".

Emphasizing on social security for the poor, the Union Minister said "more than one-third of our population still lives below the poverty line. There is an imperative need to extend some social security cover to the poorer sections of our society. I have decided to introduce a new scheme of Group Insurance 'Jana Shree Bima Yojana' under which beneficiaries will have insurance cover".

On the need for empowerment of women the Union Minister expressed "there is an urgent need for improving the access of women to national resources and for ensuring their rightful place in the main stream of economic development. Towards this objective the Government will set up a Task Force under an eminent person to review all existing legislations and Government Schemes pertaining to the role of women in the National Economy".

On population, Health and Environment the Union Minister added "Government have recently announced a new National population policy, a key objective of which is to bring down total fertility rate to replacement level by 2010. To operationalise this objective, the plan allocation through the Department of Family Welfare has been increased from Rs. 2920 crores in 1999-2000 to Rs. 3520 crores in next year".

REFERENCES

1. Amartya Sen, 1998, Address at the International Press Conference after receiving the Nobel Award, *op. cit.*
2. Government of India, 1998, Address of the Union Finance Minister at the meeting of the Parliamentary Consultative Committee attached to the Finance Ministry on 17-12-1998, Reported in *Deccan Herald* on 18-12-1998.
3. Government of India, 2000, Union Finance Minister's Budget Speech for the year 2000-2001 delivered on 28-2-2000 and reported in *Economic Times* on 1-3-2000.

10

STRATEGIES FOR ACCELERATING RURAL POVERTY ALLEVIATION

By strategies we mean the ways in which actions have to be initiated to fulfil the objectives of the programme speedily and effectively. Hence strategies to be used in rural poverty alleviation must keep these purposes in mind. Experience of handling rural development programmes in various developing nations have suggested a number of useful things to be kept in view for effective implementation of the programmes. Some important strategies have been suggested in the following paragraphs.

10.1 BALANCED APPROACH FOR DEVELOPMENT

This strategy has been explained by the World Bank (1975) as follows:

> "This requires emphasizing growth of the modern sector economy as well as uplift of the traditional sector consisting of the rural poor. Past strategies in most developing countries have tended to emphasize economic growth without specifically considering the manner in which the benefits of growth are to be distributed. The assumption has been that increased growth *per se* would lead to a reduction in poverty as the benefits of an expanding economy spread among the people. Accordingly, the emphasis has been on increasing the rate of growth with a corresponding concentration of efforts on the 'high growth' modern sectors of the economy—to the

virtual exclusion of the traditional sector where the small holders, tenants and landless make up the bulk of the rural poor. Although in the long run, economic development for the growing rural population will depend on expansion of the modern sector and on non-agricultural pursuits, too strong an emphasis on the modern sector is apt to neglect the growth potential of the rural areas. Failure to recognize this has been the major reason why the rural growth has been slow and rural poverty has been increasing. At the other extreme, a few governments, occupied with promoting social equality in the rural areas, may have discouraged investments in growth to the point where economic stagnation has resulted. With the rapidly growing population, per capita incomes in the rural areas have declined, even though the range of differences in incomes is much narrower than it was".

"A strategy for rural development aimed at raising growth rates and distributing the fruits of growth more fairly implies greater interaction between the modern and traditional sectors, especially in the form of increased trade in farm produce and in technical inputs and services[1]."

10.2 THE PROGRAMME OF RURAL DEVELOPMENT SHOULD INCLUDE A WIDE RANGE OF ACTIVITIES

According to the World Bank Report (1975) "The operational goals of rural development for poverty alleviation extend beyond any particular sector; they include improved productivity, and thus higher incomes for the target groups, as well as minimum acceptable levels of food, shelter, education and health services. Fulfilment of these objectives calls for an expansion of goods and services available to the rural poor, and institutions and policies that will enable them to benefit fully from the whole range of economic and social services. In order that the development be self-sustaining, it is of special importance that the members of the target groups participate in the organization of the programme. A programme of rural development must embrace a wide range and mix of activities, including projects to raise agricultural output, to improve health and education, to expand communications and to improve housing. The mix of activities will vary with the requirements of a region and the priorities assigned to components within a programme at particular times and at particular stages of development. The programme may be based on the series of sequential projects—first health, then education, then agricultural development. Or it may attempt a broad based multi-sectoral approach whereby a series of activities are to be undertaken almost simultaneously. In all cases, the constituent elements should be complementary and reinforcing".

"Most of the low income groups in the rural areas depend heavily on agriculture for their livelihood. It follows that many of the programmes intended to raise rural incomes must centre on agricultural development[1]".

10.3 THE PROGRAMME MUST AIM AT SUSTAINABLE DEVELOPMENT AND EQUITY IN GROWTH OF THE RURAL POOR

The progress achieved must be sustainable and the gap between the rich and the poor must not increase over a period of years. This can be possibly provided if specific attention is bestowed on this aspect while developing and implementing the programme. Unfortunately this is not happening at present in India. The VIII Plan document accepts this lacuna by stating "experience indicates that while poverty alleviation programmes have been successful in providing a certain quantum of employment to people and have led to the creation of some durable assets in the village, there is a perception that the achievements have not been commensurate with the resources spent on them[2]". Under the IRDP, the very fact that about half the number of beneficiaries have overdue, raises doubts about their ability to come out of the debt syndrome. This, it is argued, is due to low level of assistance which does not generate enough income to repay the loan and for subsistence However, banks are reluctant to raise the credit limit because of skepticism regarding the repayment capacity of the target group. It is estimated that about one-third of them did not even have the original asset that was given to them. The beneficiaries may be forced to sell the asset as they require the money. What is more, even those who have generated sufficient additional income to cross the poverty line may relapse into the category of poor, with additions to the family, loss of assets and non-viability of the activity chosen by them[2].

It is, therefore, necessary to enhance Credit to be made available to the intended beneficiaries to help them to attain sustainable development by increasing their income adequately. They also need assistance by way of providing loans for recurring expenditure over a period of years in addition to the existing assistance for acquiring assets for development.

10.4 LOCAL PLANNING SHOULD BE THE FOCUS FOR A SUCCESSFUL STRATEGY

This strategy is explained as follows by the World Bank (1975): "Ideally, the planning and implementation of rural development programmes involve adequate regional planning, strong central coordination, effective local level organization, and the participation of the rural people in the planning and implementation processes. Few countries have been able to come close to this ideal. Regional planning is desirable both because rural development cuts across all sectors and because rural programmes need to be framed to meet regional conditions. Inter-regional allocations of technical and financial resources must be decided in relation to resource endowments, the domestic and foreign funds available, a balance of equity and growth considerations, and mutually acceptable arrangements for sharing responsibilities between the central and local authorities. All these elements should be brought together into an internally balanced rural development plan. However, the lack of a comprehensive rural development plan should not prevent the evolution of programmes on a local level[1]".

10.5 NEW TYPE OF DECENTRALIZATION IS NECESSARY FOR A GOOD STRATEGY OF RURAL DEVELOPMENT

As advocated by David Leonard, "Rural development requires a new type of decentralization. What is needed is not power for either central government or local organizations, but complementary strength in both. Central government agencies, intermediate organizations and local groups all possess resources and capabilities that are needed by the others. The challenge is to link these institutions together in such a way that their weaknesses are counter balanced and their comparative advantages are used. By so doing, the contribution can be made to development which neither local nor national organizations could achieve alone[3]".

10.6 PROMOTE PARTICIPATORY APPROACH AS A STRATEGY FOR RURAL DEVELOPMENT

The consultative discussion on poverty eradication sponsored by the United Nations at Delhi in October 1996, pointed out that "It is not so much lack of resources that has inhibited poverty eradication as attitudinal blinkers and a mistaken notion that the people cannot know what is best for them. This consultative discussion therefore sought to highlight empowerment of the community as a strategy. In this discussion it was also pointed out that it is not money that is the primary bottleneck in poverty alleviation, but the mind set the top down approach which fails to involve the people[4].

Out of participatory approach to empower local people, has emerged a new emphasis on finding solutions to poverty that are locally based and that involve both economic and social development. The ESCAP publication, "The Rural Poor" has made out a strong case for participation as given below. Among the justification that have been putforth for this participatory approach are the following:

(a) More will be accomplished,
(b) Services can be provided at lower cost,
(c) Participation has an intrinsic values for participants,
(d) Participation is a catalyst for further development efforts,
(e) Participation leads to a sense of responsibility for the project,
(f) Participation guarantees that a felt need is involved,
(g) Participation ensures that things are done in a way

appropriate to the local circumstances,

(h) Participation involves the use of indigenous knowledge and expertise,

(i) Participation means less dependence on professionals, and

(j) Participation leads to "conscientization".[5]

10.7 A SOUND STRATEGY OF RURAL DEVELOPMENT DEMANDS DUE FOCUS ON AGRICULTURAL DEVELOPMENT

A Commonwealth Consultative Group held in Colombo in 1992 has identified that neglect of agriculture is one of the important problems in attacking rural poverty[6]. India is a classic example of this deficiency. Inspite of our tall talks about food self-sufficiency, India has been very slow in its agricultural development. The High Powered Committee appointed by the Government of India in 1990 on agricultural programmes and policies in its report has pointed out that "the fastest, surest and the most effective way for reducing poverty, unemployment and disparity in India is to tap the vast unrealized potential of Indian Agriculture. The aim should be to double our agricultural production within the next 15 years, that is to attain an average growth rate of 4.7 per cent per annum. It is not difficult to achieve this growth rate; our neighbouring countries namely; Pakistan (4.92%), China (4.94%) and Burma (4.98%) have been at higher growth rate between 1979-81 and 1986-88. The only reason why India has lagged behind others is that our agriculture has been starved of capital[7]".

10.8 DEVELOPMENT OF RURAL GROWTH CENTRES

Rural growth centres for every 300 sq. kms. should be provided which should have atleast four aspects of development.

1. A fully developed primary school,
2. Rural dispensary with hospital facilities,
3. A branch of the rural bank, and
4. A multi-purpose supply store for foodstuffs and agricultural inputs[7].

These institutes should be provided with Government transport which should be made available for the rural poor for their travel to the growth centres from their residence and back on fixed days.

10.9 STOP SUBSIDY SCHEMES

The ESCAP publication, "The rural poor" (1985) in concluding paragraph comments on the subsidy scheme as follows. "When nations are faced with burgeoning millions who are caught up in oppressive poverty cycle, their plight is seen as insurmountable. Indeed, providing sufficient government assistance to these populations is clearly beyond the meagre fiscal resources at the command of even the more prosperous nations. Nor does foreign aid seem to provide the answer, as governments often lack the absorptive capacity to make effective use of such aid or, as is sometimes the case, exhibit a remarkable capacity to absorb the aid before it reaches the designated target groups. Under the circumstances it seems likely that programmes that enable the poor to become economically viable using loan capital instead of grant will be the only acceptable alternative. Fortunately, the S.F.D.P. has clearly demonstrated that such an approach is not only possible but also well received by the target groups who were previously the recipients of more paternalistic programmes which tended to promote a dependency on government rather than the self-reliant ethic that is imperative under the circumstances[5].

10.10 STAGE-WISE DEVELOPMENT OF THE AREA TO BE PLANNED

The World Bank policy paper has suggested that the mix of activities to be included for rural developments will vary with the requirements of a region and the priorities assigned, the components within a programme at particular times and at particular stages of development. The programmes may be based on a series of sequential projects from health, then education, then agricultural development etc. Since most of the low income groups in villages depend mostly on agriculture and allied occupations for their livelihood, it is desirable that many of the programmes needed to raise rural income must concentrate on agricultural development[1].

According to Mellor, "the basic policy needs a good strategy on a commitment to technological change in agriculture as the engine of growth, to investments in the rural infrastructural facilities including roads and electricity on a massive scale and to fostering small scale rural industries[8]".

In agriculture, the development should be in stages, first development of foodgrain crops, then focus on increasing non-food grain agriculture to create more employment and last to development of subsidiary industries to support agriculture.

10.11 ENLIST THE SUPPORT OF THE BASIC VILLAGE INSTITUTIONS IN RURAL DEVELOPMENT WORK

The government has spent lot of money in developing the three Basic Institutes at the rural level during the last 50 years. Schools, Panchayats and the Co-operative Societies are these three Basic Institutes. At present the services of these institutes are not adequately used in promoting rural development work in villages. These institutes having work points in villages have enough staff who have more contact with rural people. The earlier philosophy of using these basic institutes in development work remains unfulfilled and as a result, there is no direct involvement of these institutes in the rural development work. Since these institutes can play an important role in organizing village meetings, conduct social surveys, assist rural poor in providing access to services, assist the extension services in educational work, help in organizing training programmes and village visits to the rural poor etc., the active support of these institutions in rural development work should be solicited.

10.12 USE OTHER CATEGORIES OF RURAL PEOPLE TO GENERATE EMPLOYMENT TO RURAL POOR

It is not necessary that all efforts to generate additional employment to rural people should be done only by government. If people other than rural poor in the villages develop their assets and resources, there can be additional source of providing employment to rural poor of their villages. Hence some programmes should be taken up for improving the income of these rural people in addition to the special programmes meant for the rural poor. This will be a cheaper way of providing employment to the rural poor[1]. This will also help the rural people other than the rural poor to get satisfaction from the government programmes of rural development[1].

10.13 DEVELOP SUITABLE ORGANIZATIONS FOR IMPLEMENTING RURAL DEVELOPMENT PROGRAMMES AT LOCAL LEVELS

The type of organizations required to plan and implement programmes for rural poor depends on the activities undertaken. The existing government organizations at the block level cannot be expected to implement all kinds of programmes to be developed in different areas. Considering the type of programmes which should be developed for the rural poor, the primary requirement is that the organization has local knowledge of men, material and environment. Hence a monolith style of organization is ruled out. An organization which can work on the basis of decentralized authority and responsibility and a centralized information system may be more appropriate one. The feasibility of involving the voluntary organizations existing in the local area for rural development work should also be explored. An authority at central level, namely the district or the block, should co-ordinate the work of different organizations implementing various programmes[9].

10.14 PROVISION OF SAFETY NETS TO THE RURAL POOR IS A MUST FOR ANY GOOD STRATEGY

The rural poor will not be attracted towards income generating new projects if there is any kind of risk involved in the technology. Thus government policy to provide safety nets to the rural poor to reduce uncertainty and to increase poor people's ability to absorb risk, is important to improving income of the rural poor. The important point to be noted is that simply providing access to credit may not be a sufficient condition for poor people's active participation in income increasing technology adoption. Any effective strategy, to help the rural poors development projects, must carefully examine this issue and provide the necessary safety nets by way of insurance, risk free technology, cost effective technology to minimize the uncertainties and guaranteed purchase price to eliminate risk in selling the produce etc[8]. In dry farming areas even the use of fertilizers is beset with risky situations due to drought conditions which may occur in any season. Labour intensive technologies are normally intensive in the requirements of working capital and risks of uncertainty from way of insects and diseases effect of yields and production instability tend to be rather high. Thus periodically the rural poor often avoid the labour intensive enterprise combinations which on the surface seem better suited to them. The policy needs in such cases should provide adequate safety nets by way of (1) Research emphasis to relieve uncertainty of labour intensive enterprises through greater control tolerance to weather fluctuations, (2) To improve credit facilities to meet the high risk conditions of such enterprises, and (3) Improve marketing and processing facilities to reduce price fluctuations and risks[8]. Nobel Laureate Amartya Sen (1998) emphasizes the provision of safety nets in the following words "Economic development without providing safety nets to the rural poor is meaningless [13]".

10.15 INSTITUTIONS MEANT FOR PROVIDING SERVICES TO THE RURAL POOR MUST THEMSELVES REACH THE POOR

It is not sufficient to establish various kinds of institutions to provide services to the rural poor. Majority of the rural poor will not be able to utilize the services of these institutes by themselves. It is, therefore, necessary that the institutions themselves should develop the philosophy to reach the poor in the villages and make available their services at the rural people's doors in villages. In this new task, these institutes should take the assistance of the Basic Village Institutions already existing in the rural areas namely, the School, the Panchayat and the Co-operative Society and promote NGOs to involve them in this work.

A good example of this kind of strategy followed by Nicaragua (Bathrick, 1981) is given below which indicates how the institutions should reach the poor to provide services[9]

Services provided by credit institutions in Nicaragua

1. Organising meetings of all interested participants and complete the filling of application forms at the community level.
2. With the help of Community Board, reviewing the accuracy of the data provided in applications.
3. Processing loan applications related to selection of beneficiaries.
4. Assurance of contract providing applicant with the 5-year loan of credit and listing the total eligible amount.
5. Disbursement of multipurpose credit.
6. Making available basic production inputs.
7. Providing marketing assistance.

10.16 CO-ORDINATION AT ALL LEVELS IS IMPORTANT

A strong co-ordination at the National and State levels is essential to the successful implementation of all rural development programmes. A special co-ordination officer is needed at central level, having responsibility for the definition of target groups, co-ordination of national and State efforts and integration of the activities of national sub-agencies. It is also to ensure that policies of all departments are commensurate with rural development objectives.[10] Co-ordination at the local level is emphasized because of the growing evidence that multi-sectoral programmes can be implemented most effectively through a substantial increase in decentralization. Community involvement which is essential to sustained development process is greatly facilitated by local rather than centralized control. The special point is that the problems of the local area as perceived by local committee's representatives and those suggested by local officials tend to be more easily reconciled. Coordination at the operational level is very important since the responsibilities for different activities needed for rural development are entrusted to different departments like credit supply services etc.[11]

10.17 ASSISTANCE TO RURAL POOR TO GET ACCESS TO SERVICES IS A MUST

There is a belief in the country that the government's responsibility will be over by establishing various kinds of institutes to provide different kinds of services to the rural poor. With this in mind various institutions to help the rural poor, have been established. For example, Rural Banks, have been set up. Farmers Service Societies have been established. Franchise centres in rural areas have been supplied with inputs, Extension Services have been strengthened at local levels. But with these institutions, the rural situation has not changed satisfactorily. The rural poor are still to get access to these various institutions for their help. The pertinent point is that in addition to these services it is absolutely necessary to provide a special kind of services called as management services to help the rural poor. The World Bank in their publication "Poverty 1994" states. "In general the poor have less access to publicly provided goods and infrastructure than the other groups"[11]. On the whole the Governments fail to reach the rural poor. Even in urban areas poor neighbourers are less well supplied with services than the well-to-do ones.

Assisting the rural poor to have access to the services has not been given much attention perhaps. Coombs and Ahmed (1974) have commented on this topic as follows :

> "The cause as well as the symptoms of the rural under-development is that facilities for provision of services and supplies are absent, not adequate or do not function effectively. But even when the provisions are made, they cannot be made to function adequately and effectively without a mechanism for management, co-ordinate and adopt at the local level; it is

in this matter of management where larger farmers have a crucial advantage. But small farmers find it difficult to manage the services and supplies at their place of residence. Governments in varying degrees have been providing engineering, technical, economic and social services but rarely have they even tried to provide assistance; in management services. In the absence of any integrated, a systematic view of the farmers overall situation, each rural support services has been viewed as an independent factor and each organization has gone its own way. The need for management services to tie them together as rarely have been recognized. Management services for small farmers combined with the development of participatory institutions would help them break away from subsistence life and give them a chance to move into the modernizing agricultural world. We therefore, consider this to be an extremely vital approach that wants much more attention and resources"[12].

Providing management services to rural poor refers to the degree to which rural poor get assistance in getting training, supplies, services, loans, subsidies and help in processing and marketing of produce etc.

10.18 IDENTIFICATION OF RURAL POOR AND PREPARING AREA MAPS

Steps should be taken to identify the rural poor in an objective way and indicate their number in different villages and a map prepared giving this information. Local people should be involved in this work and transparency ensured in the process followed for identification. This work should not be left completely to the discretion of officials. The target group identified should be used to find out the categories of rural poor so as to classify them into various segments. This classification should be developed on the basis of their physical abilities, potential skills, management talent, interest of motivation. These basic information should be the starting point for developing separate programmes for different segments based on their requirements. The list of rural poor prepared need to be revised once in 5 years in order to update the information.

10.19 INTRODUCE TRANSPARENCY IN GOVERNMENT SUPPORTED PROJECTS

This is necessary to minimize the possible mis-appropriation of funds and also to minimize corruption. It is generally agreed that the sizable percentage of government's funds meant for rural development work, is not properly used and lot of mis-appropriation of government money is also seen yielding to corrupt practices. The national level consultative discussion held in October 1996 at New Delhi, which was sponsored by the U.N. bodies, has also revealed this lacuna in operation of rural development programmes[4]. Common examples of such corrupt practices like the use of muster rolls having names of persons who are not living and payment of money to companies which do not even exist are available. The strategy needed to check such corrupt practices is to have a complete transparency of government records when public funds are spent for rural development programmes.

10.20 EMPOWERMENT OF WOMEN IN RURAL DEVELOPMENT

It is high time that we recognize the role of women and the youth which offers the best hope of greater effectiveness in implementing the rural development programmes. More attention shall be given to organize groups of rural poor women and provide them greater legal aid to enable better participation and meaningful involvement at the community level. Practical methods should be found out to accelerate this process of empowering rural women belonging to rural families.

REFERENCES

1. World Bank, 1975, Rural Development—A Sector Policy Paper, *op. cit.*

2. Government of India, VIII Plan Document, 1992, *op. cit.*

3. Leonard, David; Dale Marshall; Jose Garzon; Stephen Peterson and Sven Steinmo, 1981, Linkages to Decentralized Units, Mimeographed paper, Project on managing decentralization, University of California, Berkeley, USA.

4. Narasimhan, Sakuntala, 1996, *The Failure of Poverty Eradication, op. cit.*

5. United Nations Economic and Social Commission for Asia and Pacific (ESCAP), 1985, *The Rural Poor, op. cit.*

6. Common Wealth Secretariat, 1993, Action to reduce poverty, proposals for needful instructions developed by a Common Wealth Consultation on Rural Poverty Alleviation, Colombo, Sri Lanka, 5-9 October, 1992, *op. cit.*

7. Government of India, 1990, Report of High Powered Committee on Agricultural Policies and Programmes, *op. cit.*

8. Mellor John, W., 1975, *The Impact of New Agricultural Technology on Employment and Income Distribution—Constraints and Policies, op. cit.*

9. Bathrick, D.D., 1981, *Agricultural Credit for Small Farm Development. Policies and Practices,* West View Special Studies in Social-Political and Economic Development. West View Press, *op. cit.*

10. Dantwala, M.L. and Bermeda, 1991, Rural development, approaches and issues in Dantwala, M.L. (Editor), *Indian Agricultural Development since Independence,* 2nd Edn. *op. cit.*

11. World Bank, 1994, Poverty, World Bank, Washington, D.C., USA.

12. Coombs, P.H. and Ahmed, M., 1974, *Attacking Rural Poverty, op. cit.*

13. Amartya Sen (1998) Globalization without safety nets for poor is absurd. Press report published by the *Deccan Herald* paper on 2-6-1998 (p. 7).

11

METHODS AND TECHNIQUES FOR PROMOTING WELFARE OF THE RURAL POOR—I

11.1 PREAMBLE

There need not be any disillusionment on the prevailing belief that rural poverty cannot be eliminated in India although it is true that rural poverty alleviation programmes have not shown the expected progress over the years. If we carefully examine the methodology followed and pursued in the past and also look at the few success stories achieved in some places, both in India and other developing countries, it will be clear that there is no need for despair. The problem of rural poverty can be handled more effectively than before, provided a pragmatic and practical methodology, is followed in place of the one that is now being practiced in India. In other words, there is a need for change in the methods and techniques used. The present day top down, subsidy oriented approach, with a wrong belief that people cannot know what is best for them, should be changed to education oriented method, highlighting, empowerment of the people aided by loans and safety nets to be provided by the government to the rural poor in place of subsidy. According to Nobel Laureate Amartya Sen, the programme should be people-oriented and not commodity-oriented. This new methodology requires that it is necessary to involve the rural poor actively in the programme to put their own efforts in income generating activities which they themselves have to choose. This new methodology will succeed only if the rural people's needs, their societal environment and their cultural values become the corner stone of the programmes being offered to them. There are some essential components which govern the success of this new methodology.

First and foremost, it is necessary to understand and use some important guidelines drawn from the good work done in some rural areas in developing villages. Many of these guidelines also are supported by the findings of recent research and case studies experiences of intensive village work done by agencies etc.

There are innumerable research studies which have reported that rural people's participation in extension educational activities is low as compared to other non-poor rural people. Many of these studies have also wrongly concluded that the rural poor are backward in outlook and less progressive. However, very few of these studies have gone into the details to find out why the rural poor's participation in educational programmes is low. A close look at the profile of rural people, as outlined in the earlier chapter of this book, and also the way in which educational activities are conducted with rural poor people will help us to find out the answer. Pioneering experimental study by Muniraju (1976)[1] has revealed the real reasons for the low participation of rural poor in development education activities. This research has also reported that when developmental educational activities are conducted at the place and time convenient for the rural poor, the educational participation of the rural poor is almost at the same level as that of the other non-poor rural people. Subsequent case studies reported by ESCAP[2] and other empirical data available in the intensively undertaken village production programmes like village adoption programmes, collaborate with these new findings. This is an important lesson for following a new approach in educating the rural poor.

Another required aspect of educating the rural poor is to develop their motivation towards the programme activities. The existing nature of development activities, conducted by development workers, lack in providing the requisite education for motivating the rural poor. Unfortunately a policy of giving subsidies and distributing few free items like seeds, fertilizers and chemicals, are followed without actively involving the rural poor in motivating them for action. A classic Ph.D. research conducted by Nandapurkar (1980)[3] has clearly revealed why the rural poor do not take active part in development programmes and do not adopt modern technology and fail to take up income generating activities successfully. One of the important facts identified is the need to develop the entrepreneurship ability, especially to arouse their achievement motivation level.

Educating and promoting motivation of the rural poor are, however, only necessary conditions for promoting action but not sufficient conditions. There are other related factors which influence action on the part of rural poor.

Rural poor are not able to help themselves to get the advantage of rural services provided by government institutions and organisations to obtain training, credit, supply and services etc. This has been described as the "rural vacuum theory" by Mosher[4]. Lot of outside assistance is, therefore, required for the rural poor to get these services which work is now popularly called as providing management services.

Intensive work should be done with a few selected rural poor families in every village and get them lifted above the poverty line, so that they will become examples for other rural poor to follow.[5] This strategy is seldom undertaken. Therefore, what is needed is, to initiate rural development programme with intensive work, with a small number of rural poor, in all areas of the country on a massive scale, instead of the present approach of selecting a handful number of villages, for intensive work as show pieces, by injecting all kinds of extra resources, which cannot be readily multipliable in all areas. The touch and go system of developmental educational work as exemplified by the current T and V system should also be changed for a better intensive developmental work with a few selected rural poor in all villages simultaneously.

Promoting new kinds of limited informal local level organisations to help involvement of the rural poor in development programmes is another necessity. Right from independence, a static policy of promoting only the formal co-operative institutions in villages as registered societies has been taken up. A recent study undertaken by the International Development Centre at the University of California, Berkeley Campus, USA, has recommended for organizing these limited informal local level organisations in addition to the co-operative institutions.[6]

Although local planning involving village people has been accepted as the ideal method in rural development, this has been completely ignored in India's Rural Development work all these years. Atleast some good beginning has to be made to follow local planning atleast at implementation stage on a number of activities. An appropriate methodology for use in this local planning work is, therefore, required.

Role of Voluntary Local Organisations (NGOs) is equally important in the development work. India's Planning Commission has pointed out that such organisations are required to get local people's co-operation and participation in the implementation of the development programmes. This Commission is also clear about the emphatic role of NGOs as providers of welfare measures and as mitigators of hardships of weaker sections. In this pragmatic methodology we are more concerned with the mitigation role of non-governmental voluntary organisations.

India has built three basic village institutions since the beginning of the Plan Era. These are : (1) The village Panchayats, (2) The village Co-operatives, and (3) The village Schools

These are the three legs of a tripod on which the future of rural India is to be laid to bring about the socio-economic transformation of rural India. The Panchayat is to provide the much needed leadership, both through elected and informal leaders, for the rural development programmes. The co operative is to look after the various needs of the community and the school is to function as the centre of educational and cultural activities. Besides, these three institutes other associated institutes of the village, if in existence, like the youth clubs, Mahila Samajas etc. are to be involved in the development programme.

Rural Development work also requires the active support of informal voluntary local leaders.[7] They will be able to multiply the efforts of development personnel manifold and that too without any extra cost to the government. Unfortunately, this aspect has not been given enough attention all these years. In this pragmatic methodology as special mention has to be made about using the informal local leaders in rural development work.

Empowerment of rural women and youth especially those belonging to the poor families is another need for accelerating rural development programmes. Women labour force participation and their relative contribution to total family are rather higher in households with lower economic status. The poorer the family, the more it depends on the earnings of its female members. In very poor households, women's capacities to work, their health, knowledge and skills are often crucial for family survival. Women's economic productivity is particularly critical to 50 million Indian households which live below poverty line. Women may be the main or only earners in these households. Over 35 per cent of households, below the poverty line, are headed by women. Hence, greater attention to the creation of employment opportunities for poor women and efforts which will increase the productivity of women workers, particularly those in the primary sector, are needed urgently.[8] Special methods to empower rural poor women in this is absolutely essential to speed up the welfare of rural people.

Besides, the above mentioned components, for the new methodology, this chapter also closes by making a brief reference to some related ideas which are part of the Government policies and strategies needed to promote the welfare of the rural poor. These are (1) Providing safety nets to the development of the rural poor, and (2) Infrastructure facilities to be provided in rural areas especially in the field of education and health. Unless these are provided by the government, it will be difficult to accelerate the progress of rural development programmes as recently clarified by the Nobel Laureate Amartya Sen.[9]

11.2 SOME IMPORTANT GUIDELINES FOR VILLAGE DEVELOPMENT

A collection of 32 important guidelines has been made in this regard and summarised as follows :

1. Availability of social services by selfless people with devotion

for village work will accelerate the progress of rural development programmes.

2. Discussion with villagers on the problems to be tackled in the villages are always advantageous to convince the local people about the need for that work.
3. The key to rural development is to identify and start work on projects satisfying the immediate needs of the local people.
4. People's co-operation in the developmental efforts is very important and it is available for projects that fulfil their immediate needs.
5. There are many voluntary social service organisations working in the field of rural development. Quite a number of them are doing this work not for money or personal gains but out of dedication and intensive social commitment. If the Government makes use of such organisations to assist it in the implementation of various schemes, it would have saved a lot of money that is now being spent in administrative establishment, sometimes to the extent of 60-70 per cent of the funds presently allocated.
6. Problems which are common to majority of villagers are to be taken up first.
7. Projects which satisfy the immediate needs of the people of the village should be taken up first in implementing rural development programmes.
8. Since rural women generally hesitate to contest elections to local institutes like Panchayats and Co-operatives, they can be nominated as members of these Bodies. It is observed that when rural women have been nominated to take up such responsibilities they have proved to be efficient in managing the affairs.[10]
9. No village work will succeed without the full and active involvement of the village people. Unless there is unanimity of opinion, no project is to be started. Once villagers' opinion is solicited and approval by the Village Assembly obtained, there will be generally no interference or any trouble on the decision taken.

10. Really selfless work with devotion should be done without looking to the immediate results. If we look at the immediate results, many times we may face criticisms, will not be praised by all in the village and thus we may get frustrated. What is necessary is to follow the principle stated in the *Bhagavad Geeta* — *"Karmanye Vadhikarasthe Maphaleshu Kadachana"*. Hence it is necessary to do your duty without expecting the results. Keep on going with your work as long as you feel it is good for the village. Do not worry about the criticisms and difficulties which are bound to come. You simply continue your good work.

11. A voluntary worker has to be very particular about the transparency in all his dealings, particularly those having financial outlay. With this transparency he can pursue his goal steadfastly without being disturbed by criticisms or humiliations by others in the process.

12. The success of the projects to benefit the rural poor are dependent on a set of the following positive actions by them

    (a) Their participation in project, decision making which appears more significant in the implementation stage.

    (b) Their willingness to contribute labour and money to the development efforts.

    It was observed that those development projects, which took time and effort necessary to build in an active and co-operative role for the rural poor, were significantly more successful than other projects which merely follow the externally dominated development approach.

13. Studies with the rural poor have revealed that money factor though important in Project success with the rural poor did not actually turn out to be so, especially the degree of subsidies offered for adoption of new technology was not, suggesting that the rural poor will adopt new technology without further incentives, if it appears in their interest to do so.[11]

14. There are numerous success stories of individual and group activities among the rural poor and the re-counting of these experiences by the people themselves, who had undertaken those projects, in the presence of their peers, would be one of the most effective ways to promote similar self-reliance activities elsewhere.

    The philosophy behind the above mentioned methods is that people at the village level in developing countries have a great deal to teach their own people and that they themselves are the best teachers. In following the "farmer-trains-farmer approach", there are three requirements to be met with namely; (1) Choosing successful rural people who have completed the projects with success, (2) The experience to be reported should be replicable by other rural poor who listen to the success story and are protected on to carry out similar activity with the resources available to them in their villages, and (3) It is essential that the persons who have achieved success must be the ones making the presentation.

15. Participation of village people by contributing free labour for development activities (*shramadan*) is possible and should be encouraged as the basic method for achieving self-reliance and self-sufficiency. It is possible to take up construction of roads, school buildings, hospitals, watershed development works etc., through this method. In addition to this method, outside contributions can be used to speed up the project undertaken with the help of *shramadan*.

16. Government Grants or subsidies by themselves do not produce results in rural development work. The active cooperation of the people concerned is important for the success, in implementing rural development programmes.

17. The village assembly (Grama Sabha) shall have the authority to decide about the priorities in the village development process. The Grama Panchayat should be the only executive authority and should be responsible to the Grama Sabha. The panchayat would be accountable to the Grama Sabha to achieve the real devolution of power as part of the democratic process. When this is followed, there will be less village

frictions and internal fights which when developed will undermine the pace of rural development.

18. The first important step in rural development work is to organise a systematic discussions of common felt needs by village people. It is only when discussion about any problems are systematically arranged, eventhough very few representative villagers participate in them, important common felt needs are brought out.

19. Village people should be encouraged to carry out the first self-help project which has been selected by method of systematic discussion. This step is important to mobilise the community to do something for itself.

20. To accomplish the self-help project it is necessary to have mobilisation and harnessing of physical, economic and social potentialities of local village groups.

21. To initiate one self-help project after another and harnessing the development of group aspirations. This will help team spirit *esprit de corps,* patriotism or in other words group sentiments.

22. Providing management services consists of operational activities to help the rural poor to get easy access to government provided services like education, training, supplies, services, credit etc.[12]

23. Rural poor directed, limited, local level organisations also help to facilitate the greater integration and administration of services.

24. The experience of the rural poor who have already tried new technology in their homes and have got experience as paraprofessionals was one of the cost effective ways to spread new technology.

25. In circumstances of high risk and particularly when large cash costs are involved, various risk sharing plans, ranging from crop insurance to input provisions, output sharing arrangements, should be provided in rural projects.

26. Successful rural development requires commitment to a basic policy—Commitment to technological change in agriculture

as an engine of growth, to investment in rural infrastructure including roads and electricity on a massive scale, and to foster small scale rural industries.[13]

26a. By and large, group repayment responsibilities provide for better repayment rates and other benefits than old programmes in which the rural poor were individually responsible for repayment.

27. While recommending technology to rural poor, proper method should be followed namely the technology systems approach. This approach requires that technologies have to be recommended to each poor rural family, considering the available cafeteria of technology practices.

28. In Rural Development, a development worker is a person who lives among the group of rural poor and gets intimately acquainted with what they are doing, what prevents of their welfare to get more productivity and income and thus helps them to do whatever needs to be done to move forward.

29. Any technology to be recommended to rural poor for their benefit even when tested locally should indicate the complementary pre-requisites of capital, land, required inputs, marketing services which may accompany the new technology.

30. To promote rural poor's participation in development programmes, it is necessary to conduct development education activity at the place and time convenient for the rural poor.

31. Promoting action by the rural poor will be facilitated by developing the entrepreneurship ability of the rural poor, and instilling among them achievement motivation by educational methods and technologies.

32. The rural poor often have difficulty in obtaining capital necessary for the application of new technology. But even more important they face serious problems of risk and to be resistant aversions.

REFERENCES

1. Muniraju, A., 1976, A study on extension participation of farmers in Bangalore District of Karnataka State, Unpublished M.Sc. thesis, Dept. of Extension, University of Agricultural Sciences, Bangalore.
2. United Nations Economic and Social Commission for Asia and Pacific (ESCAP), 1985, *The Rural Poor, op. cit.*
3. Nandapurkar, C.G., 1980, A study on entrepreneurial behaviour of small farmers, Unpublished Ph.D. Thesis, Department of Agricultural Extension, University of Agricultural Sciences, Bangalore, *op. cit.*
4. Mosher, A.T., 1978, An introduction to agricultural extension, Agricultural Development Council, New York, USA.
5. Government of India, 1990, Report of High Powered Committee on Agricultural Policies and Programmes *op. cit.*
6. Leonard, David; Dale Marshall; Jose Garzon, Stephen Peterson and Sven Steinmo, 1981, *Linkages to Decentralized Units, op. cit.*
7. Taylor, Carl *et al.*, 1965, *Steps in Local Group Action op. cit.*
8. World Bank, *Gender and Poverty, op. cit.*
9. Sen, Amartya, 1998, Address at the First Press Conference after getting the Nobel award, *op. cit.*
10. Hazare, Anna, 1997, Ralegaon Siddhi, A veritable transformation, Ralegaon Siddhi Pariwar Prakashan, Ralegaon Siddhi, Dist. Ahmednagar.
11. Elliott R. Morss, John K. Hatch, Donald R. Mickelweit and Charles F. Sweet, 1975, Strategies for small farmers development, an empirical study of rural development projects. Development alternatives Inc., Washington, D.C., USA.
12. Coombs, P.H. and Ahmed, M., 1974, *Attacking Rural Poverty, op. cit.*
13. Mellor John, W., 1975, *The Impact of New Agricultural Technology in Employment and Income Distribution—Constraints and Policies, op. cit.*

12

METHODS AND TECHNIQUES FOR PROMOTING WELFARE OF THE RURAL POOR—II

12.1 PRAGMATIC METHODOLOGY FOR EDUCATING AND INVOLVING THE RURAL POOR IN DEVELOPMENT PROGRAMMES

The rural poor have to be assisted in group discussions to identify the programmes themselves

An important factor in the new methodology consists of developing faith of the rural poor in the programmes to be taken up for their welfare so as to enable them to participate effectively. This can be achieved, provided the following items of work, are carried out effectively.

(i) The rural development/extension workers study the local situation and prepare brief notes about the same, summarizing the situation relating to the rural poor in a meaningful way. This local situation should then be compared with some new activities carried out by similar rural poor in the same area or similar areas indicating how the new activities have helped them to come out of the poverty line.

(ii) Systematic discussion sessions should be organized involving the rural poor where the situational information and the success stories of new activities carried out by other rural people are identified and presented. This item is very important because when discussion about villagers' problems are systematic, even though, among a relatively few representative persons or families, important community felt needs are revealed.

Specific financial budget allotment is required to carry out these items. The rural development department should provide budget for these and make them available to each rural development worker. Funds can also be sought from donations to be raised in the villages from the well-to-do farmers and village and taluk level institutions. A specific provision should be made to earmark some percentage of the budget of the village cooperative society, Panchayat and the school for this purpose.

Care should also be taken to see that the success stories are presented by the farmers themselves who have already had sufficient experience with new technologies in their farms/villages. The narration of such successful instances by the small farmers themselves, in the presence of their peers, would be one of the most effective ways to promote similar self-reliant activities elsewhere. The philosophy behind this activity is that "people at the grass-root level in developing countries have a great deal to teach to their own people and that they themselves are the best teachers"[1].

Classify the rural people according to their interest in different projects

It is generally observed during discussion meetings that all the rural poor are not equally interested in all new programme activities. A good strategy to be followed at the time of assisting the rural poor in selecting the programme areas, is that all of them cannot be considered as a homogeneous cluster with uniform programmes for the amelioration of their misery. They need to be grouped in different segments to undertake different programmes suitable to their varying requirements. Hence, the rural poor should be classified on the basis of their physical abilities, skills, managerial talents, motivations etc. Different programmes should be developed for each group, e.g. for physically able beneficiary persons, programmes for road and house construction, digging roads and wells, soil conservation, afforestry work will be suitable. For such of the rural poor with some lands, programmes like poultry, dairy and artisan work may be more useful. For small farmers, multiple cropping, dairy farm and other farm based occupations will be appropriate. The segment with managerial talent can be helped to develop small enterprises[3].

Educating people interested in different programmes to develop their own entrepreneurship and to motivate them for active participation

This step is necessary to promote participatory approach needed for the success of the programme[2]. People interested in different project groups require to be educated through group work to develop their entrepreneurship behaviour and also to get motivated for active involvement in the programmes. Research has indicated that the entrepreneurial behaviour of the rural poor mostly influenced by the following five important factors[4]:

1. Decision making ability,
2. Innovativeness,
3. Getting assistance of management services,
4. Achievement motivation, and
5. Ability to coordinate activities.

Hence while educating them, these areas should be focused intensively. It is particularly stressed to give more attention on promoting achievement motivation which is a special value that emphasises desire for excellence, in order to enable an individual to attain a sense of personal accomplishment. Fortunately, this value can be developed in individuals by providing the required education. Since the entrepreneurial behaviour of the rural poor is greatly influenced by achievement motivation, more attention is needed in educating people to foster this value. Narrating other farmers' achievements, participation in field trips to successful farmers' areas and group discussions by involving those local people who are successful in new programme activities are some of the techniques which will help to increase achievement motivation of the rural poor towards new activities to be implemented. An important point to be noted in this step of educating people and motivating them is that the government field workers of the rural development department should play the role of catalysts and not teachers themselves and encourage successful rural people whose success stories are to be presented to take responsibility for providing technical expertise or advice to the interested rural people. This will help to create an opportunity for learning from farmer to farmer. Successful rural people have proven to be the ideal teachers of their peers and the best examples of successful change agents.

Some pre-requisites for successfully carrying out this step

Since rural poor people are always busy doing work for earning their livelihood, it is necessary that they are contacted for their education only during their spare time. Night meetings are the best methods for this purpose, when the rural people are free from their day's work. In case they are to be taken for trips outside the villages, it is desirable not only to meet the cost of the travel but also necessary to pay compensation fee for the loss of their daily wages which they have to forego in order to participate in the field trips. Financial provision has, therefore, to be made in the budget of the rural development programme for these items.

12.2 SELECTING TECHNOLOGY SYSTEMS

It is necessary to treat each rural family as a separate unit for guiding on the needed technology for each family to enable it to cross over the poverty line. This procedure of treating each family separately and assist it in finding out an appropriate technology suited to that family is popularly known as "technology systems approach" mentioned by Kasseba (1989).[5] The basis for this approach are explained as under.

"In most of the developing world, extension systems are still evolved around top-down supply driven extension approach which do not adequately address the socio-economic solutions of the resource poor small holders, producers or their requirements. The major challenge in this context is, therefore, to develop appropriate technology transfer systems in developing agricultural economies which in turn takes into account the small holder's perceptions and requirements". This philosophy has been further supported by Jazairy (1989), who has stated "Extension services based fundamentally on the delivery of research and technology concerned and developed within the agricultural centres of the industrialised countries, cannot always be applied successfully for the developing world. This is especially true when extension services are required for remote, unschooled, impoverished and often subdued rural small holders or landless farmers, in marginal lands subject to flood, drought, disease and insect invasions. Thus the challenge is to find out what the people need and how it can be delivered best."[6]

Since this new kind of procedure is a clear deviation from the presently practiced system of technology transfer, intensive training is required for the field staff of the development departments to enable them to carry out their work properly. Further, when such technology systems are to be developed for each rural poor family, the support of specialised staff should be made available to each field extension worker. Again adequate time has to be provided to meet each family and have discussions with them in order to educate the family members on the technology systems suited to their needs.

Care to be taken in selecting the technologies

(i) *Cost effective and sustainable technologies to be given preference :* Out of the technologies available, cost effective technologies should be selected for the use of rural poor which should also be of sustaining nature. Such technologies should ensure resource neutrality by substituting non-monetary or inexpensive inputs for high cost inputs and minimising yield fluctuations[7]. For example, if two kinds of seeds are available, one the hybrid type and the other the synthetic one, it is desirable to include the synthetic one for recommending to the rural poor, since it is more cost effective and sustainable as compared to the hybrid seed. The synthetic type can be used for a number of years without the need of purchasing new seed every year as in the case of the hybrid type.

(ii) *Technology to be recommended should be thoroughly tested locally before recommending the same to the rural poor :*

(iii) Thorough testing of technologies under the locally prevailing conditions over a period of years is a must to avoid risky situations of aberrationary or dry weather conditions and menace of insect pests and diseases. The rural poor cannot take risk and they would prefer technologies which are safe as compared to those which may produce more yield but are risky. Only if risk free situations are available by providing insurance, we may even recommend the said technologies but such environment is not yet available in India, since farm insurance schemes have not developed adequately to help the rural poor.

12.3 ASSISTING THE RURAL POOR TO GET ACCESS TO SERVICES

The government have provided four important kinds of services for assisting the agricultural and rural development programmes. These are (1) Engineering, (2) Technical, (3) Economic and (4) Social services. Under the existing programmes most of these four essential services are being strengthened. But these services are not reaching the rural poor, especially the credit supplies and marketing services. The main reason for this is that affluent sections of the rural communities appropriate such benefits for themselves. However, in the case of the rural poor, some special types of assistance is necessary. In more specific terms, it could be stated that the rural poor require one more crucial service with assistance of integrated management services in operational forms so that the above mentioned four types of government services are able to reach them[8].

Management services for the rural poor include more detailed operational activities to get benefit of the four kinds of services at the village level on continuing basis. Providing such management services to the rural poor is an emerging concept cited in recent literatures. It can be defined as the degree to which the rural poor get assistance at their village level in getting access to training, supplies, services, loans, subsidies and help in processing and marketing the produce etc. through a set of special operational activities.

Some examples of operational activities to provide management services to the rural poor are listed below :

Example 1 : Operational activities used by INVIERNO project of Nicaragua (Africa) to provide easy access of credit and inputs to rural poor[9] (This has been explained in Chapter 10 under strategies)

Example 2 : Operational activities included in a scale to measure the extent of management services provided to rural poor[10].

(a) Help in providing technical advice at the local level

(i) Helping small farmers to see demonstration plots established in the locality either by the government or by other organisations to understand the importance of technology promoted.

(ii) Assisting small farmers in getting technical information through village meetings/training programmes/distribution of literature etc.

(iii) Assistance in motivating the rural poor in respect of superiority of new practices by exposing them to the economic aspects of the new practices.

(iv) Helping the rural poor to know the technical information at various important stages of the project at farm or at village level.

(b) Help in getting inputs at the local level, e.g., seed

(i) Assisting in finding out the seed requirement of individual small farmers.

(ii) Help in getting seed at the village level.

(iii) If the seed is not available at the village level, assisting in getting the seed from outside sources.

Fertilizers

1. Assisting in finding out fertilizer requirements of small farmers.
2. Help in getting the fertilizers from the nearest sales point or depot.
3. If the fertilizer is not available in the nearest sales point or depot helping small farmers in getting the same from other outside sources.

Assistance in getting access to credit

(i) Encouraging small farmers to know the importance of new technical programme and giving details of the loan amount required in implementing the programme.

(ii) Distribution of loan application to small farmers to enable them to get the application without any problem.

(iii) Assisting small farmers at the village level in getting the loan application filled up.

(iv) Help in sending the loan application to the finance agency.

(v) Getting the loan application processed through the agency.

(vi) Help in getting the loan sanction order.

The effectiveness of the programme depends upon this important factor. There is no one way to carry out these activities. The following examples illustrates, the various ways in which this can be done.

Example 1 : In intensive village adoption programme, these requirements are fulfilled by carrying out work developed by the various agencies involved in the programme implementation. An example of how this was done in the Block Demonstration programme undertaken in Karnataka State in 1972-73 can be cited as a good illustration. The co-ordinated activities consisted of the following details of work done.[11]

(i) Farmers meetings were organised by extension workers in villages two months before the season to discuss about the advantage of using new practices by farmers. As a result of these meetings several farmers were motivated.

(ii) Listing out various requirements of those farmers in respect of seeds, fertilizers, chemicals, credit etc.

(iii) Extension workers belonging to various organisations such as Karnataka State Department of Agriculture, University of Agricultural Sciences, Farmers Service Societies, Commercial Banks, shared these responsibilities and assisted participant farmers in getting their requirements.

Example 2 : In government sponsored co-operative societies like co-operative Dairy Project of the Anand model, dairy co-operative societies are set up in villages to help its member farmers on the following items of work[12]:

(i) Milk receiving and testing,

(ii) Providing first aid,

(iii) Purchase of milk,

(iv) Channelising inputs for milk production,

(v) Co-ordination with the various functions of milk unions, and

(vi). Providing chaff cutting machines.

Government can at the most demonstrate the contribution of such management services in few selected villages where intensive development programmes are taken up like, village adoption programme, community demonstration etc. But, it will not be possible as revealed by various case studies to continue to provide such services on permanent basis by government organisations. It is only the co-operative organisations and NGOs established in villages which can take up responsibility of providing such management services on a permanent basis.

12.4 NGOs ROLE IN PROVIDING MANAGEMENT SERVICES TO RURAL POOR

Success stories reported from few villages regarding village development have many lessons for implementing rural developmental activity. One important lesson is that there are many voluntary social services-oriented NGOs working in the field of rural development in a number of villages. Quite a number of them are doing this important work not for money or personal gains but out of dedication of intensive social commitment. It should be a wise policy to use such NGOs actively for village development work. So, promoting, developing and using NGOs will be the most important feature for accelerating progress of rural development programme[13].

In some villages, non-government organisations have started rural development programmes and help the rural families with required services. For example Sri Kshetra Dharmasthala Rural Development Project undertaken by Sri Kshetra Dharmasthala of Ujire in Mangalore[14] district of Karnataka State has the following system to assist the rural poor farmers under their development projects. The project now has a band of dedicated workers who act as catalytic agents of the villagers. These are the trained Seva Niraths who guide 250 to 300 beneficiary families each and have greatly succeeded in improving the economic and social conditions of the beneficiary families. The beneficiary puts his hard labour, the project gives food for his subsistence, all other supports of full guidance for his complete blossoming as a self-sufficient person. Thus the project gives assistance for on-the-farm permanent development such as digging of wells, tanks, putting up bunds, land levelling, raising perennials such as coconut, arecanut, rubber, cashew etc. Project distributes seed material and fertilizers to the needy. Project also takes care of other aspects of the family members such as health, education, family welfare, cleanliness, sanitation, thrift and the like. The beneficiaries are helped in getting loan from the financing institutions. Thus the project takes care to see that the beneficiary families are helped directly as well as indirectly.

12.5 DEVELOPMENT OF THE POOR FAMILIES IS NOT A ONE SHOT AFFAIR AND REQUIRES SYSTEMATIC WORK OVER A PERIOD OF YEARS

The present method followed in promoting income generating project for the rural poor is that the beneficiary families are identified, subsidy and loan according to the prescribed norms are provided and then the development workers move to the other beneficiary for similar work. Development of the poor family cannot be a one shot activity like this. What is required is continuous guidance and assistance to the family for a period of years, say 3 to 5, till the family becomes self sustainable to increase its income level. During these years timely technical guidance followed by other assistance to get the various kinds of services are required. So what is needed is to concentrate on a few selected poor families in every village rather than follow a one shot activity with many families. In this connection, it is worthwhile to consider the recommendation of the 1990 High Power Committee on Agricultural Policies and Programmes[15] made in their report, which reads as follows :

> "For improving the economic lot of small farmers, more attention will have to be paid to cash crops and supplementary enterprises. There is no lack of technologies of production even for dryland and small farmers, which can generate more incomes and employment in villages. But these cannot be adopted by small farmers unless the necessary services to support these enterprises in the form of backward and forward linkages are first provided. Rural India will remain poor so long as (1) New techniques of production are not adopted, (2) Adequate capital in the form of loans for adoption of the new techniques is not provided, and (3) Efficient marketing arrangements for the produce are not made. All these will have to be provided simultaneously in a package and not in unplanned manner as hitherto"[15].

> "It will not be possible to provide all the services needed to support the different enterprises everywhere, it is advisable that farmers in every development block of the country, be provided an opportunity to select one cash crop or enterprise most suited to their areas. After this decision has been made every assistance, technological, financial and managerial, should be provided for that particular crop or enterprise, through co-operative and panchayat effort. Concerted localised programmes, for promotion and production of horticultural and animal husbandry products will in course of time also promote agro processing industries and export of such production."[15]

12.6 GROUP EFFORTS ARE NEEDED TO HELP THE UNORGANISED RURAL POOR

Recently a special method is being suggested called the group effort. The beneficiaries having common purposes are assisted to form small groups with group leaders to assist them in getting these services and the extension agent is entrusted with the job of promoting such groups and provide guidance. Since the village Co-operative Societies which are primary organisations to provide this kind of assistance to farmers have not been performing well, alternate methods are suggested for organising other kinds of co-operative organisations to carry out such functions.

Promoting group action by the rural poor while undertaking income generating projects

The basic strategy of this method is to help the rural poor in organising themselves into small (10 to 15 persons) in formal, socially and economically homogeneous groups around common income generating activities so that they may benefit from the larger scale of operating. By exerting group influence in the community, the groups will gain better access to production resources and to receive a more equitable share of development benefits which hitherto had escaped them as individuals.

According to Subramaniyam, (1982, pp. 16 & 17) [16]

"Numerous opportunities for co-operative action by compact groups of rural poor in their mutual interest can be envisaged. In activities like soil conservation, water management, creating irrigation facilities, use of productivity enhancing equipments, raising nurseries, in weed and pest control, in storage and marketing, in provision of mutual guarantees for credit to mention, but a few."[16]

"The size of the group and its method of operation will vary depending on the immediate purpose in view. Hence this type of activity cannot be put in a straight jacket of a rigid programme whose parameters are determined and prescribed from above. A great deal of flexibility and local initiative will be called for if this approach is to succeed."

The same principle of group action can be resorted to, for enabling the weaker sections of society to organise themselves and protect their interest through strengthening their bargaining positions vis-a-vis the more powerful and entrenched interests. From the purely social aspects of village life, for say, the Harijans, access to common facilities like drinking water, education health services etc. to more economic phenomena such as tenancy terms or wage rates, group action can be a salutary instrument at the hands of the weak in their dealings with the powerful. There are enough examples in the country and elsewhere to show how this approach can facilitate in the cause of equity.

Organising such self help groups in gaining importance in recent years as a main strategy to provide government loan to rural poor, it has been observed that when groups are formed to obtain credit for their members and repayment responsibility rests with the group, it is easy to obtain loan from the organisations of the government. It is also seen that the rural poors' repaying capacity is improved when they are part of the group.

Apart from formal co-operative organisations, it is also necessary to promote informal local level organisations based on co-operative spirit. According to International Development Association of the University of California, Berkeley campus, USA, such informal local level organisations are needed, keeping in view the following aspects[17] :

"There are some distinct features of such informal local level

"There are some distinct features of such informal local level organisations as mentioned below:

1. They are organised around a concrete goal, which can be achieved in a limited time period and would not necessarily require the organisation thereafter. Though the organisation may continue and expand into other activities, once the concrete goal is achieved, the farmers perceive themselves as organising to achieve this one goal and not to create an organisation.
2. They start with one task and not several.
3. That task can be carried out with an organisational form that minimises the need for non-farmer skills, such as book-keeping. Examples are the building of infrastructure projects, the application for credit as a group, the distribution of water on a small scale.
4. Co-operation is required around a task that cannot be done on an individual level, i.e., certain kinds of irrigation, construction of an access road, obtaining credit available only to groups. Examples of tasks that are problematic because they can be done on both a group level and an individual level are marketing and community farming.
5. They produce goods or services for which there is a proven desire on the part of the small farmers involved.
6. The groups are small and unconnected to other groups. Group success has often gone along with the smallness and isolation from other groups because (1) Rivalry with outsiders is important in getting some groups to form and in keeping them together; (2) Smallness allows for peer pressure to induce group cohesion and loyalty, and (3) When groups are successful, they tend to become exclusive.
7. The task can be carried out by relatively informal, unsophisticated and familiar organisational forms.

The key features of these informal local level organisation is the simplicity which ensures local control and allows them to evolve or terminate if necessary".

12.7 METHODOLOGY FOR ENLISTING PEOPLE'S PARTICIPATION IN POVERTY ALLEVIATION PROGRAMMES

People's participation in rural development can be effectively enlisted provided informal local leaders' involvement is actively promoted

In recent years, there has been an understanding that for successful Rural Development, people's participation should be enlisted. However, methods to be used for successful participation by rural people are not clearly spelled out. People's participation cannot be accomplished by involving only the leaders of elected village panchayats. It can be at the most a first step in this direction. For enlisting effective people's participation in the programme, it is essential to promote active involvement of informal local leaders of the rural area.

Local leaders' contribution to rural development is invaluable. There will be no cost to the government to utilize local leaders. Local leaders will multiply the efforts of paid government workers many times, for example; if the rural development worker contacts ten local group leaders, each local leader will in turn contact atleast ten rural people. This will result in increasing the people's contact by ten times.

There are other advantages of using local leaders. These leaders speak the language of local people who have more trust in their local leader than in paid rural development worker. Rural people are convinced about the new things more easily if these local leaders communicate with them regarding the innovations. The two steps flow of communication works in these cases. In the first step rural development workers communicate with the leaders. In the second step these leaders communicate with their group members.

A classic example of successful group work through leaders has been cited by Carl Taylor (1956)[2], who reports as follows :

> "The reason for citing the particular case is because it is so completely parallels what India must do if she expect to

accomplish the outstanding increase in agricultural production which she desires and needs, in the immediate future. Experts in the field of conservation in the United States began more than 75 years ago to express the need for soil conservation practices. They were, however, voices crying in the wilderness for almost 50 years. About 25 to 30 years ago the need for such conservation had become apparent to enough farmers and public leaders that a soil conservation programme was launched. The methods for promoting the programme were typical extension methods. As many individual farmers as possible were induced to adopt various soil conservation methods. High powered propaganda of all kinds was employed to promote the use of these methods. During the depression of the 1930s, civilian conservation camps by the hundreds were established and operated. Unemployment was great and thousands of unemployed youths, both rural and urban, were employed in these camps at subsistent wages. At that moment a soil conservation programme was largely a public works programme. But, the methods of inducing individuals to adopt soil conservation practices was continued. Progress by use of this method alone was still slow. Soil deterioration and erosion was probably actually gaining ground."

"The next step in the conservation battle was an extensive programme of subsidies, paid to farmers to practice conservation methods. This undoubtedly hastened the adoption of improved practices, but there is little doubt that many farmers practiced the methods partly atleast, in order to collect their subsidy payments."[2]

"It was less than ten years ago that some of the leaders of the soil conservation programme finally became convinced that group methods might help. It is important to record that they asked for the assistance of persons who have specialists in group formation and community mobilization. These specialists taught them how to identify and delineate natural neighbour groups and discover the natural leaders of these groups. Today there are 75,000 such groups in the United States. Soil conservation on private farms is now all done under the initiative and responsibility of these groups if for no other reasons than because they cannot find time to serve individual farmers who are not members of groups, soil conservation specialists now work only through these groups. These specialists are probably no better soil and engineering specialists than they were 10 years ago, but they have added to their knowledge of scientific practice a knowledge of the practices of group formation and group responsibility. Each local group selects its own leader and carries on for more than 90 per cent of its work without the expert being present."[2]

"No other country in the world is heroically attempting to develop hundreds of millions of local people and hundreds of thousands of local communities by democratic methods as in India. The magnitude of this undertaking should not obscure the basic fact that the successful processes for the developing one local community after another are the same, whether there are thousand or five hundred thousand communities to be developed. The providing of trained local workers, the development of local groups to accept responsibility and the development of local leaders are the necessary components of a sound local community programme everywhere in the world."[2]

The greatest asset of a community organisation that is wise enough to enlist the co-operation of all groups, which exist in the village, is that it thereby discovers and uses a great many group leaders. It tries to usurp the roles of other groups, it restricts the roles of their leaders and very often incurs their enmity. It should be taken for granted that there are hundreds of thousands of local group leaders in Indian villages. Nothing is more important in rural development programme than to identify, use and develop them".

12.8 INVOLVING BASIC VILLAGE INSTITUTIONS IN THE POVERTY ALLEVIATION PROGRAMME

In the earlier community development days the three local institutes viz., the panchayat village schools and village co-operatives were assigned some specific functions in the promotion of village programme. Since the start of rural development programme, these local institutions have remained in the background and are not actively involved. The publication "Three Basic Institutions", brought out by the Government of India (1959)[18] had described the role of these institutes in community development and the following paragraphs are based on this publication.

In implementing the rural development programme, the following roles can be performed by these three basic institutes.

Village Panchayat

1. Undertaking rural planning as per the needs of the village and put up to village assembly for approval.
2. Execution of the approved plan as per time table.
3. Pooling of all available village resources, material and money needed for rural development.
4. Stock taking of the work done and its evaluation from time to time as per guidance of the village assembly.
5. Help in consolidation of land holdings in villages by educating people.
6. Bringing waste land under cultivation by developing the scheme with the approval of village people.
7. Promoting the construction of pucca irrigation projects like tanks and Bandharas.
8. Raising village forests, grazing lands and orchards for common benefit of village people.
9. Encourage villagers to grow improved seed to meet local demand with storage facility.
10. Responsible for all community undertaking such as : construction, maintenance and repairs of roads, drains, bunds, culverts and bridges and construction work of public buildings and village market.
11. Look after village water supply and sanitation and preventive measures against diseases.

12. In the socio-cultural field the panchayat can help in the following activities:

    (a) Spreading education and encouraging better attendance in schools.
    (b) Ensure the follow-up of medical advice.
    (c) Establish recreation centres, libraries, village theatres and community centres.

In order to enable the panchayats to carry out these activities, it is necessary to make adequate provisions in the existing act to enable the panchayats to raise its own income by levying some taxes, fees and cess for different items, besides giving some share from the taluk and district funds allotted by the State Government.

It is also necessary for the Panchayat to take the assistance of knowledgeable persons available in the village by nominating them as members of the Panchayat sub-committees or designate them as leaders for various programmes and activities.

The village school and rural development

The village school through its extra curricular activities can play an active role in rural development programmes of the village. The following activities can be entrusted to the school:

1. Organising village meetings at the school premises to discuss development activities.
2. Conducting village surveys to find out local situational facts from time to time.
3. Demonstrating new farm practices on the school farm and on the farms of parents of school students with the co-operation of the development departments.
4. Promoting projects as a part of school work like tailoring spinning, weaving, typing etc.
5. Conducting periodical lectures and discussion sessions in collaboration with the development department.

6. Organising youth clubs on the pattern of 4H clubs of the USA type to instil in the minds of students scientific approach.
7. Conducting school trips for students and their parents to model farms of the locality to enable students and their parents to see new ideas and practices useful for the village.

The school can also render useful services in promoting social and cultural revolution in the village. Since students of all castes and creed attend the school and stay together and read together, we can train them to run common kitchen which helps to break the caste barriers in the villages.

The schools can also run a library service useful not only for the students but also for the village elders.

In order to enable the school to perform the above mentioned activities related to rural development, there should be a system of collecting donations by the school for performing major rural development services with approval of the village Panchayat and village people.

In sum, it could be said that for carrying out effective rural development programme, neither the school can remain aloof from the village community norms nor the community can carry out rural development programme without the help of the village school.

Role of village co-operative in development programmes

The co-operative society of the village is the third basic village institution, which can play a dominant role in the rural development activities. A co-operative can assist in the economic development of the village. It shall provide the organisational, financial and technical guidance for the development of the economy. It is not enough if the co-operative is organised only for providing credit for members and distributing food article under PDS scheme. It should have broader functions and if necessary should develop subsidiary wings to help different sections of the rural community such as, weavers, artisans, transport and building workers, brick makers etc.

Work through co-operative society will bring the advantage of economies of scale by resources of individual members. Co-operatives can help in pooling the farm produce of members, storing it when market prices are low and selling at the proper time when the prices start improving in the market. The various kinds of inputs required by villagers like seed, fertilizer, farm articles, stationery and other equipments can be handled by the co-operative and made available to the members and other villagers.

Honest selfless hard work is required to make the co-operative society a really successful one. Majority of co-operative societies established in villages have failed to serve the members for lack of such people to provide leadership in the traditional co-operative societies.

12.9 METHODOLOGY FOR PROMOTING LOCAL PLANNING FOR IMPLEMENTATION OF PROJECTS

Although under the present day system, it is difficult to take up local planning in rural development programmes, it is still possible to take up some kind of local planning for implementing some of the community projects which benefit a large number of these people. A method based on work carried out in a number of such successful village works including village development activities in the Ralegaon Siddhi village of Ahmednagar district in Maharashtra State under the leadership of Anna Hazare[19] can be stated as follows :

1. Any community village project to be implemented in a village has to be discussed and approved by the village assembly or the Grama Sabha.
2. Before placing the item before the village assembly, the details of the project to be implemented must be worked out and presented before the village assembly meeting. In order to work out the details it may be necessary to formulate the local committee consisting of knowledgeable persons of the village to be nominated by the Panchayat and also include the representatives of the concerned development

departments to which the project is concerned. This committee should study the local situation and prepare the required details of the project.

3. While implementing programme in the village it is not desirable to work out a master plan to include all kinds of projects in one document. What is needed is to have details of the first project to be undertaken. Only when this project is implemented and successful results are seen, the next project is to be taken up after consideration. In order to help in taking up the more important projects it is necessary to list the possible programme items. And out of this list, the most important should be selected first. When the first programme is carried out and starts giving the result, the village people will be easily motivated to participate in the second project to be taken up.

4. Detailed information on the project should include the following items :

    (a) Situation details about the need of the project indicating clearly the possible advantage of the Project.
    (b) Spell out the important objectives of the project to be undertaken in clear-cut terms.
    (c) Methods needed to implement the programme and the responsibilities to be entrusted to different sections of the village people giving details of who to implement, what to implement, when to implement and how to implement?
    (d) Approximate time required for implementing the project.

REFERENCES

1. United Nations Economic and Social Commission for Asia and Pacific (ESCAP), 1985, *The Rural Poor, op. cit.*

2. Taylor, Carl, 1956. A critical analysis of India's Community Development

Programme. The commonly projects Administration, Government of India.

3. Desai, D.K. and Hariprakash, 1974, Strategy for Rural Development for Weaker Sections in Seminar on Rural Development for Weaker Sections, Seminar series XII, The Indian Society of Agricultural Economics, Bombay in collaboration with Centre for Management in Agriculture, IIM, Ahmedabad, p 153-159.

4. Nandapurkar, C.G., 1980, A study on entrepreneurial behaviour of small farmers unpublished Ph.D. thesis, Department of Agricultural Extension, University of Agricultural Sciences, Bangalore, *op. cit.*

5. Kesseba, Abbas M. 1989, "Introduction" in *Technology Systems for Small Farmers*, Ed., Abbas M. Kesseba, Westview Press, USA and UK.

6. Jazairy Idriss, 1989, "Foreword" in *Technology Systems for Small Farmers*, *op. cit.*

7. Swaminathan, M.S., 1985, Achieving rural urban Harmony in Agricultural Development, Guest hectare series No. 3, Institute of Rural Management, Anand, Gujarat.

8. Coombs, P.H. and Ahmed, M., 1974, *Attacking Rural Poverty, op. cit.*

9. Bathrick, D.D., 1981, *Agricultural Credit for Small Farm Development Policies and Practices, op. cit.*

10. Narayanaswamy, B.K., 1994, Management services for small farmers development, Unpublished Ph.D. thesis, Department of Agricultural Extension, University of Agricultural Sciences, Bangalore.

11. Department of Agriculture, Karnataka State, 1972, Block Demonstration Programme.

12. Anonymous, 1980, Karnataka Cooperative Milk Producers Federation (KMF), mimeographal bulletin.

13. Government of India, Planning Commission.

14. Anonymous, 1982, Sri Kshetra Dharmasthala Rural Development Project (SKDRDP), Belthangady, Dharmasthala.

15. Government of India, 1990, Report of High Powered Committee on Agricultural Policies and Programmes, *op. cit.*

16. Subramaniam, C., 1982, Seminar on Indian Agriculture, Theme paper, Rajaji International Institute of Public Affairs and Administration, New Delhi.

17. Leonard, David; Dale Marshall; Jose Garzon; Stephen Peterson and Sven Steinmo, 1981, Linkges to Decentralized Units, *op. cit.*

18. Government of India, 1959, *Three Basic Institutions*, Ministry of Community Development and Cooperation, New Delhi.

19. Hazare, Anna, 1998, Ralegaon Siddhi, A veritable transformation, Ralegaon Siddhi Pariwar, Ahmednagar dist, Mahrashtra State, India.

13

METHODS AND TECHNIQUES FOR PROMOTING WELFARE OF THE RURAL POOR—III

13.1 PRAGMATIC METHODOLOGY FOR SUSTAINABLE EMPOWERMENT OF RURAL POOR WOMEN IN AGRICULTURE

In India, women's economic productivity is rather critical to 60 million households (one-third of the households of the country) whose family members live below the poverty line. This is because women are the only main earners in these 60 million households, according to the information furnished in the World Bank Report (1995).[1] Thus, the empowerment of poor women is vital for attacking rural poverty in India.

The Government of India launched the project for Development of Women and Children in Rural Areas (DWCRA) which was commenced in 1982 as an exclusive scheme for women, covering 161 districts out of 446. The scheme operates with 28,000 women groups (each group consists 12-15 women) covering 4.6 lakh women. As pointed out in the Eighth Plan Document (of Government of India), the operation of the scheme had inadequate impact and, therefore, failed in organizing cohesion within and among the groups to identify the activities that could generate sustained income.[2]

It took about almost nine years to reach half of the country with the programme (240 out of 446 districts). It was only during the year 1995 the programme could cover all the districts of the country. Even then the number of villages covered was not at all satisfactory. The target fixed for the programme was to involve 7500 groups of rural poor women each year. Assuming that a minimum of one group of 15 rural poor women is organized in each village, 7500 villages would be reached with the programme each year. There are 5,59,000 villages in India and it will naturally take (5,59,000 divided by 7,500) 74 years to cover every village in India. Hence, the programme of this kind which depends on entirely outside finance and that too on a limited level, has inherent weakness in not reaching a majority of rural women. The very idea of developing such programmes by only utilizing outside finance will come in the way of expanding the programme to cover every village.

The present day paradigm itself is based on providing one time grant and subsidies, depending on top down approach, taking the short view for the success of the programme and need for additional staff to be created for operating the programme and all contributed only for hindering the programme.

It is our conviction that, the existing infrastructure in the villages and the Government staff like, Gramsevaks, Gramasevikas, Agricultural Assistants and Anganawadi workers etc., are quite adequate to develop and implement empowerment programme in every village, targetting the rural poor families. This programme has to be a co-ordinated one, combining rural poor women's health and family planning services, education and training, developing entrepreneurship and motivation of the beneficiaries and making available loan needed for undertaking the projects through self help groups.

There is no need to give honorarium to group organizers. What is needed is to inspire voluntary efforts by the group leaders instead of creating a band of workers who only aspire for remuneration, instead of working for rural poor women. There is ample availability of voluntary leaders in rural communities. Only they have to be identified, trained and used for this task of empowerment of rural poor women. The voluntary group promoter has to be trained for undertaking the following activities (i) identifying eligible participants, (ii) assisting them to organize themselves into small groups around some income generating activities, (iii) helping them to obtain needed credit from the revolving fund or from institutional credit, (iv) obtain and services from concerned agencies, and (v) guiding the group towards self reliance.The group promoter will also be responsible for monitoring, analyzing and documenting the overall performance of the group. Such an approach for using voluntary group leaders has been reported by ESCAP in its publication *The Rural Poor* published in 1985.[3]

A new pragmatic approach is essential to reorient the programme so that every village will be reached immediately. Methodology recommended for this pragmatic approach has to lay emphasis on the important factors enumerated below :

Participatory approach

This is a reverse of the presently followed top down approach. The participatory approach is essential for the success of the projects like empowerment of rural poor women.

Promoting and using SHG based on limited local organisations

The second important feature of the pragmatic approach is to provide a different kind of group approach for fulfilling their needs. This is what is known as "limited level social organization" recommended by Tendler (1976)[4] and Korten (1980).[5] This, differs from traditional co-operative approach which have to be registered for their functioning and have complicated procedures. The features of this local level limited organisations have already been explained in the previous chapter.

Involvement of rural poor women in selecting viable projects

For involving rural poor women in undertaking viable projects, it is necessary to undertake intensive educational efforts preferably through night meetings. This will also help to enlist their participation in the empowerment programme. In these educational meetings the rural development worker should play the catalyzer's role entrusting the main job of educating people to their own representatives, who have already started such projects in the rural areas. The motto should be farmer to train farmer. These meetings should also help people to decide particular projects in which they are interested and to form different groups for different projects.

Developing Entrepreneurship and achievement motivation

The rural poor women who indicate their inclination to join the particular project group require further intensive education to assist in motivating them for action and also help them to develop their entrepreneurial ability. Research on rural poor has identified five important components which influence their emtrepreneurial behaviour.[6]

Hence, in this intensive educational programme entrepreneurial aspects have to be focused. Narrating achievements of the rural poor who have already undertaken such projects, organizing visits to their projects and holding group discussion with those successful rural people, are some of the techniques which will help in increasing achievement motivation of rural people towards an activity.

Self-help supported by small loans

Promoting self help among the group members, who have joined the particular group, is the most important requirement of this pragmatic approach of empowering rural poor women. The hitherto followed subsidy-cum-loan approach,[7] has to be modified into self help and loan approach. The subsidy approach has really created more problems as compared to the assistance provided to the rural poor. Research conducted by USAID has indicated that subsidies are not important factors in promoting projects work with rural poor as believed earlier. ESCAP (1985) has recommended that programmes that enable the poor to become economically viable, using loan capital instead of grants, will only be acceptable alternatives. Small farmers developments programmes undertaken by the ESCAP has clearly demonstrated that such an approach is not only possible but also well received by the target groups, who were previously the recipients for more paternalistic programmes, which tended to promote dependency on governments rather than a self reliant ethic that is imperative under the circumstances. What is needed is the loan amount required to undertake the projects successfully. Rural women have to be provided with small amounts of loan. Hilary Clinton is reported to have said that "the small loans as low as $125 could change the lives of poor people around the globe and urged expansion of small lines of credit to them", during her visit to SEWA, an NGO in India.[8] The same point was stressed by Lady Clinton in her address at the Micro Credit Summit held at Washington DC in USA in Feb 1997.[9] The experience of Mohammed Unis, in Bangladesh, in his Grameena Bank Movement for the poor in 1970, has also supported this micro credit programme.

Recently an intensive empowerment programme for rural poor women has been successfully undertaken in Hunsur (Ta) of Mysore district, Karnataka, India. In this programme self help supported by small loans has assisted women groups in 187 villages involving 7000 rural poor women. A detailed report on this work has been written by R. Srikanth and published in the Kannada weekly *Sudha* in April 1999 under the caption 'Strishakthi', The following paragraphs give summarised information of this article.

Promoting and using local leaders for multiplier effects

Local leaders have to be actively involved in any rural development work. Without the use of local leaders there cannot be the expected level of multiplier effect of rural development programme. As pointed by Carl Taylor[10] as early as in 1956, it should be taken for granted that there are hundreds or thousands of local groups leaders in Indian villages. Nothing is more important in empowerment programme of rural poor women than to locate, use, and develop these local leaders for rapid multiplier effect of the programme.

Utilizing existing infrastructure like basic village institutions

At present these basic village institutions have not been provided with any active role in promoting empowerment programme for rural poor women. Therefore, it is necessary to utilize the services of these infrastructure facilities for effective implementation of the programme. The pragmatic methodology pinpoints the need for this approach.

Initiating empowerment programme by targetting young women through 4H ideas

It is necessary that the rural women empowerment work should be started with young women of the villages. This programme should be based on 4H club work carried out successfully in the USA. Project work is the fundamental approach through which young women will learn by doing. The educational experiences which young people gain through these projects and activities, give them an introduction for accepting adult life responsibilities. They provide avenues for character building, good citizenship development and leadership growth. This work can be initiated first in the village schools as an extra curricular activity with the support of interested teachers and village leaders. What is needed is a bold policy to promote the idea.

Use of NGO's which are small and flexible with local roots and contacts

India's Planning Commission has pointed out that NGO's are required to get people's co-operation and participation in the implementation of development programmes. Rural women's empowerment programme is no exception. Hence, it is a firm belief of this pragmatic methodology to promote and use NGOs which are small and flexible in their approach. Successful village work in India reported from few villages is primarily attributed to the active involvement of NGOs in the development programme. This kind of work can also be promoted without any extra funds. Primarily NGOs assistance is required in assisting rural women to get access to several services provided by the government and other organizations.

Nomination of poor women for managing rural organizations

We are only pleading for getting reservation for women in different areas of work including reservation in Parliament. But involvement of women in the management of their village institutions can be achieved if the villagers simply nominate women to take over the responsibilities of these institutions. The work carried out by Anna Hazare who has spearheaded the village upliftment programme in Ralegaon Siddhi village of Ahmednagar district of Maharashtra, India, is a classic example of how women could be assigned responsibilities of managing village institutions.[11] Under his guidance, the village Panchayat has nominated women as its office bearers and all these women have carried out their work satisfactorily.

Based on the article published in Kannada weekly in March 1998 under the caption 'Strishakthi',[12] a case study has ben prepared and the following paragraphs give summarized information regarding this case study.

13.2 A CASE STUDY ON SELF HELP GROUP APPROACH BY AN NGO (PARIVARTHANA) IN THE SOUTHERN PART OF INDIA

Since several decades, Hunsur Taluk, Mysore District (situated in the southern part of India), has been considered as the bowl of Ragi, a staple food of the majority of poor people in rural areas. This is also famous internationally for teak wood. Earlier, here farmers, tribes, backward class and SCs and STs have led a happy and prosperous life. Farmers from several parts of the State used to come here and stay for few months with their livestock for grazing. The thick and beautiful forest was a calm and peaceful place for leading a happy and contended life.

In the beginning of 1970 farmers here have started cultivating tobacco in their fields. This has resulted in losing the productivity of their lands. Thereafter there was a gradual decline in the area under forest, existing trees in the fields and community forest near village. As a consequence of this, once Hunsur which was famous as the "prosperous land of Ragi", has now become a "land of diseases".

On an average, this region used to receive 45" of annual rainfall. But now it is receiving only 13" to 20". Out of the 26 different basic sources of water for the well known river "Laxmanthirtha" of this region. Presently we have only five sources. The river has therefore dried up and made the people in Hunsur to cry even for drinking water. The health condition of the people living in the villages has deteriorated due to poor nutrition, unhygienic conditions and poverty. A majority of the villagers are illiterate and have become habitual drinkers of the low quality, highly intoxicating drinks supplied at cheaper rates by the Government agents. There is an enormous growth of population in the villages leading to cut-throat fight for available resources and the services provided under Government programmes are not yielding any significant improvement in any sphere of life of these people.

During lean periods of agriculture, the poor people from several villages of the taluk, migrate to nearby coffee plantations for short periods in search of employment along with their family members including school-going children. Because of these reasons the conditions of living of these villagers was miserable and there was no sign of improvement.

How it started

Under the concerted efforts of 'Parivarthana', an NGO, revolutionary work was initiated in motivating and organizing the poor rural women in these villages, and the women have established an Association of their men.

Here is the story of the Hunsur taluk Narasimha Swamy Shanthi Mahila Sangha. "The Sangha has started in unique way by the inspiration of the Organization for the Development of People (ODP). About 5 years back, this organization was distributing nutritious food for ladies and children. In the process, the nuns of this organization inspired the ladies to form a union. In the beginning the illiterate and ignorant women were reluctant, to do so. Later due to constant persuasion and inspiration from these ODP nuns, 10 to 12 women joined and formed the Shanthi Mahila Sangha.

In the beginning it was very difficult even to collect all women members at one place for discussion. Gradually this burden of collecting them at one place vanished when they formed "Self Help Groups". The important objectives of this self help group were :

1. To build confidence and independence among rural poor women through cooperation of one another.
2. Encouraging small scale savings among the members.
3. Inspiring through education and by using savings compensated with credits to start sustainable small enterprises.

Through these self help groups, each member used to save, depending upon her capacity, to a tune of rupees 10 to 20 in a week and they kept this accumulated amount as deposit and each member became eligible to get two and half times more amount as credit.

The self help group which is a part of the Shanthi Mahila Sangha has gradually grown and started silently motivating other poor women in the village to join their hands. The members of this self help group have started their own independent activities based on their own capabilities. For example,

	Name of the member		Activity started
1.	Poojarama	:	Crushing stone for construction of houses
2.	Jayamma	:	Marketing of citrus fruits
3.	Rahmath Unnisa	:	Petty shop
4.	Kalamani	:	Bangle store business
5.	Yashodamma	:	Tailoring

Rural poor women who have availed hundred or two hundred rupees as credit in the beginning have started taking loan upto 10,000 rupees after five years. Their per week saving which was 10 to 20 rupees has reached, few thousand rupees. Presently there are 50 members in this 'Self-Help-Group' and they are availing more than 2 lakh as credit and also repaying regularly. There is not a single incidence or misuse of money by the members of the group.

Changes that have taken place in the village after the formation of the Shanthi Mahila Sangha, as explained by the members are :

1. Earlier their husbands use to beat them for petty reasons. Now that has stopped, and they have started behaving properly.
2. Improvement in the social and spiritual norms in the village.
3. Change in neglected or sarcastic attitude to respectful attitude towards rural poor women by all the members of their families and villagers.
4. Husbands have started taking loan from their wives for production purposes.
5. Rural poor women who were afraid even to walk in the villages alone have developed courage to attend night meetings after completing their family responsibilities and discuss about their problems and possible ways for their economic and social improvement.

In addition to these, they have purchased a site for the Sangh by paying 15,000 rupees. These women, through their agitations, have fought with Government Departments and got sanctioned a Community Drinking Water Scheme. Under that, construction of a water tank is in progress in the village. Also, they have diplomatically succeeded in getting a post office and a police station in the village.

There are today 187 such Sanghas which are functioning effectively in 33 taluks of Mysore, Mandya, a Coorg district. All these 187 Sanghas have been federated with 'Mahilodaya-Mahila Sangha" which is located at Mysore. Presently, there are 700 members enrolled in these 187 villages Mahila Sanghas.

Education and Training, Motivation and Organizing, and Independence, are the three strong themes on which this federation has been laying more emphasis.

REFERENCES

1. World Bank, 1995, *Gender and Poverty.*

2. Government of India, VIII Plan Document, 1992.
3. United Nations Economic and Social Commission for Asia and Pacific (ESCAP), 1985, The Rural Poor, *op. cit.*
4. Tendeler, Judith, 1979, New Directions for Rural Roads, Washington, DC: Agency for International Development, Office of Evaluation.
5. Korten, Frances E. and Sarah Young "The Mothers Clubs of Korea" *Managing Community Based Population Programmes*, Kuala Lumpur. International Committee on the Management of Population Programmes.
6. Nandapurkar, C.G., 1980, A study on entrepreneurial behaviour of small farmers, *op. cit.*
7. Leonard, David; Dale Marshall; Jose Garzon; Stephen Peterson and Sven Steinmo, 1981. *Linkages to Decentralized Units, op. cit.*
8. Clinton, Hillary, 1997, Statement made after visiting SEWA as reported by *The Times of India*, dated February 5, 1997.
9. Clinton, Hillary, 1998, Address at the Micro credit summit held at Washington DC, USA in February 1997 reported in *Deccan Herald.*
10. Taylor, Carl, 1956, A critical analysis of India's community development programme. Issued by the Community Projects Administration. Government of India.
11. Hazare, Anna, 1998, Ralegaon Siddhi, *op. cit.*
12. Special article in weekly magazine *Sudha* titled "Shree Shakthi" written by Srikanth and published in March 1998.

14

PROGRAMME OBJECTIVES OF RURAL DEVELOPMENT

Objectives are expressions of the ends towards which our efforts, through various programmes, are to be directed. In other words, the term 'objective' indicates the direction of movements. Objectives are generally expressed at different levels from very broad level to specific level like : (1) Fundamental objectives at the broadest level, (2) General objectives which define the important areas on a broad enough level, and (3) Specific objectives with clearly stated programme areas which are related to the workable aspect i.e., directly related to the area of operation.

14.1 KINDS OF OBJECTIVES FOR RURAL DEVELOPMENT

Rural poverty, the world over, has re-emerged as one of the critical issues on the International Arena of Development during the 1990s. All International Development Agencies have expressed their concern and further proclaimed their strong commitment to reducing rural poverty in the world. The World Bank President, Lews T. Preston, has also stated that the fundamental objective of the World Bank is sustainable poverty reduction.

Programmes for alleviation of rural poverty have been included under important objectives of India's Planned Development from the beginning of the plan era. It is reported that ever since the inception of planning, the objectives and programmes are being designed and redesigned, keeping this cardinal principle in mind. It was realized that a sustainable strategy of poverty alleviation has to be based on increasing the productive employment opportunity in the process of growth itself. The First Five Year Plan document stated in clear terms that "the backwardness of India's economy is primarily due to its unbalanced occupational structure itself, since a sizable majority of the working population was dependent upon Agriculture for its occupation."[1] This Plan document, therefore, stressed that a change in the occupational patterns in the direction of a greater employment in the industrial sector and in services is clearly necessary if the associated phenomenon of mass poverty and unemployment is to be effectively tackled. Based on this background, increasing the GDP to a satisfactory level has been kept as the most important objectives of National Programme of alleviation of rural poverty in India.

It is not sufficient if the objectives are stated only at a very broad level as is done now in India's Plan Documents. What is needed is to formulate operational objectives keeping the broad objectives in mind, so that suitable programmes of activities can be chalked out to fulfil the operational objectives of alleviating rural poverty. It is here that much needs to be done. In all our Plan documents, including the VIII Five Year Plan, the alleviation of rural poverty has always occupied an important base in the list of States over all objectives. Broad statements like, promoting of employment opportunity and allocation in the proportion of income wealth, have been observed in all these Plan publications. However, in operational terms, these objectives are given a rather scant attention and as a result, no clear cut set of operational objectives were clearly stated, and identification of well defined programme areas under each programme objectives, have not been spelled out (Kamta Prasad, 1985)[2]. This has naturally, resulted in not carrying out the needed activities to alleviate rural poverty effectively.

The purpose of this chapter is to highlight this aspect and make out a case for formulation of clear cut, specifically stated, operational programme objectives, which provide guidance to poverty alleviation in the years to come and to development of an inventory of needed programme areas under each programme objective which may lead to effective implementation so as to reach the objectives.

14.2 STRATEGIES IN DESIGNING NATIONAL OBJECTIVES OF RURAL DEVELOPMENT

The objectives of rural development include sustained increase in the per capita output and incomes, expansion of productive employment and greater equality in the distribution of the benefits of growth. This implies reducing poverty and the human misery by increasing profitability of the rural poor and providing them greater access to goods and services and also enabling them to take advantage of the safetynets to be provided by the government. Rural development aimed at target groups must constitute a major part of a developmental strategy, if large segment of the poor in greater need are to benefit.

Past strategies, as in most developing countries, have failed to emphasize economic growths without operationally considering the manner in which the benefits of growth are to be distributed. A strategy in designing objectives for successful rural development should be aimed at raising growth rates and distributing the fruits of growths more fairly to reach the rural poor. This further implies greater interaction between the modern and traditional sectors of development, especially in the form of increased trade in farm produce and in technical input and services. In operational terms this broad strategy thus needs not only concentration of objectives to putforth efforts on the high growth modern sectors of the country's economy by increasing the GDP at a satisfactory growth rate on an assumption that this increased growth *per se* would automatically lead in the long run, through trickle down effect to a reduction in rural poverty; although this kind of modern growth is necessary for rural development it cannot be a sufficient condition for eradication of rural poverty, unless concomitant attention is paid and corresponding, concentration is given to keep objectives to reach the traditional sector population of rural poor, including small farmers, tenants and agricultural labourers and artisans. Failure to recognize this strategy in formulating programme objectives has been a major reason why eradication of rural poverty in most of the developing countries has been slow and rural poverty has not been satisfactorily alleviated, in spite of years of work carried out in this regard, even with the massive assistance from world bodies.

14.3 COMPLEX NATURE OF NATIONAL OBJECTIVES FOR RURAL DEVELOPMENT

Since Rural Development is aimed at alleviating poverty, it must be clearly planned and designed to increase production and raise productivity not only of the country in general but of the rural poor in particular. National objectives of rural development should also recognize that the improved food supplies and nutrition, along with other basic services such as health and education, are not only necessary for direct improvement of the well-being and better quality of life of the rural poor, but also are essentially required to play an important role to enhance their productivity and their ability to contribute to the nation's economy. The operative objectives of rural development are rather complex in nature and extend beyond any particular sector. Besides increasing the national income and productivity to attain a satisfactory GDP, they should include improved productivity and thus higher income for the target groups of rural poor simultaneously, as well as a minimum acceptable level of food, shelter, education and health services. Fulfilment of these complex nature of objectives causes an expansion of goods and services available in the country, with particular reference to the rural poor and build institutions and promote policies that will enable the rural poor to benefit fully from the whole range of economic and social services, so that the development attainable will be self-sustainable. In order that this should happen, it is necessary that the target groups be properly identified and encouraged to actively participate in the organization and implementation of the programme.

14.4 WIDE RANGE OF OBJECTIVES TO ENCOMPASS MIX OF ACTIVITIES

It has already been made clear both under the concept and issues as well as in the earlier discussion of this chapter that the rural development objectives extend beyond any particular sector and they encompass a mix of activities. It is necessary to list out major kinds of activities in a brief way so that these can be accommodated while formulating detailed rural development programme objectives.

The objectives of rural development besides including projects to improve agricultural output generate new employment opportunity, provide proper health and education facilities, expand communication (World Bank, 1975)[3].

One of the important obstacle related to a country's development is said to be its immobility from one area to the other. 'Transport facilities are necessary conditions for economic development of any area. It is, therefore, no wonder that countries like India with low standard of living are also characteristically the countries with poor facilities of roads and transport. If the physical barriers and costs of transporting goods to and from local markets are too high in the absence of good roads, marketing facilities will be very costly to the villagers. Hence the development of roads in the rural areas is very crucial. It is absolutely clear that the growing rural unemployment cannot be reduced unless cottage and village industries and modernized small industries are encouraged to develop in the rural areas.

Rural poverty is not only due to lack of resources, but also due to sub-human living conditions, ill-health and under-development of minds. To overcome this, social amenities such as sanitary facilities, potable drinking water, hospitals and schools etc., should be provided in the rural areas. If a poor family has access to these, it makes determined efforts to improve its economic conditions, but when poverty is accompanied by the absence of these facilities, road to progress is totally blocked.

Objectives of rural development besides including projects to improve agricultural output, generate new employment opportunities, provide proper health and education facilities, expand communication and improve housing. Despite increase of migration to urban areas, the rural population is growing approximately at the rate of two per cent per year. The consequent worsening of the man-land ratio means that diminishing land resources of the rural poor require that increases in production and income must come primarily from higher yields per hectare and cultivation of more cash giving crops or enterprises. To achieve such gain depends upon objectives with programmes promoting modern sustainable technology and availability of capital and safety-net and utilize it without risk and uncertainty.

These programmes in turn require programme objectives to provide the needed assistance to the rural poor for getting access to the various services of the variety of institutions set up in the country for the welfare of the rural poor. Again objectives, to provide special programmes to help the rural poor to participate and contribute more fully to and increase in output are required. There is also a need for programmes which include the provision of infrastructure and on-farm improvements.

The identification of specific target groups of the rural poor for specific rural development programmes for their welfare is an equally important requirement for which programme objectives must give due attention. In the absence of clear cut objectives on this, the benefits meant for the rural poor may be grabbed by the non-poor rural people who may be influential and politically strong.

Objectives of rural development programmes must also be clearly spelled out for organizing, planning and implementation of the programmes involving adequate local planning, strong co-ordination at all levels of administration, including the operational level, creation of effective local level organizations and active participation of the village people including the rural poor in both the planning and implementing process.

Since sizable number of farm families of the rural poor are headed by women, special attention needs to be given for their active involvement to speed up the progress of development and this aspect has to be specifically stated as one of the important objectives of the programme of alleviation of rural poverty.

There is need to create employment opportunities for the rural unemployed and under-employed at their doors. This can be done by developing cottage and village industries and supporting enterprises[4].

In order to help the rural poor to increase their production and income, it is necessary to assist them to improve their existing resources and also encourage them to acquire new assets. Hence asset development and asset availability are two objectives important in any programme for alleviating rural poverty.

14.5 OBJECTIVES OF RURAL DEVELOPMENT AS VISUALIZED BY PIONEERS

The objectives of rural development visualized by pioneer and national leaders help us to take a pragmatic look at the formulation of the programme objectives for the years to come. This will also serve as useful guidelines for developing the needed philosophy behind formulation of the rural development programme. A brief account of these objectives as visualized by our pioneer national leaders is given in the following paragraphs.

Rural poverty has been a bane in India from times even before independence. Attempts have been made to alleviate this deficiency starting from the period prior to independence. It was Gandhiji who initiated moves to increase rural employment and production in the countryside by starting village development work as an important aspect of building the country. At the same time Rabindranath Tagore also started work to increase rural employment and production programme in the rural areas. In those days when every educated man only thought of development related to big towns and industries, Gandhiji gave a mission to the country stating frankly that what is required is to build India through the villages. His ideas of village reconstruction programme which he called the "Vidhayaka Karyakrama" was primarily meant to alleviate poverty in villages and increase employment for rural people both men and women.

Gandhiji's dream of India's development was intensely rural. He saw India's greatness not in highly industrialized cities, but in intelligent, independent and contented millions in its villages. He was appalled by the ignorance, disease and poverty of rural people and visualized village reconstruction programme that would fire the imagination of rural poor and lead them through self-help to ensure ample food for all, adequate health protection and medical services, free education, local self-government and self-employment through cottage industries[5].

The principle planks of his programme were (1) communal harmony, (2) removal of untouchability, (3) prohibition, (4) use of khadi, (5) promotion of village industries, (6) uplift of young, privileged class and women, (7) full development and utilization of local resources, (8) promotion of economic equality, (9) self-sufficient village economy, (10) self-reliant village community. In this programme he had focused attention on the importance of developing the rural people and rural areas.

Gandhiji's ideas about rural poverty and its alleviation and also his thinking regarding village development based on local people's involvement have been summarised in the following paragraphs. As far as possible these ideas have been stated in Gandhiji's own words as available in various publications.

Objectives of rural development as visualised by Gandhiji and his ideas about Rural Poverty and its Alleviation

Analyzing the poverty situation in India, Gandhiji said : "I have been travelling through India. I cannot bear the heart rendering cry of the poor. The young and old all tell me, we cannot get cheap clothes. We have not the meals. Everything is dear, provision, cloth and all. What are we to do and they heave a sigh of despair. It is my duty to give these men a satisfactory reply"[6].

Gandhiji explained the cause of poverty in the following words: "We have 21 crore farmers. My own experience and the experience of authoritative writers shows that they have four months of the year lying idle on their hands. This is a huge economic waste. No wonder that they are poor"[6]. *Young India,* August 20, 1919 quoted in the book the "Village Reconstruction" (p. 303)[6].

Gandhiji's suggestion to alleviate rural poverty

Gandhiji said : "The hungry millions ask for one poem; invigorating food. They cannot be given it. They must earn it and they can earn only by the sweat of their brow ....".

... To the people famishing and idle, the only acceptable form in which God can dare appear is work and a promise of food as basis". Gandhiji further says : "According to me the economic constitution of India and for that matter, that of the world should be such that no one under it should suffer from want of food and clothing. In other words, everybody should be able to get sufficient work and to enable him to make the two ends meet. This ideal can be universally realised only if the means of production for elementary necessities of life remain in the control of the masses"[8] (*Young India*, dated 15-11-1928) quoted in the book "*The Village Reconstruction*", p.29[6].

Gandhiji's ideas about economic equality

"Economic equality must never be supposed to mean possession of an equal amount of worldly goods by everyone. It does mean however that everyone will have a proper house to live in sufficient and balanced food to eat and sufficient 'Khadi' with which to cover himself. It also means that the cruel inequality that operates today will be removed by purely non-violent means (*Harijan*, 18-8-1940). Quoted in the book *Selected Works of Mahatma Gandhi*, p. 340, Vol. 6)"[7]. "The contrasts between rich and poor today is a painful sight. The poor villagers are exploited. They produce the food and go hungry. They produce milk and their children have to go without it. It is disgraceful. Everyone must have balanced diet, a decent house to live in, facilities for the education of one's children and adequate medical relief, that constitutes my picture of economic equality", quoted in the book "*Selected Works of Mahatma Gandhi*", p. 340[7].

Remedy for poverty

"The millions must have a simple industry to supplement agriculture. Spinning was a cottage industry years ago and if the millions are to be saved from starvation, they must be enabled to reintroduce spinning in their house and every village must repossess its own weaver" (From page 4, "The Village Reconstruction" : from an article in *Young India,* July, 21, 1920)[6].

Economics required

"The economics that inculcates Mammon worship and enables the strong to amass wealth at the expense of the weak, is a false and dismal science. It spells death. True Economics on the other hand stands for social justice. It promotes the good of all equally, including the weakest and is indispensable for decent life. Adam Smith in his *Wealth of Nations* after laying down certain principles according to which economic phenomena are governed, went on to describe certain other things which constituted the disturbing factor and prevented economic laws from having free play. Human element was one of them. Now, it is this human element on which the entire economics of Khadi rests and human selfishness, Adam Smith's pure economic motive constitutes a disturbing factor that has got to be overcome" (From *Harijan* 21-9-1934; also from *Selected Works of Mahatma Gandhi,* page 322)[7].

Work for masses

Gandhiji said : "No scheme of irrigation or other agricultural improvement that human ingenuity can conceive, can deal with the vastly scattered population of India or provide work for masses of mankind who are constantly thrown out of employment. Imagine a nation working only five hours per day on an average and this is not by choice but by force of circumstances and you have a realistic picture of India". (*Young India*, November 3, 1921 and also page 12, in *The Village Reconstruction*.

"I have abundant proof now to support my statement that a spinning wheel will solve the problem of economic distress in millions of Indian homes and it constitutes an effective insurance against famines. India does not need to be industrialized in the modern sense of the term. The people are rooted to the soil and the vast majority are living hand to mouth life. There is no doubt that millions are living in enforced idleness for atleast four months in a year. Agriculture requires a supplementary industry. The most natural is the introduction of spinning wheel and not the handloom. The latter cannot be introduced in every home whereas the former can, and it used to be so even a century ago. It was driven out not by economic pressure but by force deliberately used as can be proved from authentic records.The restoration, therefore, of the spinnning wheel solves the economic problem of India at a stroke" (From *Young*

India, April 6, 1922). Quoted in the book *The Village Reconstruction, p.* 14.[6]

Khadi and other industries

According to Gandhiji : "Khadi is the 'sun' of the village solar system. The planets are the various industries which can support Khadi in return for the heat and the sustenance they derive from it. Without it the other industries cannot grow but during my last tour I discovered that without the revival of the other industries, Khadi could not make further progress for villagers to be able to occupy their spare time profitably. The village life must be touched at all points. Other village industries come in as a hand made to Khadi. They cannot exist without Khadi and Khadi is robbed of its dignity without them. Village economy cannot be complete without the essential village industries such as hand grinding, hand pounding, soap making, paper making, match making, tanning, oil pressing etc. *(Selected Works of Mahatma Gandhi,* page 396-99)[7].

Government's role in promoting village industry

Gandhiji specified the role of Government in promoting village industries. He recommended : "The Government should notify the villagers that they will be expected to manufacture Khadi for the needs of their villages within a fixed date after which no cloth will be supplied to them from outside. The Government in its turn will supply villagers with cotton seeds or cotton wherever required at cost price and the focus of manufacture also at cost to be recovered in easy instalments payable, that is to say for five years or more. The villages will be surveyed and a list prepared of things that can be manufactured locally with little or no help and which may be required for village use or for sale outside"[7] (From *'Harijan'* 28-4-1946) quoted in the book Rebuilding Our Village (p. 100)[8].

Other measures for poverty alleviation

Gandhiji added : "I am thinking of ways and means of improving the condition of the people through rehabilitation of agriculture, cattle breeding and all other village industries" (Ref : *"Selected Works of Mahatma Gandhi"*, pp. 401)[7]

Self sufficiency

Gandhiji's view about self sufficiency are explained as follows : "My idea of self sufficiency is that villagers must be self sufficient in regard to food, cloth and other basic necessities. To be self sufficient is not to be altogether self contained. In no circumstances would we be able to produce all the things we need. So though our aim is complete self sufficiency, which we shall have to get from outside the village what we cannot produce in a village. We shall have to produce more of what we can in order thereby to obtain in exchange what we are unable to produce. As for food, India has plenty of fertile land. There is enough water and no dearth of manpower. The public should be educated to become self reliant. Once they know that they have got to stand on their own legs, it would electrify the atmosphere (Ref : *Selected Works of Mahatma Gandhi*, pp. 349; *Harijan*, 19-10-1947)[7].

Planning

While explaining planning, Gandhiji said, "Local planning consists in the best utilization of the whole manpower of India and the distribution of raw products of India in numerous villages, instead of sending them outside and rebuying finished articles at fabulous prices. I heartily endorse the proposition that any plan which exploits the raw materials of a country and neglects the potentially more powerful manpower is lopsided and can never tend to establish human equality. Every human being has a right to live and, therefore, to find the wherewithal to feed himself and where necessary to clothe and house himself. But for this simple performance we need no assistance from economists or their laws" (Ref : *Selected Works of Mahatma Gandhi*, pp. 323)[7].

Use of outside money

According to Gandhiji : "You cannot bring a model village into being by a magic wand of money. When money is given it can only do harm. It has got to be earned when it is required. I am convinced that the American and British money which has been voted for missionary societies has done more harm than good (Ref : *Rebuilding Our Villages,* pp. 8 and also *Harijan,* 26-12-1936)[8].

Gandhiji on decentralization

"The centre of power now is in New Delhi, not in Calcutta and Bombay, in big cities. I would have it distributed among the 7,00,000 villages of India (Ref : *Selected Works of Mahatma Gandhi*— The Last Phase, Vol 2, 158, pp. 614)[7].

Village Panchayats

"True democracy cannot be worked by 20 men sitting at the centre. It has to be worked from below by the people of every village.

In my opinion, there is no law which can stop a Panchayat from functioning wherever the people want it. Every group (of villages) or its member can have the Panchayat system whether the rest of India has it or not. True rights come as a result of duty donc. No one can snatch away such rights. The Panchayat is there to serve the people in a village. Even if one village wants Panchayat Raj, which is called republic in English, no one can stop it" (Ref : *Harijan,* 18-1-48, pp. 519)[10].

"Independence must begin at the bottom. Thus, every village will be a republic or Panchayat having full powers. It follows, therefore, that every village has to be self sustained and capable of managing its affairs even to the extent of defending itself against the whole world" (Ref : *Harijan,* 28-7-46, pp. 236)[11].

The greater the power of the Panchayats, the better for the people. Moreover, for Panchayats to be effective and efficient, the level of people's education has to be considerably raised (*Harijan,* 5-6-1937)[14].

Gandhiji on Education

Craft, art, health and education should all be integrated into one scheme. Nai Talim is a beautiful blend of all the four and covers the whole education of the individual from the time of conception to the moment of death. Instead of regarding craft and industry as different from education, I will regard the former as a medium for the latter (Ref : *Harijan,* 10-11-46, pp. 394)[12].

Our system of (basic) education leads to the development of the mind, body and soul. The ordinary system cares only for the mind (Ref : *Harijan*, 9-11-47, pp. 401)[13].

Educating villagers

"If we want to impart education best suited to the needs of villagers, we should take the 'Vidyapith' to the villages. We should convert it into a training school in order that we might be able to give practical training to leaders in terms of the needs of villagers. You cannot instruct the teachers on the needs of villagers through a training school in a city. Nor can you so interest them in the condition of villagers (Ref : *Harijan,* 5-6-37, pp. 130)[14].

Objectives of rural development as visualised by other pioneers

Rabindranath Tagore involved himself in rural improvement as part of his Sriniketan programme. Gurudev became mindful as to how to eradicate the evils and extricate the helpless villagers from the bondage of poverty. He explained his philosophy of village reconstruction as follows :[15]

"From the very beginning I was convinced that any attempt to help the villagers from outside would be the most unreal thing. It would only amount to serving the present at the cost of the future. With a spirit of self-reliance, one can discover a source of sustenance. Even in a desert, such a fountain can never go dry. We have to find out at the fountain of strength in the hearts of villagers themselves. The first step towards that would be to create faith in their own strength and particularly in the strength of co-operative endeavour".

Rabindranath Tagore actually started village reconstruction work in selected villages under Sriniketan programme. Without Government assistance, work began in a quiet manner. At first the villagers were sceptical about the intended motives of the band of workers. They, however, soon realized that they themselves would benefit by the spread of education and sanitation and they readily co-operated in the work of reconstruction of their villages. During leisure hours the women folk started learning different crafts and became adept in cottage industries, began to flourish and villagers got some amount of relief from poverty by selling their products.

The First President of India, Dr. Rajendra Prasad[16], termed Community Development as the *yagna* and advocated a clear cut policies for eradicating under-employment, unemployment and poverty in the villages. According to him, the village people mostly the poor, have idle time for atleast half of the year and this has to be used by providing additional employment by alternate occupations, like cottage industries which can be provided, which will not require continuous operation but could be interrupted and taken up again without imposing any serious dislocation or loss. Rajendra Babu also stressed the role of scores of village leaders who have a measure of initiative and pride in this work.

The First Indian Governor General, C. Rajagopalachari[17], called Community Development as the *Grama Kalyan*. His concept of *Grama Kalyan* (1952, p. 7) included, improved methods of agriculture and contained the following ideas. Reclamation of all available land and the utilization of all local resources. Good feeder roads must be made for easy and speedy transport and to link up neighbouring villages. It also includes education, sports and entertainment. The projects also should envisage facilities for fuller education of working children and vocational and technical training for those who have no family craft to follow. Also they will seek to do all that is necessary to improve public health in those areas especially in the matter of good drinking water and proper disposal and utilization of human and animal refuse. Special attention needs be given to what is woefully lacking now namely, proper medical attention for those who need it. The development of cottage and small scale industries to absorb all those who are now a burden on rural family was an important part of *Grama Kalyan*. Efforts should be made to provide and create satisfactory housing conditions.

Pandit Jawaharlal Nehru, the first Prime Minister of India,[18] who is the father of the Community Development Programme as well as the planned development in the country, said about the programme as follows :

"Nothing can be more important than building Indian Humanity. It is in the growth and betterment of our peasantry that the future of India must necessarily depend. The great number of them have barely one or two acres of land to cultivate. It is possible and necessary to increase the yield of the little patches of land and then to better somewhat the conditions of the peasants. But there is a limit to do this, the limit laid down by the smallness of that holding. There are too many people in India subsisting on land. This means that many people must take to other activities and occupations. Some of these can be whole time and some part time to agriculture. Herein is the importance of cottage and small scale industries programme. No doubt as large industries grow up, some people from the rural areas will be attracted to them. But, however, speedy the growth of large industries, the major problems of unemployment and other occupations will not be solved by them. There are far too many backward people in the country. As a matter of fact you can safely say that 95 per cent of the people of India are economically very backward. I hope that the communities of the country will not merely pick out the best and most favourable persons and help them to develop but also try to work out problems of the other spots which are backward, economically and socially and in other respects. And they gain a wealth of experience of various types and conditions in India, so that the tremendous problem of backwardness may be tackled in the best and quickest way possible.

14.6 DELINEATING PROGRAMME OBJECTIVES OF THE RURAL DEVELOPMENT WORK

It is essential to spell out important programme objectives for attacking rural poverty as a pre-requisite for determining the various programme areas involved. Similarly, after a careful examination of these aspects the following programme objectives for a pragmatic rural development programme in India have been formulated.

Objective No. 1	:	Identification of beneficiaries
Objective No. 2	:	Using the existing resources available
Objective No. 3	:	Increasing agricultural production
Objective No. 4	:	Encouraging the rural poor to take up non-foodgrain agriculture and subsidiary enterprises and cottage industries to increase their income.
Objective No. 5	:	Generation of employment in the rural areas to provide jobs for unemployed and under-employed.
Objective No. 6	:	Promoting small industries in the rural areas to generate employment for the rural poor.
Objective No. 7	:	Undertaking rural works programme
Objective No. 8	:	Intensive social welfare programme to provide improved infrastructure consisting of cheap food, clothing, shelter, health and educational facilities.
Objective No. 9	:	Creating infrastructure to improve communication, transport, marketing and other facilities.
Objective No. 10	:	Assisting rural poor to get access to services
Objective No. 11	:	Creating an effective organization for administering rural development programme
Objective No. 12	:	Providing safety nets to rural poor
Objective No. 13	:	Undertaking programmes for development of rural women and youth.
Objective No. 14	:	Promoting people's participation

Objective No. 15 : Encouraging non-government organizations and local institutes to participate in the programme of rural development.

REFERENCES

1. Government of India, First Five Year Plan.
2. Kamata Prasad (1985). *Planning for Poverty Alleviation op. cit.*
3. World Bank, 1975, *Rural Development Policy Paper, op. cit.*
4. Mellor, John, W., 1975, *The Impact of New Agricultural Technology on Employment and Income Distribution—Constraints and Policies, op. cit.*
5. Ravi Varma, R., 1967, Ramrajya and Community Development, *Kurukshetra*, A Symposium Publications Division, Government of India, pp. 30.
6. Bharathiya Vidya Bhavan, Bombay, 1966, *The Village Reconstruction.* M.K. Gandhi, Edt. and Pub. Hindorani.
7. Navajeevan Trust, Ahmedabad, 1968, *The Selected Works of Mahatma Gandhi*, **6**, Voice of Truth.
8. Navajeevan Publishing House, Ahmedabad, 1956, *Rebuilding Our Villages* by M.K. Gandhi.
9. Navajeevan Publishing House, 1966, *Village Industries* by M.K. Gandhi, Compiled by R.K. Prabhu.
10. M.K. Gandhi, *Harijan*, 18-1-1948.
11. M.K. Gandhi, *Harijan*, 28-7-1946.
12. M.K. Gandhi, *Harijan*, 10-11-1946.
13. M.K. Gandhi, *Harijan*, 9-11-1947.
14. M.K. Gandhi, *Harijan*, 5-6-1937.
15. Das, S.R., 1967, Tagore—A Pioneer in Village Reconstruction, *Kurukshetra*, A symposium, pp. 520, *op. cit.*
16. Rajendra Prasad, 1952, The Yajna Broadcast from All India Radio, Delhi, October 2, 1952, Published in *Kurukshetra*, A symposium, pp. 1, *op. cit.*
17. Rajagopalachari, 1952, Gram Kalyan, October, 1952, *Kurukshetra*, A symposium, pp. 6, *op. cit.*
18. Government of India, 1958, Publications Division, *Jawaharlal Nehru on Community Development.*

15

FROM PROGRAMME OBJECTIVES TO PROGRAMME AREAS

15.1 NEED FOR DELINEATING PROGRAMME AREAS

Listing detailed programme objectives is only the first essential step which helps to formulate more specifically stated programme areas for action to be taken in implementing the rural development programme. The action oriented programme areas are required to be enunciated for each programme objective, after looking to the urgent needs of the particular local region, taluk or unit.

An inventory of the possible programme areas which can be thought of at the present day requirements of India's rural development programme, has been developed and is enclosed in the next chapter.

15.2 SOME GUIDELINES FOR DEVELOPMENT OF PROGRAMME AREAS

Based on the experience of working of poverty alleviation programmes over the years, the following guidelines are suggested for the development of programme areas relevant to programme objectives.

1. Separate programme areas have to be formulated for each programme objective

The purpose of programme objective cannot be served unless

specific action is taken by formulating the required action oriented programme areas under each objective and implement action accordingly.

2. Programme areas must relate to both the modern sector and the traditional sector development

Laying emphasis only on modern sector development that is, increasing the National Income alone (GNP), will not be adequate to tackle the problems of the rural poor in India. Similarly, stressing only the Targetted Approach to help the rural poor, without co-ordinating with other sections of development of modern sector, will also not help in the matter. What is needed is a judicious combination of both the sectors that should reflect in the formulation of specific programme areas under the programme objectives.

3. Programme areas should consider and indicate the stepwise development needed in the area concerned, so that priority programmes can be set up accordingly

It is expected that without satisfactory agricultural development, it is not possible to encourage employment increase in any area. Similarly, increase of foodgrain must be followed by increasing non-foodgrain agricultural and allied enterprises and rural industries. The programme areas must indicate the particular stage of development for the concerned area for which local plans are to be prepared. A single carpet like plan, for entire country, will not be of much use in undertaking programmes for alleviating rural poverty.

4. Programme areas for promoting small industries must include supporting policies

Improved infrastructure for better work in markets, imports of capital intensive raw materials and intermediate products and easy availability of working capital and raising consumer income, are all required for development of small industries. Specific programme areas must provide this environment.

5. Programme areas to promote development of the rural poor, must also provide measures to reduce risk and uncertainty

The rural poor face a lot of problems of risk and uncertainty in using additional inputs, which have to be purchased from outside. Unless these risks are covered under specified programme areas, it is rather difficult to expect the rural poor, to use the additional inputs for increased production. Government policies of insurance, guaranteed purchase at minimum price announced etc., can come under this category of programme areas.

6. Programme areas must also include re-orienting research to reduce risk and uncertainty, in development of technology to facilitate sustained agricultural practices

The research techniques at present do not emphasize this aspect of developing technology to reduce risk and uncertainty and also to provide income stabilization. New programme areas on this aspect are, therefore, needed.

7. Programme areas should cover activities to provide access to services for the rural poor

Without special programme to help the rural poor in obtaining the services of the various institutions, the poor will not be able to utilize the services from these institutions.

8. Programme areas must pay attention to providing economic infrastructure scheme

For effective eradication of rural poverty, it should be recognized, that rural areas have a poor share of infrastructure facilities like protected drinking water, electricity and waste disposal. Even where these facilities are available, their access to the rural poor are rather inadequate. Hence programme areas for each region must specify these requirements.

9. New programme areas are required considering the limitations of the existing co-operative societies considered in the rural areas

Depending only on the traditional co-operative society for helping the rural poor has not been found to be really effective. New programme areas should be formulated to promote what are called as limited local level organizations for getting access to various services for the rural poor outside the co-operative society, using the co-operative spirit.

10. Programme areas must consider specific needs of each local area

Programme areas to be developed for a particular region should be based on recommendation that the mix of activities will vary with a particular requirement of the area and also based on the priority assigned to component suited at a particular time and stage of development. It is, therefore, necessary to follow local planning to formulate programme areas which will help in creating employment opportunities by the efforts of the local people themselves.

11. Programme areas must focus attention on projects for involvement of rural women actively

Since in nearly 60 million rural households in India, women may be the main or only earners in the family and because 35 per cent of the rural households of the rural poor are headed by women, it is necessary to emphasize on special programme areas involving women and children in every locality. Empowerment of rural poor women must be given priority in designing programme areas for each locality.

12. Programme areas must indicate the responsibilities to be entrusted to the Basic Rural Institutions, namely, the School, the Panchayat and the Co-operative Society

These three Basic Rural Institutions, which have been set up to play an important role in the development of rural areas and hence their involvement in the various programme areas must be clearly indicated while formulating the areas.

13. Programme areas for alleviating rural poverty need not depend only on subsidies

In recent years, a philosophy has been developed in the country that all programme areas to be initiated for rural poverty alleviation, require the support of government subsidies. This naturally puts limit on the coverage of the programme to the extent of Government's ability to provide funds for meeting the cost of subsidies. Thus, a majority of the rural poor are kept out of the programme areas over the years. Further, this provision of subsidies has also resulted in various kinds of misuses, even leading to possible misappropriations.

13a. This philosophy, that subsidies are essentially required for programmes of rural poverty alleviation is really not correct. Research studies conducted by the U.S.A.I.D. in a number of third world countries have revealed that the degree of subsidies offered for the success of rural poverty alleviation projects was not necessary for the success of the projects and that rural poor will adopt new technologies even without such incentives if the technology appears beneficial in their view.[2]

14. Selecting programme areas need not necessarily involve large quantity of material resources

As a corollary to the idea stated in unit No. 13, it could be said that the material resources required for rural development need not be disproportionately large. In many successful schemes, the capital cost per beneficiary, has been quite low. Although low capital cost per beneficiary is not by itself a criterion for a good project, it is an important element in designing projects, to teach large number in the target groups. Rural development schemes benefiting large number of people can be as productive and economically attractive as schemes of a conventional kind, directly benefiting only fewer people.[1]

REFERENCES

1. The World Bank (1975), Rural Development Sector Policy Paper.
2. Morss, E.R.; Hatch, J. K.; Mickeelwait, D. R.; Sweet, C.F.; (1975),*Strategies for Small Farmers Development. op. cit.*

16

PROGRAMME AREAS FOR RURAL POVERTY ALLEVIATION

It has already been mentioned under previous paragraphs about the need for identifying programme areas, under each programme objective. An attempt is made in this chapter to list out programme areas under each of the 15 programme objectives already formulated for Rural Development. Under each programme area, current situational facts and action suggested with innovative measures wherever available have been mentioned.

16.1 PROGRAMME AREAS FOR OBJECTIVE – I : IDENTIFICATION OF BENEFICIARIES

Identification of Target Groups

Current situation

Even after completing Five Year Plans after starting the National Rural Development Programme in the VI Plan, all the rural poor families have not been still identified and listed in villages of India. It is primarily because the IRDP is required to work only with the selected small number of rural poor every year according to the limitation caused by the allotment of subsidy to be distributed and provided in the budget. Further, most of the rural poor in villages are not aware of the programme benefits. Also the procedure for the identification and listing of the rural poor has become very complicated. The local village organisations have not been given any responsibility in identifying these families. As a result, most of the advantages meant for the rural poor are generally grabbed by a sizable percentage of people who are really not eligible to benefit from these programmes. It is revealed that atleast 15 to 20 per cent of the so called beneficiaries do not belong to the rural poor category. Hence, to that extent, the government funds are totally misused. Further, there is no coordination beween the financial agencies like Banks and Cooperatives and the Rural Development administration in preparing the list of eligible beneficiaries under the programme.

Action suggested

(a) Make the selection procedure for identifying the rural poor a simple one, (b) Give specific responsibilities to the Basic Village institutions namely, the Panchayat, School and Cooperative Society in this work of identifying the rural poor along with the responsibility to be entrusted to village/taluk officials, (c) Ensure that this work of identifying the rural poor in all villages is completed before the close of the Ninth Five Year Plan, (d) Give wide publicity in all villages through local mass media like posters, pamphlets and drum-beat to inform village rural people about their entitlements of the IRDP and the need to register their names under the rural poor category within the stipulated period.

Revising the target group list periodically

Current situation

At present there is no clear cut procedure laid down to revise the list of the Rural poor (target group) once it is prepared. It is quite likely that even after a poor family once listed shows development and comes above the poverty line, it may still continue to be in the list under the poor category. Further, new names of the rural poor who might now come under the target group may not be identified.

Action suggested

(a) See that instructions are issued to the concerned to revise the list of the target group before the next Five Year Plan programme starts, (b) The list should be published in each village for the information of village people including the rural poor and objections if any, solicited for correcting the list, (c) A village Gramasabha should be empowered for approving the revised list of the poor people, (d) A map of the village should be prepared indicating the number of poor families still continuing in the villages, (e) The copy of the revised list should be supplied to all the financial agencies, banks, cooperative societies and to the offices of the Rural Development Administration.

16.2 PROGRAMME AREAS FOR OBJECTIVE — II USING EXISTING RESOURCES

Enforcing ceiling laws and continuing the distribution of surplus lands to the rural poor

Current situation

Imposition of ceiling and redistribution of surplus land is advocated on the ground that in the absence of an egalitarian asset distribution, particularly land ownership, which determines a political equation, the root cause of poverty and exploitation will not be eliminated (Dantwala, 1991)[1]. It is assumed that redistribution of surplus land obtained after imposing ceiling will not be more than 16.4 crore hectares, while the total number of agricultural workers without land is more than 18 crores. Even if the entire surplus area is equally distributed amongst them, each will not get more than 0.9 hectare which at the present level of production and prices can neither support a family above the poverty line level nor provide adequate employment (High Powered Committee, 1990)[2]. There is also another view point about land ceiling potential for redistribution, according to this view presented by Haque (1988)[3] "Land is still the single most important asset in rural area and given the present state of agricultural technology even a small farm can be viable both in terms of employment and income of a family". Hence, this work should not be allowed to stagnate. The work of land legislation is now almost more than 50 years old. The land legislation was started in all States of India before independence. If such action cannot be completed over such a long time, we are not competent to do anything else.

Action suggested

The task of land reforms still remains unfulfilled. The objectives of land reforms are as follows[4] :

1. Restructuring of agrarian relations to achieve egalitarian social structure,
2. Elimination of exploitation in land relations,
3. Actualization of the goal of "Land to the tiller",
4. Improvement of socio-economic conditions of the rural poor by widening their land base,
5. Increase in agricultural productivity and production,
6. Facilitating land based development of rural poor, and
7. Infusion of greater measures of equality in local institutions (VIII Plan document).

The following actions as recommended by the Eighth Plan document should be taken up immediately.

On the question of land ceiling, the two aspects needing urgent attention are : (a) Detection of surplus lands hitherto unavailable because of recourse to evasive methods like *benami* transfers, partitions, fraud, collusion with official machinery etc., and (b) Ensuring that the allottees retain possession and there is severe penalty for dispossession[4]. The lacuna in the laws will have to be removed so as to help resolve both these issues.

Consolidation of holdings

Current situation

The rural poor who are having small sized land have also got these in scattered pieces. Unless these pieces are consolidated, they cannot cultivate the land economically. It will also not be possible to introduce new technology on these fragments. There is no uniform progress on consolidation work in the country. Only 15 States have passed legislations to enforce consolidation. The only States where consolidation of holdings has been successfully carried out are Punjab and Haryana and Western UP. In these States also the success is primarily due to more focus on educating the farmers and not only due to compulsion. The Sixth Plan document expressed the view that the implementation of the consolidation legislation has been extremely patchy and it continues like that even now[5].

Action suggested

(a) Two aspects need immediate attention in respect of consolidation of agricultural holdings. These are : (i) smaller farmers harbour strong apprehensions about getting a raw deal in the process of exchanging parcels of land towards consolidation of holdings, and (ii) the process of breaking up of holdings is a continuous one and a one time settlement does not really solve the problem. The solution will, therefore, lie on making the farmer recognise that it is advantageous to share income from land rather than the land itself.

(b) It is also necessary to take up intensive educational work in all villages to propagate the advantages of consolidation of holdings.

(c) Consolidation should not be undertaken in a mechanical manner. The opportunities provided should be explained in practical way.

(d) Contiguous blocks of small farmers land holdings can be created while consolidating holdings, where well irrigation scheme is taken up to assist small farmers.

LAND DEVELOPMENT

Reclamation of saline or alkaline irrigated land

Current situation

India has achieved good progress in increasing the irrigated area from 19.4 million hectares in 1947 to 74.16 million hectares by the end of the VIII Plan. However, a recent study conducted by the Administrative Staff College of India has revealed that around 10 million hectares of canal irrigated land has become water logged and is not fit for farm cultivation. Further, another 25 million hectares is endangered with salinity. Thus, 68.8 per cent of the irrigated land is in danger due to salinity and alkalinity (Vasanth Desai)[6]. Although CAD Projects have been taken up as part of reclamation demonstration work, the progress achieved by this programme has not been upto the mark due to lack of cooperation and coordination from various government departments involved in the programme (Dantwala, 1991). The drainage system has not been developed along with irrigation. Commenting on this, the High Powered Committee on Agricultural Programmes and Policies (1990) stated: "Even abundance does not help a nation or even a family to improve its economic conditions, if the resources are abused and wasted. India has been very reckless in using its land and water resources. If the abuse or waste of these natural resources is not stopped, and that too with a sense of urgency, sustainability of agriculture and following that, the very survival of a nation will be in danger"[2].

Action suggested

(a) Development of drainage systems in all canal irrigated areas, especially in areas which have been presently affected by water logging and salinity and alkalinity conditions should be given top priority, (b) The entire cost of drainage on irrigated land owned by small farmers should be borne by the government initially and may be recovered in easy annual instalment over a period of 10 to 20 years, (c) Promoting inter-disciplinary and inter-departmental team work to take care of the reclamation of all alkaline and saline land should be given top most priority, (d) Vigorous educational programmes to promote farmers active involvement and co-operation in reclaiming these problem soils affected by water logging, saline and alkalinity condition should be tackled, (e) Construction of field channels for irrigation is a must to regulate the flow of water judiciously. This should be got done on a priority basis, (f) Introduction of conjunctive use of water by introducing method like Warabandi system of irrigation with a regular on and off period for irrigation is a must.

Bunding, levelling and grading of dry lands

Current situation

In India, dry land or rainfed agriculture is practiced on nearly 104 million hectares, mostly spread out in 85 districts of the country. This is nearly 73 per cent of the net cultivated area of the country. Most of the drylands are highly eroded and the problem of land shaping and soil conservation has assumed alarming proportions. The damage has extended beyond lowering soil fertility directly and due to sedimentation of the eroded soil the capacity to store water for power generation and irrigation is being seriously affected. Some examples are coated by Subramanyam (1982)[8] : (i) The storage capacity of Nizam Sagar lake of Andhra Pradesh has been reduced by 63 per cent in 44 years, (ii) Of Mayurakshi and Maithan reservoirs by 10 per cent in twenty years, (iii) Of Panshed lake by 12 per cent in 19 years, and of (iv) Bhakra by 6 per cent in 15 years. Similarly most of the village tanks have been silted up over the last 100 years and do not store the expected capacity today. Hence intensive efforts are necessary to improve dry lands by way of bunding, levelling and grading to prevent this process of high erosion which has continued for several years in the past. Although soil conservation projects are in operation in the country from 1942 onwards, the progress achieved is not satisfactory. Recently, a new high cost watershed development programme has been taken up in the country which is also aided by funding agencies from foreign countries.

Since 1982, crores of rupees have been spent on these projects taken up in selected locations of the country. Unfortunately even these have not provided the required results. Today we are looking at more than 15 years of experience in the watershed management programmes in India, managed by government departments, research institutions, NGOs or a combination of any of these.

The results of watershed projects have been rather disappointing, despite the large amount of public and foreign funds spent on these programmes so far[8]. Farmers generally do not maintain soil and water conservation (SWC) projects and do not follow the recommended practices, once the project support is withdrawn. Project practices have hardly ever spread to neighbouring, non-project areas (Barbara Adolph, 1995)[9].

The main reason for the non-success of these projects is that they are all time bound and are short viewed and ignore the long range view of the farmers. Everything is done in a great hurry to spend the budget and as a result, the requirements are not fulfilled in most of the cases. Another common belief that poor people live hand to mouth and cannot take a long view, is also not correct. The real fact is that the rural poor often seem to take the long view and preserve their livelihood assets even when faced by famine, poor people are seen planting and protecting trees on their own land and invest labour to create sustainable agriculture systems like paddy fields and terraces. We have large amount of capital available in the villages namely, rural labour and we should be able to utilise it effectively. This programme of soil conservation requires to be taken up in all villages with existing resources utilizing the human labour capital. There is no transparency in transaction related to soil conservation works. This has resulted in a lot of misuse of government money. Karnataka Agricultural minister in charge of the soil conservation programme in 1996 had this to say about the programme: "Most of the Rs. 500.00 crores spent on soil conservation work in the State during the last 5 years has gone down the drain in most places. Quality of the work was very poor and in many instances, work has not been taken up after drawing the money"[10] (*Deccan Herald* Report dated 28th July 1996).

Action suggested

(a) Soil conservation should be declared as a national programme to be taken up in every village of the country where such problems exist, (b) Programme should be promoted with local resources namely, utilizing human labour which has to be harnessed for the purpose, (c) The programme should be drawn on a long term basis giving yearly objectives of the programme and how it should be carried out, (d) Transparency is a must in these operations, to avoid possible misuse of funds.

Tapping the underground water for irrigation

Current situation

Ground water development forms a bulk of the minor irrigation programme and assumes critical importance in agricultural development of dry areas. Ground water is more widely distributed all over India and represents generally an instrument of assured source of irrigation for cultivating. Even in canal areas, ground water development provides a twin advantage of improvement on the status of irrigated crops along with the control of water logging and salinity. Another feature of ground water irrigation is that it imposes very little burden directly on the public exchequer. It is essentially the farmers' own programme to bc carried out through individual and co-operative efforts, financed largely by institutional sources by providing loans. Underground water utilisation is a real boon to the eastern States of India. These areas are literally floating on the water in the sense, that there are vast resources of under ground water in these States. Considering the cost of creating irrigation potentials, the minor irrigation system is far more cost saving as compared to major and medium irrigation systems. The cost of creating irrigation potential through major and minor irrigation works increased from Rs. 1200 per hectare during 1951-56 to Rs. 35,000 during 1985-90 and during 1990-95 it was estimated at Rs. 50,000 per hectare. In the case of minor irrigation, though the cost has gone up, it is not to the same extent. During

1985-90, estimated cost of creating irrigation potential through minor irrigation was estimated at Rs. 7331.00/ha as against the estimate of Rs. 35,000 per ha for major and medium irrigation works[2].

The budget spent on minor irrigation is also far less than the money earmarked for major and medium irrigation works.Table 16.1 gives comparison.

Table 16.1 : Plan-wise expenditure on major and minor irrigation works

(Expenditure in crores of rupees)

Sl. No.	Period	Major & medium irrigation works	Minor irrigation works
1.	I Plan 1951-56	380	76
2.	II Plan 1956-61	380	142
3.	III Plan 1961-66	581	328
4.	Annual Plans 1966-69	434	326
5.	IV Plan 1969-74	1237	513
6.	V Plan 1974-79	3399	868
7.	Annual Plan 1979-80	1079	280
8.	VI Plan 1980-85	7570	1979
9.	VII Plan 1985-90	11856	2805
	Total	26916	7317

Source : CMIE (1989), Ref. Table 2 in Sawanth S.D., 1991.[11]

Thus, ground water development through minor irrigation has not received much attention all these years though it is known that it imposes very little burden directly on the government spending.

Action suggested

(a) In dry area, exploiting the use of underground water through wells should be given top priority in the rural development programme, as an important step to eradicate poverty, because one hectare under well irrigation is enough to help a poor farmer's family to come above the poverty line, (b) The budget allocation presently made for major and medium irrigation and the minor irrigation should be revised and reversed, (c) De-silting of tanks and ponds in the villages should be taken up at Government cost only, when people's participation is ensured on priority basis, so as to promote better recharge of ground water to increase minor irrigation potential and in this work no machines should be used but available human labour to be harnessed to provide more employment to rural poor. The programme may be a long range one requiring many years to complete, (d) Poor farmers should be given priority in providing sanction of the loans for digging wells for irrigation as compared to non-poor farmers, (e) Vigorous educational programme should be taken up to involve large number of poor farmers on well digging programmes so as to help them come above the poverty line.

Distributing cultivable waste land for the rural poor

Current situation

In India, a large per cent of cultivable land is available under the class culturable waste. It is possible to develop such land and allot it to the landless and/or small farmers to build up their assets. Waste Land Development Scheme was started in the Seventh Plan to satisfy this objective. However, the progress achieved so far of the scheme is far from satisfactory. A large portion of this waste land is still left undistributed. In 1950-51, the extent of this culturable waste land was 22.9 million hectares out of the total geographic area of 328.7 million hectares, constituting 7 per cent of the area. Even after 30 years i.e., as on 1991-92, the extent of the land still remained undistributed was 15.11 million hectares i.e., only 7 million hectares was distributed during the period. Due to lack of financial support, even major portion of such waste land allotted has not really been developed to assist the allottees to increase their income. The government is also finding it difficult to get the required resources for developing such waste land.

Action suggested

An innovative method based on experience of several other

countries can be followed to accelerate the distribution of culturable waste land and to develop it. This method is to allot the land to persons who undertake improvement of the land, using their own resources and after developing the land, on willing to return 50 per cent of the land back to the government, which can then be redistributed to the rural poor. The High Powered Committee appointed by Government of India on Agricultural Policies and Programmes, in its report presented in 1990, has recommended this method for speedy disposal of the culturable waste land[2].

16.3 PROGRAMME AREAS FOR OBJECTIVE—III: INCREASING AGRICULTURAL PRODUCTION OF THE COUNTRY

Increasing agricultural production to the potential available

Current situation

This area is very important considering the alleviation of rural poverty in India. No country in the world, except mineral oil producing countries of the Gulfs, have been able to eradicate poverty without first attaining development in the field of agriculture. Somehow, the Government of India and the planners have not paid much attention to this aspect so far. They are content by taking satisfaction of having achieved some sufficiency in food production. The consultative group of Common Wealth countries, in its meeting, held at Colombo in 1992, has also pointed out that 'neglect of agriculture' is one of the important reasons as to why many countries of Asia, have not been able to alleviate rural poverty[12].

There is lot of potential in India to increase the per hectare yields of a number of crops, from the current low yields. A study by Indian Agricultural Research Institute (IARI) has given information regarding the potential available in respect of a number of crops. Table 16.2 gives these details.

Table 16.2 : State-wise unrealised potentials of Indian Agriculture

(Million Rupees at 1970-71prices)

Sl. No.	State	Actual gross returns at prevailing level of adoption of new technique in 1978-79	Returns possible with adoption of recommen-ded level of technology in 1978-79
1.	Andhra Pradesh	13210	43252
2.	Assam	2362	7904
3.	Bihar	10076	31220
4.	Gujarat	11483	27980
5.	Haryana	7292	14349
6.	Himachal Pradesh	1034	1306
7.	Jammu and Kashmir	1032	1385
8.	Karnataka	11308	27672
9.	Kerala	5702	9257
10.	Madhya Pradesh	10861	56394
11.	Maharashtra	14663	41758
12.	Manipur	196	378
13.	Meghalaya	161	540
14.	Nagaland	81	368
15.	Orissa	6129	20696
16.	Punjab	13453	17253
17.	Rajasthan	8761	60076
18.	Tamil Nadu	10861	27597
19.	Tripura	357	1654
20.	Uttar Pradesh	24085	59626
21.	West Bengal	10758	30828
22.	Union Territory	650	1916
	Total	164695	473409

Note : Actual returns of the country is only 35 per cent of the returns possible (of the potential difference between the price and the actual returns)
Unutilized potential = 473409–164695 million rupees
= 308714 million rupees
= half of the national income (approximately)

Source : Technology assessment and Research Imbalances by Dr. Druva Srivastava and T. Haque, IARI, New Delhi quoted by High Powered Committee (1990).[13]

The High Powered Committee on Agricultural policies and programmes in its report of 1990, has remarked as follows regarding the potential and performance of Indian agriculture: "When a factory or industry produces considerably less than its rated capacity, it is said to be sick and all corrective measures are taken to restore it to health. But the fact, that Indian Agriculture has been sick for a long time, producing much less than its potential or capacity, has not been even noted by our policy makers, leave alone take any steps to bring it back to health and achieve its full potential. All that has been attempted in the past was to achieve self sufficiency in foodgrain, and that too at the subsistence level of consumption. A country that has all the potential of emerging as No.1 agricultural power in the world, has been aiming merely at survival and in achieving even this modest goal, it has failed, as is evident from the fact that during the last 38 years (1950-51 to 1988-89), India has imported foodgrains in as many as 31 years and attained subsistence level of foodgrains consumption (181 kg of foodgrains per capita per annum, the minimum recommended by nutrition experts) in only four years"[2].

The low percentage crop yields of Indian Agriculture are also evident as earlier indicated in this chapter on "Causes of Rural Poverty" where the average yields of Indian Agricultural crops were compared with the average yields of other countries of the world. The summary of this is given in Table 16.3.

Action suggested

(a) The High Powered Committee on Agricultural Policies and Programmes appointed by the Government of India, in its 1990 report, has suggested to take various steps to realise the potential of Indian agriculture. The report has further indicated the following constraints that come in the way of cultivation. These can be grouped into the following three categories[2].

Ecological constraints

(a) Weather
(b) Pollution
(c) Desertification

Production constraints

(a) Lack of high yielding varieties (HYVs) and quality seeds
(b) Weeds
(c) Pests and diseases
(d) Non-availability of inputs in time and inadequate quantity
(e) Soil sickness
(f) Poor weather management
(g) Inadequate and inappropriate farm machinery
(h) Poor post-harvest technology

Table 16.3 : Summarized information regarding per hectare yields of important crops grown in India and the Ranks assigned comparing the yield obtained in other countries.[17]

Sl. No.	Crop	World area (in '000 ha)	Area in India (in '000 ha)	Rank among the world countries based on area	Per ha yield in kg		Rank assigned to India based on per ha yield
					World	India	
1.	Rice (Paddy)	146452	42034	I	3651	2817	VII
2.	Wheat	215921	24431	III	2445	2420	VIII
3.	Maize	131528	6000	V	4730	1750	IX
4.	Sorghum	43718	12800	I	1394	977	V
5.	Pulses	69270	23951	I	847	607	XI
6.	Soybean	52653	3950	V	2182	835	XI
7.	Groundnut (in shell)	21781	8500	I	1308	988	VI
8.	Safflower	1168	900	I	685	478	VI
9.	Cotton (with seed)	31118	7670	I	1712	898	XI
10.	Millets	37710	14700	I	689	708	III
11.	Potatoes	18191	1000	V	14591	15000	IV
12.	Coffee	10535	840	III	515	545	IX
13.	Onion (dry)	2023	390	I	16087	11111	VI
14.	Cabbage	1713	200	II	23496	16500	XII
15.	Sugarcane	17606	3578	II	61108	77178	IV

Source : FAO Production Year Book, 1994.[17]

Socio-economic constraints

(a) Lack of institutions and institutional support
(b) Traditional outlook and attitudes
(c) Farmers' lack of awareness of technological advances
(d) Non-availability of credit and power
(e) Adverse terms of trade
(f) Inefficient marketing arrangements

The High Powered Committee has further suggested the following points for improving the agricultural production:

(a) Amongst all the constraints stated above, only weather is beyond human control. Therefore, while the element of risk and uncertainty cannot be altogether eliminated from agriculture, their adverse impact can be reduced, if all the other constraints are eased or removed altogether, through human effort and policy measures. In our view it is mostly the socio-economic constraints which are basically holding back Indian agriculture[2].

(b) Even amongst the socio-economic constraints, the restraining and decisive ones are the last four, namely farmers' lack of awareness of new techniques of production, non-availability of credit and power, adverse terms of trade and inefficient marketing arrangements[2].

(c) The kind of awareness that is needed for rural growth can be achieved through universalization of education in the country. It is a development tragedy of very high order that in the 1981 census, 34 years after the dawn of freedom, only 29.6 per cent were found literate in the villages[14]. No country in the world peasantry, having remained illiterate to the extent of over 70 per cent, can adopt new techniques of production and become productive. The converse is also true, that is farmers, having become literate, have not remained unproductive. Universalisation of education should, therefore, get priority over all other development programmes.

(d) In the meantime, instead of relying exclusively on government personnel for extension of new techniques of production, rural youth should be trained at the rate of atleast one in each village with a population of over 500, as model farmers, to demonstrate to the rest of the villagers what can be achieved through application of the new techniques of production[22].

In addition to the above mentioned suggestions, it is also necessary to take immediate action as follows :

(a) Let each village prepare its own plan to increase the yield per hectare of crops grown and implement the same with the help of agriculture and rural development departments. Priority for development of agriculture in each village should be identified and the most important work implemented first.

(b) A list of farmers in each village, whose average yields are lower than the village average, should be prepared and these farmers should be given top priority for providing assistance to increase the yield on planned basis.

Increasing the agricultural production of small farmers

Current situation

Since the entire country's agricultural production is at a low level, compared to the per hectare yield of crops in the world, the agricultural production of small farmers is naturally still lower. There are many reasons for this malady. These reasons can be briefly stated as follows :

(i) Small farmers are not reached by the agencies providing different services.

(ii) Their land resources, particularly in drylands, are not developed, soil erosion is rampant.

(iii) Their agricultural holdings are very small and are being fragmented year after year and have become uneconomic to cultivate.

(iv) Government policies to provide safety nets to the rural poor are not very encouraging.

(v) Small farmers are not organised in group efforts to get them the economies of scale and also to take advantage of the market facilities.

(vi) Technologies developed for large areas, are not very much suitable, for small farmers, since they are not sustainable and are not based on cost economics. These technologies are also not encouraging more labour requirement.

(vii) Government assistance to small farmers is not to the required level.

(viii) There are very few effective non-governmental organisations operating at the rural level to work for the welfare of small farmers.

(ix) Small farmers are not involved in participation of programmes for development.

The small farmer often has difficulty in obtaining capital necessary for application of high yielding farm technology, but even more important, he faces serious problems of risk and uncertainty and aversion, which make him reluctant to borrow or to innovate even when weather conditions are favourable. Thus small farmers frequently choose lower income to more stable crop combinations and technologies[15].

Small farmer earns his income from the labour of his family than from his small piece of land—he is thus in part a landless labourer and in part a land owner, but weighted towards labour. It is for this reason that the labour intensity farm is so important to the small farmer and it is here that important interactions occur with other elements of development strategy. The farm enterprises which offer greater opportunity for labour intensity—livestock products such as milk, vegetables and some types of fruits, have highly elastic demand. Unless, consumer expenditure is generally raising there will not be a favourable demand and price context for more increases in production of such commodities. Thus, the absorptive capacity of agricultural farm labour is very much influenced by level and growth of consumer incomes.

The age old system of promoting technology recommendations from top level continues even today. This is not very much suitable for the use of every small farmer.

Action suggested

(a) Technology transfer systems for small farmers must be based on Cafeteria approach, treating each farm family as an individual unit to which suitable technology should be recommended[16], (b) Small farmer family members should be actively involved in group discussions and development education, for increasing their achievement motivation, should be provided, (c) Attention on providing irrigation facilities to them, through well irrigation wherever feasible, should be given, since this step itself is adequate to bring the family above the poverty line, (d) Informal local level organizations, meant for rural poor, should be promoted to enable small farmers to take advantage of the technologies and to get benefit of economies of scale, (e) Non-foodgrains agriculture should be promoted, (f) Management services should be provided to small farmers (through some methods) so that they will be in a position to get access to the various services provided by the government, (g) In developing technologies which should become sustainable for small farmers, research efforts are needed to reduce yield uncertainty of labour intensive enterprises through greater pest resistance and control, (h) Improved credit facilities, to meet the high risk conditions of agricultural production wherever such situations exist should be available, (i) Improved marketing and processing facilities to reduce price fluctuations and risk and to provide the advantage of economies of scale should also be at the disposal of the small farmer, (j) Encouraging development of NGOs and through them, promoting agricultural development programmes for the benefit of small farmers is a must, (k) In each village, one or two rural poor small farm families should be adopted for intensive work to be taken up with them for a period of 3-5 years to bring them above the poverty line. Such small farmers will then become model farmers for the remaining rural poor people of the village.[2]

16.4 PROGRAMME AREAS FOR OBJECTIVE—IV : ENCOURAGING THE RURAL POOR TO TAKE UP NON-FOODGRAINS AGRICULTURE AND SUBSIDIARY ENTERPRISES AND COTTAGE INDUSTRIES TO INCREASE THEIR INCOME

Developing Entrepreneurship of the rural poor for taking up income generating projects

Current situation

Entrepreneurship is an economic behaviour which is essential in successfully managing any activity. It refers to the attitude of the person towards an activity and also explains the ability of the person, the needed information and other requirements needed to manage the activity. Only recently, it has been recognized that entrepreneurship is not only required for managing industries but also is essential in the field of agricultural enterprises. A Ph.D. research (1980) has revealed that, entrepreneurship of the rural poor is a composite variable and a person develops entrepreneurial behaviour by possessing some special characteristics. This research has also found out that a poor rural person having high entrepreneurial behaviour is an active participant in undertaking income generating projects.[18]

In rural development work, except in case of rural industries, practically no attempt is made to develop the entrepreneurial behaviour of the prospective beneficiaries, before enrolling them for undertaking income generating projects like dairying, poultry, piggery etc. The beneficiaries are hurriedly selected to fulfil the financial targets communicated by the Government. No preparatory work is undertaken for training beneficiaries and their entrepreneurial behaviour is not developed (Dantwala and Barmeda, 1991). As a result, a majority of the beneficiaries do not attain the objectives and have failed to get benefits from the projects to increase their income level above the poverty line.

Action suggested

(a) Before enrolling the prospective beneficiaries in undertaking the income generating projects, they should be encouraged to undergo entrepreneurial development training and only those who develop high entrepreneurial behaviour should be enlisted to take up that project. Others should be encouraged to take up other projects in which they may be interested and their entrepreneurship in those other projects should be developed before enrolling them.
(b) Rural development workers are required to be trained so as to enable them to sponsor entrepreneurial development training programmes for the beneficiaries. The entrepreneurial behaviour is a composite variable with the following 10 components.

1. Decision making ability
2. Innovativeness
3. Getting assistance of management services
4. Achievement motivation
5. Ability to coordinate farm activities
6. Risk taking ability
7. Information seeking ability
8. Cosmopoliteness
9. Knowledge of the enterprise
10. Leadership ability

The development workers must pay attention to instil these skills in the prospective beneficiaries as a part of entrepreneurial behaviour training.

(c) An Entrepreneurial Development Unit should be attached to each district rural development office to provide leadership and guidelines for the rural development staff.

Providing proper technical guidance both for initiating and for completing the income generating projects

Current situation

Proper technical knowledge is a must for the success of any income generating project taken up by the rural poor. Unfortunately in their hurry to complete the target, the development administration does not pay enough attention to this aspect. Intending beneficiaries are not given adequate training before they are provided loans and subsidies for starting the projects. In many cases, these beneficiaries had to depend only on the local farmers who have taken up similar projects earlier for the technical knowledge. As a result a majority of the beneficiaries are handicapped and are not having the required technical knowledge for initiating and completing the projects. A number of research studies on IRDP have indicated that the beneficiaries are not at all satisfied with the technical training given to them for allotting projects and also for completing the same (Ekanthạppa, 1987)[19].

Action suggested

(a) See that before any income generating project is undertaken by the beneficiaries, they are given proper technical knowledge which is essential for a successful undertaking, (b) No subsidy or loan assistance to be recommended to the beneficiaries unless they have undergone satisfactory technical training, (c) Identify the crucial stages at which technical guidance is necessary in completing the income generating projects and see that arrangements are made to provide this technical knowledge through periodic trainings, (d) Print and distribute ready to use pamphlets in the local language giving technical information about the project before starting the project.

Providing working capital for completing the projects

Current situation

The present pattern of providing assistance to beneficiaries is to make available subsidies and loan assistance at one time only before starting the project. This is called as "one shot approach".[20] Since no facilities are provided to make available the working capital, it becomes very difficult for a majority of the rural poor who have undertaken the projects to complete them satisfactorily. A number of research studies have revealed this deficiency. Another serious problem identified in some other studies is that the initial increase in income through the projects is often not sustained over a longer period, for want of working capital. In other words, the self-employment activity often deteriorates over time instead of becoming a self-sustaining viable enterprise. An interesting hypothesis is that this probably happens because the self-employed producers assume that these programmes are not assured of continuous preferential access to pledge. For example, a unit may get its minimum credit requirement in the special dispensation of the self-employment scheme, but have not similar provision is made to cater for its subsequent credit should leave, it may be difficult for the unit to survive.

Action suggested

(a) A well designed system for providing credit not just initially on a one shot basis but also on a continuing basis to meet the economically justifiable needs of the enterprise, would enable a large number of poor households to improve their own income earning capacity. If this is combined with an element of training and marketing services and also supported by possible co-operative marketing arrangements wherever appropriate, it could provide a basis for self-sustaining, viable production, which could help in poverty alleviation. This kind of financial assistance for working capital is presently provided in a few areas like dairy projects, based on the Anand model, oilseed sub-projects and in a few sugar factories. This system needs to be made applicable to all income generating projects taken up by the rural development department in all villages. A number of research studies have recommended the need for providing working capital.

Creating market infrastructure and facilities for the success of the income generating projects

Current situation

Enterprises to increase income of the rural poor are prevalent in almost all parts of the country since long and actually are supposed to be a major source of income for the rural poor wherever successful. But these enterprises generally suffer from several handicaps, especially regarding securing of raw materials, access to credit facilities for marketing etc. As a result of these handicaps there is exploitation of the rural poor carrying out such enterprises by the middlemen[6].

There are no warehouses, cold storage facilities, processing units, input depots, repair shops, to provide the required services to the poor people to undertake income generating projects[2].

Action suggested

(a) Vigorous government programmes to provide facilities to the already existing enterprises are needed urgently to help rural poor to carry out the projects successfully, (b) Establish one growth centre for each cluster of villages covering 300 sq.m area to provide the required marketing infrastructure and other facilities. It is just not possible to equip all villages in India with such facilities, (c) Develop all-weather rural roads so that each village can be made approachable. Good roads will promote the development of market infrastructure and other facilities by the private sector without any expenditure on the part of government, (d) Encourage the rural poor who have taken up income generating projects to form local level limited co-operative groups, which will assist them to pool their produce for getting advantage of the economies of scale in transporting and marketing the produce.

Providing safety nets for the projects to cover the risks

Current situation

Labour intensive income generating projects like dairying, poultry, sericulture, sheep rearing etc., which are also intensive in the requirements of working capital and the risk and uncertainty from weather and pests effects. Due to these risks, the rural poor are prone to avoid such enterprises although they are most suited to them to increase their income. For example, in dairy industry, a cross-bred cow is always superior than maintaining a buffalo. However, because of the high cost of the animal and possibly due to the risk of maintaining it in good health, the rural poor would prefer to have the buffaloes. This is happening because no safety-nets are provided to cover risk like this situation. There are also no clear cut government policies to provide assured prices to the rural poor to avoid the price fluctuations in the market from time to time. There are no insurance schemes to cover the entire cost of the projects to overcome risky situations.

Action suggested

(a) Enterprise insurance to benefit the rural poor in project work, to cover the cost of inputs to be purchased, must be initiated, (b) The government should ensure remunerative price support to the rural people, undertaking these projects, (c) Improved marketing and processing facilities to be provided to reduce price fluctuations and risks, (d) research emphasis to reduce yield uncertainty of labour intensive enterprises through greater pest resistance and control and tolerance to weather fluctuations is urgently required.

16.5 PROGRAMME AREAS FOR OBJECTIVE—V : GENERATION OF EMPLOYMENT IN RURAL AREAS

Providing all-weather roads to all villages on priority basis

Current situation

At present a majority of small villages are not connected by all-weather roads. Due to this, private sector efforts are not seen to help in providing employment to the rural poor. It is generally agreed that communication and development are inter-related and when allweather roads have connected villages to market places, private enterprise will flourish and provide employment to the rural poor by starting various kinds of enterprises.

Action suggested

(a) All villages should be connected by all-weather roads on a priority basis and this work should be completed by the end of Ninth Plan period. (b) Rural road construction work should be decentralised to enable the local government organisations to participate effectively in this task as is done in the Philippines. Appendix 'A' gives details as to how this work is being done in the Philippines.[21]

16.6 PROGRAMME AREAS FOR OBJECTIVE—VI : PROMOTING SMALL INDUSTRIES IN THE RURAL AREAS TO GENERATE EMPLOYMENT FOR THE RURAL POOR

Modernising small industries

Current situation

Inspite of promises to give priority to village industries, no concerted action has been taken in these areas to implement suitable measures to modernise them. There is a mistaken belief in the scientific sector that the village industries are only a passing phase in the process of economic development, till big national industries replace them. As a result machines used in village industries have still to be modernised. Even where some improvements have been made in selected village industries, new technology has not spread fast. For example, although the semi-automatic improved loom developed in 1972, even by 1990s 90 per cent of handloom weavers continued to use the old pit loom. No modernisation is done in the case of spinning wheel for spinning low staple cotton. Even the improved model Amber charkha is not suitable for small households which have little space to use for spinning. The KVIC experience has shown that the process of developing improved technology for village industries is very slow. There is also very little support from the National Government run and assisted industries to develop modern technology for village industries. For example, Hindustan Machine Tools (HMT) and National Small Scale Industries Corporation

(NSIC), have not been of much help to modernise tools for village industries. Even the Indian Institutes of Technology (IITs), have not made significant contribution to the development of new technologies for village industries[23]. Unless the technologies of village industry are modernised to improve the production efficiency at little cost, these village industries will not be able to compete with large scale industries, manufacturing the same type of goods. Already many small scale industries, like hand pounding of rice and thousands of handlooms, have been wiped out as a result of the competition.

Action suggested

(a) IITs and CSIR institutions must take a lead in initiating research to modernised village industries, (b) Cottage and Village Industries Commission should allot more funds for undertaking research to modernise village industries, (c) There is a need to take up collaborative programmes with the Japanese collaboration to develop research for modernising village industries in India.

Protection to village industries

Current situation

Village industries in India cannot develop unless sufficient protection is given to them by the Government to avoid competition with big industries. What has however happened over the years is that the big industries have virtually steam rolled the small industries. The classic examples are the extinction of hand pounding rice industry, country Ghanis in the villages and the handloom sector. As long as there is no restriction on the establishment of big industries, we cannot expect the small industries to develop. Years ago Gandhiji has suggested some kind of State intervention is required in promoting village industries, Sri Kamaraj Nadar requested the Government to give protection to small industries by preventing establishment of big industries and also sugested to prohibit the establishment of cotton mills in India and allow Khadi and Village Industries to manufacture cotton goods. However, this proposal was not accepted by the Government then. There are many industries like the paper manufacturing, soap manufacturing, spinning, weaving, rice milling, oil extraction industries which can be completely earmarked for the small industries sector. Thus there is supreme need to streamline *swadeshi* movement in order to produce consumer goods by giving protection to small industries. However what has happened is that only big industries have been given protection by imposing import duty on manufactured goods from other developed countries. Big industries established in rural areas have been given special concessions by way of less taxation etc. This has resulted in the collapse of small industries.

Action suggested

(a) The small industries protection committees set up by the Government of India from time to time should be asked to recommend more practical ways of protection to be given to small industries, (b) Steps should be taken by the Government of India to encourage small industries on the following programme, on the lines framed out in Japan, to promote small industries.

(i) Collective projects : raw materials needed for small industries,
(ii) Collective selling of products.

Promoting new kinds of organisations for developing village industries as is done in Japan

Current situation

In small industries there is lack of innovativeness which is necessary to improve the working of small industries. Except providing subsidies to small industries to sell their products, no other action is taken to promote the small industries sector. No attempts have been made to study the experience of countries like Japan and Switzerland to promote small industries by developing a number of organisations.

Action suggested

(a) In Japan small industries are promoted by providing new kinds of co-operative organisations namely; (i) the common facilities co-operatives, (ii) credit co-operatives, (iii) Federation of co-operatives, (iv) Joint enterprise co-operatives, similar action is needed in India. (b) Japan has followed a new system of promoting production of few products in large quantities rather than spreading resources on a large variety of products in small quantities. This approach should be implemented in India. (c) The Japanese government promoted a new policy of even merging a number of small industries into a larger one in order to have advantage of economy of scale.

Appendix 'B' gives an article by Malgaonkar with details of work done in Japan in this connection.[22]

16.7 PROGRAMME AREAS FOR OBJECTIVE —VII : UNDERTAKING RURAL WORKS PROGRAMME

Priority programme areas

Promoting Public Works Programme to improve Land Assets

Current situation

Presently public works programmes are primarily implemented to spend the budget allotted, without taking into consideration the real need for improving land assets in villages. Further no follow-up work is taken up to maintain this. The local Panchayats and village people are not consulted in developing these programmes. Most of the money was spent on road work, that too on kutcha roads, which were again washed off during the rains following the undertaking of rural work. Hence assets created were mostly not durable. Although the implementation of the schemes required preparation of shelf of projects, this has been rarely implemented.

Action suggested

(a) No public works programme should be implemented without

discussing this with the local Panchayats and Gramsabhas, (b) Assets created must have clear plans of maintenance, otherwise assets cannot become durable, (c) Assets must be developed in the lands of poor people on priority basis, (d) No land development scheme or bunding should be taken up without complete plan of levelling the land and maintaining the bund after construction, (e) Watersheds should be selected for development of land in stages, (f) Desiltation of existing tanks should be taken up in the programme as priority item, (g) Without active participation of the land owning families, no development works should be taken up.

Implementing pragmatic labour policies in rural areas

Current situation

The Government itself has enacted the Minimum Labour Wages Act, but is not implementing it faithfully in rural areas. Many labour engaging projects in rural areas are given exemptions from implementing the Minimum Wages Act. Wage revision does not take place in consideration of the rise in Wholesale Price Index (WPI) from time to time. As a result of these shortcomings, even if the rural poor are given full labour employment in rural areas, they will not be able to come above the poverty line due to inadequate labour wages earned by them.[2] Labour absorption in agriculture has not satisfactorily increased in India with the introduction of new agricultural practices, as is the case in Japan and some other South Asian Countries (SAC). Priority is not given to development of non-foodgrain agriculture, where agriculture had already developed.

Action suggested

(a) Minimum Wages Act should be enforced in all rural areas without exception, (b) The minimum wages fixed should be revised, (c) New kind of research to improve the labour absorption in agriculture should be explored on a priority basis, (d) Employment audit should be introduced in research systems so as to avoid recommending new practices which displace labour, (e) New schemes for processing agricultural products in rural areas should be taken up to increase the labour requirement in rural areas.

16.8 PROGRAMME AREAS FOR OBJECTIVE —VIII : INTENSIVE SOCIAL WELFARE PROGRAMMES TO PROVIDE IMPROVED INFRASTRUCTURE CONSISTING OF SHELTER, HEALTH, EDUCATION FACILITIES AND WATER SUPPLY

Providing minimum needs as per accepted programme

Current situation

Eleven items are included in this minimum programme of infrastructure development. These are:

1. Elementary education
2. Adult education
3. Rural health
4. Rural water supply
5. Rural roads
6. Rural electricity
7. Nutrition
8. Rural domestic cooking energy
9. Housing assistance to rural landless labourers
10. Rural sanitation
11. Public health system

Inspite of 50 years after independence most of these minimum needs are not provided to a majority of villages The budget allotment in the annual plan for these items for the year 1990-91 was only Rs. 3409.18 crores which was not adequate for the infrastructural development. In the 1995 budget speech, the Union Finance Minister stated that "there are many rural infrastructure project, I propose to establish a new rural infrastructure development fund, in the NABARD from April 1995". The Eighth Plan document made the following remarks on rural infrastructure development, "the review of the programme reveals that in most cases the physical and the financial targets have been achieved satisfactorily, except in the area of rural sanitation". However the quantitative achievements do not mean much in themselves. The following examples will help to clarify this: (a) In the case of elementary education, over 90 per cent of the children were enrolled and had access to school. However the literacy rate is only about 50 per cent. This is due to the high rate of dropouts at the primary level itself. The aim is eradication of illiteracy. Hence the achievement should be judged in terms of literacy rates and retention rates and these have to be monitored. (b) In the case of rural health there is an extensive network of primary health centres and sub-centres, but these have not been operationalised in terms of adequate staff or medicines. In any case health for all means, reduction in both birth and death rates and control of diseases. Hence the performance with respect to rural health should be judged in terms of a decline in the death rate, the infant mortality rate and the birth rate, besides the reduction in morbidity due to illness and diseases.

Even by 1998 the situation has not improved regarding allocation of adequate funds to these rural infrastructure developments. In the budget speech of 1998 the Union Finance Minister made the following statement about rural infrastructure. "Next only to water is the question of rural credit and rural infrastructure. Under the Rural Infrastructure Development Fund (RIDF) managed by NABARD, moneys are made available to the State Governments for rural infrastructure. During the past three years about Rs. 2,500 crores has been allocated to it annually and I am pleased to announce RIDF with an enhanced allocation of Rs. 3000 crores".

Probably the Union Finance Minister was unaware of the fact that even as early as 1990-91, the budget allocation of Rs. 4,509 crores was not adequate. With the inflation increasing during the last eight years, the budget allotment of only Rs. 3,000 crores for rural infrastructure is going to be inadequate. Therefore, there is a need for additional allotment for developing the rural infrastructure in the years to come.

Action suggested

(a) Atleast Rs. 6,000 crores per year should be provided for improving the rural infrastructure, (b) The money allotted to rural infrastructure should not be diverted as has happened in the past, (c) Private sector should be encouraged to participate in developing rural infrastructure facilities, (d) Special cess can be levied, at local level, to augment resources needed for developing the rural infrastructure.

Developing Rural Growth Centres

A pragmatic approach is needed to develop selected number of rural infrastructure facilities at the rural growth centres, instead of attempting to develop at each village, infrastructure facilities like schools, hospitals, market centres etc.

Current situation

The present day policy adopted by the Government of India is to attempt to develop infrastructure facilities at every village. It is all right for water supply, sanitation and housing, but it is not a good idea for developing the school, hospital and market facilities at every village, since it is practically impossible or feasible to have such developments. The pragmatic idea should be to develop the growth centres for selected groups of villages.

Action suggested

(a) As recommended by the National Committee on the Development of Backward areas, the infrastructure facilities for schools, hospitals and market facilities should be developed at focal points like weekly market places or small towns or growth centres which should have the facilities for both agricultural and non-agricultural activities, as well as social and economic services considered desirable for raising the quality of rural life. The operational set-up behind this programme is the development of suitable growth centres where farmers and artisans meet their production requisites, marketing, and banking needs within 5 kms of their living places. There should have banking centres and credit facilities, Agro-service centres, retail store for essential commodities and agricultural inputs, marketing yards, diesel and petrol pumps wherever necessary, post offices and eventually telephone facilities, hospitals, schools etc. Later according to the needs of the area, more infrastructure facilities may have to be provided like the setting up of cold storages, agro-processing facilities etc. Of course, the facilities would vary from area to area depending on the local needs and conditions.

16.9 PROGRAMME AREAS FOR OBJECTIVE—IX : CREATING INFRASTRUCTURES TO IMPROVE COMMUNICATION, TRANSPORT, MARKETING AND OTHER FACILITIES

Removing basic constraints of small farmers in marketing produce

Current situation

The present day market reforms emphasize changes in the forms of market organisation by way of solving market problems rather than taking steps to remove the basic constraints that reduce the efficiency of the system[23]. The real problems faced by the small farmers in efficient marketing are : (1) poor transport facilities from the villages to the market centres, (2) Lack of credit facilities on the produce to be lodged at the market centres, and (3) availability of up-to-date market information at the village level.

Action suggested

(a) Top priority should be given to provide all-weather roads to all villages so that private sector can assist to provide better transport to villages, (b) The Marketing Societies should have a mandatory role to provide credit to small farmers, who want to store their produce with the marketing societies to avoid distress sale during fall of market prices. Agricultural Produce Marketing Committees should be given assistance/directives to provide adequate storage and cold storage facilities to enable the rural poor to store their produce when market prices fall. Modern Marketing Information Centre should be set up by Agricultural Produce Market Committees using the latest information technology which should connect the market centre with all the villages coming under its jurisdiction.

16.10 PROGRAMME OBJECTIVE—X: ASSISTING RURAL POOR TO GET ACCESS TO SERVICES

Reaching the rural poor by institutions providing services

Current situation

It has been pointed out by World Bank and other U.N. organizations that the rural poor are not able to get access to services created by National Governments in the Third World Countries. In spite of this clear indication, very few efforts have been made by the Governments to provide the needed assistance by way of what is known as 'Management Services' to the rural poor. More concern has been the ignorance shown on the part of the Governments about the need for providing such management services. Coombs and Ahmed (1974)[24] in pointing out this situational factor, have also recommended that the success of village development work will depend upon the extent of assistance to be provided to the rural poor in getting access to services. The Governor of the Reserve Bank of India in his address[25] before the seminar group on development of rural poor, has called for evolving additional and innovative mechanisms for creating an effective credit delivery system for the beneficiaries of rural development including self-helping group.

Action suggested

(a) The Government should take steps to establish a 'Management Services Wing' at the taluk level which will take steps for providing management services to rural poor of different villages with the help of local leaders and NGOs, operating at the village level. (b) The three basic village institutions, namely the village Panchayat, the village school and the village cooperative should be given some specific responsibilities to help the rural poor in providing management services to them. (c) All the institutions meant for providing services to the rural poor should reach all villages so as to enable the rural poor to get easy access to the services. (d) More NGOs should be promoted at the village level which are small but people centered to take major responsibility in assisting the rural poor to get access to services. (e) The rural poor should be educated to organise themselves into small informal groups to enable them to have access to services.

More Franchise centres are needed in villages to reach the rural poor

Current situation

Most of the villages do not have outlets of the service providing institutes. As a result the rural poor are required to visit other villages to get the services, which becomes very difficult for the rural poor due to the time required and the cost involved for such visits.

Action suggested

(a) Growth centres should be developed in each taluk for a group of villages and all institutes meant for providing services to the rural poor should have franchise centres in such growth centres.

Single window service should be provided in each growth centre

Current situation

At present all institutes providing services to the rural poor are not located in one common place. As a result the rural poor are required to move from place to place to avail of these services.

Action suggested

(a) An innovative method to provide all services through one window service must be started as already tried successfully in Sri Lanka.

16.11 PROGRAMME AREAS FOR OBJECTIVE—XI : CREATING AN EFFECTIVE ORGANISATION

Creating an appropriate agency

Current situation

Progress of poverty alleviation programmes has been hindered for lack of an appropriate agency that should be entrusted with the responsibility of preparing and implementing the programme. There are too many programmes which are handled by a score of governmental departments. The idea of developing the Panchayat Raj system, with a three-tier structure at the village, taluk and district levels has remained unimplemented since the 1950s. Many State governments have replaced the Zilla Parishads which should have been the local centre for local development, by establishing separate agencies like District Development Boards (DDBs) or the District Rural Development Agencies (DRDAs).

Action suggested

(a) As recommended by a discussion paper, developed by the Government of India in 1985[26], immediate steps are needed to constitute Panchayat Raj Institutes, giving statutory responsibilities to village assemblies, taluk development bodies and Zilla Parishads to take charge of all aspects of planning, execution and monitoring of all poverty alleviation programmes at the village, taluk and district levels, respectively. (b) These bodies will have executive officers assisted by representatives of local bodies, like members of Panchayats and members of legislature belonging to the area, presidents of major co-operative institutes, representatives of voluntary agencies with reservation seats for women, scheduled castes/tribes. These PRI bodies will be assisted by various departmental officers, drawn from the line departments of State governments at these three levels. (c) The Constitution needs to be amended so as to have regular elections to these PRI bodies.

Decentralised planning

Current situation

Top down administration, with planning from the above is the rule at present. Local planning idea was initiated by recommending Block planning. But, even after 25 years it has remained on paper only. Without a firm grasp of the wide variations in natural endowments, soil and climate, social and cultural milieus, historical legacies and group alignments, area planning would lose much of its relevance. The 74th amendment of the Constitution requires that district planning is a must. This has not been implemented all these years. People's empowerment at the local level, provided under the 73rd amendment of the Constitution, also remains to be implemented. In the consultation group and discussion held in October 1996 at New Delhi which was duly sponsored by the Government of India and several U.N. bodies, it was pointed out that it is not the money that is proving the bottleneck in poverty alleviation but the mind-set of the top down approach, which fails to involve the people and the evil element of corruption. As a result of this faulty approach, local conditions are not studied situational data not made available, and relevant local plans are not prepared. The worst of all the local people are not involved in the planning. Local leaders and local institutions are not associated. Centrally prepared plans are forced from the top, which have not helped the communities of the local areas.

Action suggested

(a) 73rd and 74th ammendments of Constitution should be implemented forthwith. The executive officers of the poverty alleviation programmes should be personally held responsible, if these are not followed, (b) No regional plan should be prepared unless the local situational data is collected systematically and such reports are made available. This step is necessary to make the plans realistic and practical oriented, (c) The three basic village institutions, namely the village Panchayat, the village school and the village co-operative, should be actively involved in preparing the required development plans, (d) NGOs present in local areas, should be encouraged to participate in the plan preparation, (e) Local leaders should be identified, trained and used in this task of rural planning, (f) No carpet plan should be imposed from above and used for the local areas. Instead, local areas like the taluks should be assisted to prepare their own local plans, taking into consideration the pertinent requirements of the area, (g) The taluk plans should be prepared duly compiling information for the different areas to suit the particular requirements of different villages.

Local control with central supervision

Current situation

For the success of poverty alleviation programmes, it is essential to have community involvement which will be facilitated by administration with local control, instead of the presently followed central control. This local control is being advocated since the publication of the Balwantrai Mehta Committee report in the 1950s from the Community Development days. However, the implementation of this step has been soft pedalled and the governments have been slow in transferring the rural administration to local level organisations. Immediate action is necessary for deligating this authority to Panchayats

Action suggested

The consultative discussion held in October 1996 at New Delhi on poverty alleviation programmes has recommended that the Panchayats must have greater powers instead of being merely carriers of projects handed down from district levels. They should have greater accountability and must function as rallying points for citizens participation. Immediate action is necessary to delegate to this authority to Panchayat and other PRI bodies.

New type of decentralisation

Current situation

There is lot of difference of opinion regarding decentralisation. Government organisations at the district and State levels feel that they are quite competent to know the problems of the rural areas and they can design useful rural development plans. People at the local level feel that their co-operation and participation are not required by the Government. This kind of tussel is going on for the last 40 years or so without any feasible solution. Even constitutional amendments are not implemented satisfactorily. A new knowledge or decision is needed. As explained by Leonard *et al.*[27] "the construction and maintenance of rural roads involves links between community organisations and intermediate levels of sub-national Government. The local group is needed to organise voluntary labour for construction and to oversee and/or provide maintenance. It also can make extremely helpful contributions at the planning stage in order to ensure the optimal fit between local use and road layout. On the other hand, the engineers to design the road and the earth moving equipment, to do heavier construction work must be found in a supra-local organization. Rural work projects function best when each is communicating with and is in support of the other".

Actions suggested

Rural development and poverty alleviation needs a new type of decentralization. What is required is not power for either State or central governments or local people's organizations but complementary strength in both. Central Government agencies, intermediate organizations and local groups, all possess resources and capabilities that are needed by others. The challenge is to link these institutions together in such a way that their weaknesses are counterbalanced and their comparative advantages are used. By so doing, a contribution can be made to development which neither local nor national organizations could achieve alone.

Co-ordination at all levels including the operational level

Current situation

The U.N. Rural Survey published in 1997[28] has reported that in India most of the poverty alleviation programmes were agency driven and were unresponsive to the real needs of the poor and lacked coordination among the multiple agencies which led to duplication, friction and unutilized synergies. As a result, many poverty alleviation programmes have not been successful, as expected, because of lack of integrated planning of related functions and coordination between different agencies involved. Coordination at all levels is not done especially at the operational level. The existing coordination mechanisms, district coordination committees and the local bodies, are not proving equal to the task.

Action suggested

(a) At the taluk level, a representative co-ordination body consisting of representatives of all development departments should consider each project of different departments to be implemented in the taluk and suggest ways and means of coordinating the same at the planning stage[34]. It should include consideration of horizontal and vertical linkages of individual projects, with a view to making them mutually reinforcing and thereby reduce overall material and manpower costs, so as to maximise the total benefits and their proper distribution. (b) For enabling the action stated under (1) above, there is a need for a planning body at a decentralized level like the district level which should have authority to adjust plans of different government agencies. (c) Members of all departments, whose efforts have to be coordinated at the taluk level, should have clear understanding about the details of coordination efforts required before the start of the project.

Accountability and transparency in Government dealings

Current situation

Financial dealings involved in implementing programmes, like wage employment programme, soil conservation programmes are at present not known by the public. As a result, there is scope for misappropriation of public funds. In the national consultative group discussion held in October 1996[29], it was pointed out that in many States, the governments have sunk crores of rupees, in supposedly rehabilitative programmes. The poor continue to remain poor, because the money gets siphoned off at various levels and never reaches them. Bogus companies get contracts and receive payment in thousands for construction work that seldom take place. In one example, where the villagers who asked for money for building a pucca road connecting a neighbouring town, were informed by a district officer that their request cannot be looked into because that road has already been built three times according to the records available.

Action suggested

(a) Transparency is needed while dealing with financial transactions or while implementing poverty alleviation programmes. (b) The village assembly (Grama Sabha), in whose jurisdiction the project is to be implemented, must be given all details of the project. (c) The records kept pertaining to the projects should be kept open for inspection by the public.

16.12 PROGRAMME AREAS FOR OBJECTIVE—XII : PROVIDING SAFETY NETS TO THE RURAL POOR

In any programme of rural poverty alleviation, when target groups of rural poor are identified, it will be necessary to provide some kind of safety nets to these categories to take care of unforeseen circumstances beyond their control. Lack of providing safety nets has been identified by Nobel Laureate Amartya Sen (1998) as the most important deficiency in the rural development programmes of the third world countries[30]. The following important programme areas are suggested.

Insurance support for rural poor to take care of unexpected losses due to vagaries of season, insect pests and diseases etc.

Current situation

At present no special insurance supports are provided for the rural poor to take care of unforeseen losses due to vagaries of season, insect pests and diseases. As a result the situation has aggravated so much as witnessed from 1998-99 by several cases of suicides committed by poor farmers who could not repay the loans due to losses beyond their control.

Action suggested

(a) To start with, at least a limited insurance scheme, to cover the cost of at least the inputs purchased by the rural poor, while taking up enterprises to increase their income, should be provided[8] as suggested by C. Subramaniam (1982), page 21. (b) A comprehensive scheme of providing insurance for the rural poor to cover the entire cost of out of pocket expenses is required for the income generating projects and this scheme may be taken up as a pilot work in selected areas to find out the effect. (c) Before recommending any new idea or practice to the rural poor more care is necessary to find out the possible reasons for any failures and see that research practices are tested thoroughly before recommending them to the rural poor.

Guarantee to provide minimum support price in the income generating projects

Current situation

At present guarantee to provide minimum price is provided only in few cases like milk production in the milkshed areas, sugarcane grown by farmers in the area covered by sugar factories. Beyond this no Government scheme is provided to provide price support to other commodities like vegetables, food-grains etc. As a result poor rural people suffer the most in times of sudden fall in the market prices.

Action suggested

(a) In all income generation projects promoted in rural development, government must provide minimum support price to the produce of rural poor,

(b) All Agricultural Marketing Societies should be able to provide advance on the produce of the rural poor and store the produce when market prices fall so that poor rural people need not engage in distress sales.

Providing credit on terms which reduce risk and uncertainty

Current situation

Credit system prevalent now will not take case on farmers risk due to vagaries of season or pest infestation. At the most their instalment to repay the loan may be extended.

Action suggested

There is a need for improving the credit facilities to provide small farmers access to credit on terms which reduce risk and uncertainty. Only then it will increase the farmers ability to absorb risk.

Research emphasis to reduce risk and uncertainty

Current situation

Inadequate attention given to small farmer management has increased production cost and risk. Because of these risks, small farmers are reluctant to adopt high cost new technologies.

Action suggested

Research scientists must devote more attention to enhance the resource neutrality of new technology by substituting non-monetary or inexpensive inputs in place of high cost inputs. In order to minimize fluctuations caused by weather aberrations and pest epidemics.

Improve marketing and processing facilities to reduce price fluctuations and risks

Current situation

There is no system presently in the market to help the poor farmers to face untimely price fluctuations when prices fall suddenly. There are no facilities for farmers to store their produce in the present market system and to provide them advance for the same. They cannot get loan for keeping their produce which they could repay when they sell their produce later when prices improve.

Action suggested

(a) All agricultural market committees should be made to provide adequate funds to improve the market system to arrange for storage facilities to help the poor farmers to store their produce when market prices suddenly fall. (b) The market system should provide loans to farmers who desire to store their produce with market committees to face the situation due to sudden fall in the prices.

In the PDS system, coarse grains should be stocked

Current situation

At present in most of the PDS centres only rice and wheat are made available. The rural poor mostly consume coarse cereals like Jower, Maize, and Ragi which are not available through PDS. As a result poor rural people will not get much benefit from the PDS.

Action suggested

All PDS centres should get regular quota of coarse grain for use of rural poor.

Village grain banks should be established for the benefit of rural poor

Current situation

At present there is no system of village grain banks to be established in villages. The rural poor have to depend only on PDS shops for their requirements of purchasing foodgrains when they need. Since the PDS will not stock coarse grains required by them. Hence they are much handicapped.

Action suggested

Some innovative efforts have been made by some NGOs to establish village grain bank using local initiatives. Anna Hazare has established the village grain bank in Ralegaon Siddhi village in Ahmednagar district of Maharashtra.[31] The method adopted in establishing this Village Grain Bank has been given in Appendix C which should serve as a model for other villages.

16.13 PROGRAMME AREAS FOR OBJECTIVE—XIII : EMPOWERMENT OF RURAL WOMEN ESPECIALLY BELONGING TO POOR FAMILIES

Improve Women's access, especially of those belonging to poor category, to vocational training, science and technology and development education, in all villages on priority basis

Current situation

At present very limited opportunities are available to rural poor women and especially young women, re-entering the labour market to develop skills, to meet the needs of the changing socio-economic context for improving their employment opportunities. Although U.N. organizational funded schemes like DWCRA are in operation since 1982-83, these schemes are not able to reach all villages to help poor rural women and their families.

Action suggested

(a) Rural poor women's development education work should be started in every village of India with the help of the existing Government staff, with the co-operation of village leaders and voluntary agencies. No subsidy is required to enroll the group organizer. What is needed is encouragement for local leaders to take up such responsibilities. (b) Design educational and training programmes for women who are unemployed in order to provide them with knowledge and skills that will improve their employment opportunities including self-employment and development of their entrepreneurial skills. (c) Self-help groups should be promoted in every village to involve the rural poor women.

Availability of credit for rural women for project work

Current situation

Credit facilities are generally not available to women since they can offer little by way of collateral and women are regarded as an appendage to their husbands in terms of their financial and social positions rather than as independent individuals in their own right.

Action suggested

(a) Rural women who are members of the self-help groups and who show their ability to save part of their earning through thrift, should be given credit by the financing agencies for help in their income generating activities. It has been shown by the Grameen Banks in Bangladesh that provision of small credit schemes are the most important element in any successful attack on poverty and the most liberating force for poor women. (b) Provide rural poor women with access to savings and credit mechanisms and institutions. (c) New credit and saving methodology that are effective in reaching women in poverty and innovative in reducing transaction cost and redefining risk.

Programmes to liberate rural poor women from constant fear, illness and premature death are necessary

Current situation

At present, no accurate health care services are provided for rural poor women and their families at village level. There is extremely high rate of maternal mortality in the poor women ranging up to 420 deaths/100000 deliveries as compared to only 24 maternal deaths/100000 in industrial countries.

Action suggested

(a) Provide free family planning service in all villages for the benefit of rural poor women. (b)Provide free transport to hospitals in rural growth centres for the benefit of rural poor women.

Supporting the empowerment programme of rural poor women by targetting the young women through 4-H method

Current situation

There are no facilities in villages to train young women of poor families with project work of the 4-H type. The village schools are not given any responsibility to train the rural youth in projects of 4-H type. As a result, there is no scope for character building, development of good citizenship and leadership among young rural women.

Action suggested

(a) A department of rural service should be started in each rural school and some teachers should be trained to take up the responsibility for training rural youth. (b) In line with the craft subjects, the rural youth, who join project work of 4-H type offered by the Rural Service Departments should get the required credits for exam. These projects will help the rural youth to earn while learning and also learn by doing.

16.14 PROGRAMME AREAS FOR OBJECTIVE—XIV : PROMOTING PEOPLE'S PARTICIPATION

Empowering Grama Sabhas to take leadership in poverty alleviation programmes

Current situation

At present in most of the Indian States Grama Sabhas i.e., village assemblies, are practically non-existent. Only in Maharashtra and Kerala the Grama Sabhas are empowered with the following responsibilities: (a) All village development work should be undertaken by the Village Panchayats only under the overall guidance of the Grama Sabhas. (b) Grama Sabhas should employ a full time secretary to look after the village development programmes especially those dealing with poverty alleviation. (c) Village Panchayats are to be treated only as executive functionaries of the Grama Sabhas. The Grama Sabhas have power to relieve the Panchayat if the latter's work is found unsatisfactory by the Grama Sabha.

Action suggested

(a) All the States should empower their Grama Sabhas complete authority for planning and implementing poverty alleviation programmes and empowering them with authorities as already done in Maharashtra and Kerala as explained in the current situation in the paragraph mentioned above. (b) All Grama Sabhas should conduct monthly meeting to consider planning and implementing programmes of poverty alleviation. Especially the work of mobilizing, organizing, utilizing human resources of the village in various commonly oriented programmes should be considered by the Grama Sabhas. This should help in the development of local initiative and responsibility on the part of local people especially the local leaders. (c) Before starting any rural development programme relating to poverty alleviation, it should be obligatory to take the approval of the Grama Sabha before implementing the programme.

Identifying, developing and utilizing local leaders for rural development program

Current situation

There are various kinds of groups in villages each group having its own group leader. These group leaders are interested in helping the groups to perform their group functions effectively. At present these groups and group leaders are not effectively used in promoting rural development programmes.

Action suggested

(a) If necessary identify the existing groups in each village and also find out a group leader.

(b) These group leaders should be trained to perform their group functions more effectively.

(c) Urge the group leaders to do more and better work related to rural development in which the groups are interested.

(d) Motivate the group leaders to continue their group functions recognizing their good work done in public functions and not by paying remuneration for the work done by them.

16.15 PROGRAMME AREAS FOR OBJECTIVE—XV ENCOURAGING NON-GOVERNMENTAL ORGANIZATIONS AND LOCAL INSTITUTIONS TO PARTICIPATE IN THE PROGRAMMES FOR RURAL DEVELOPMENT

Promoting developing and using NGOs having village roots for the success of the rural development programmes

Rural development requires assistance of local leaders and local voluntary institutions like NGOs. India's Planning Commission had pointed out that small and flexible NGOs having village roots are required as providers of welfare measures and mitigators of hardships to the weaker sections.

One important lesson on the work reported from rural development is that there are many voluntary social service organizations (NGOs). Out of these NGOs, there are only few having village roots and established because of dedication and intense social commitment to serve the villagers with selfless work. The example of NGO working in Ralegaon Siddhi village of Ahmednagar district of Maharashtra State led by Anna Hazare has been in the lime light to highlight the importance of such village rooted NGOs.

Current situation

There are some NGOs established in villages for assisting in implementation of the rural developmental programmes. However many of them have no village roots. Most of them are established with headquarters away from villages where they operate. The work of majority of NGOs is similar to the work of government departments, since they are having paid workers. They shift from one village to other after working for four to five years in a particular place as a result there has not been any appreciable impact on the rural development programmes.

Action suggested

(a) A new approach to establish small village rooted NGOs are providing voluntary services for the upliftment of the villages is essential. This requires widespread campaign as village levels requesting for voluntary action by the village leaders.

(b) Interested voluntary leaders who are desirous of starting new NGOs at the village level should be taken on field trips to Ralegaon Siddhi village of Maharashtra to get clear idea of importance of work by a village oriented NGO in rural development.

Encouraging Village Basic institutions to actively participate in planning and implementation of poverty alleviation programmes

Current situation

While developing community development programmes in 1950s three basic village institutions were established namely village panchayats, village schools and village cooperatives, with an idea to utilize these institutions in the development of village programme and encourage people's active participation. A special booklet was prepared explaining the detailed roles to be played by these institutions. In the methodology chapter-12, pages 197 to 201, we have already provided details of this information. However in the present rural development programmes these basic rural institutions have not been assigned with required roles to be played by them.

Action suggested

(a) Roles to be played by these basic institutions as specified in chapter-12 have to be reallotted by introducing the necessary constitutional amendments without any further delay. This step is necessary in getting people's active participation in poverty alleviation programmes.

REFERENCES

1. Dantwala, M.L. and Barmeda, J.N., 1991, Rural development approaches and issues, pp. 426-449 in Edt. by Dantwala. *Indian Agricultural Development since Independence, op. cit.*
2. Government of India, Report of the High powered committee on agricultural policies and programmes, 1990, *op. cit.*
3. Haque, T., 1988, Role of technological change in improving the economic conditions of marginal farmers and landless labourers in India, paper presented to the seminar on inter-relationships between Science and Technology for eradication of poverty, September 1-3, 1988, Convened by Indian Association.
4. Government of India, Planning Commission, VIII Plan document, 1992.
5. Government of India, Planning Commission VI Plan document, 1981.
6. Desai, Vasant, 1994, Fundamentals of Rural Development, Himalaya Publication, Bombay, p. 19.
7. Sundaram, T.R., Role of agriculture in the Indian National Economy, pp. 17-49, in the *Indian Agricultural Development since Independence*, Edt. by Dantwala, 1991, *op. cit.*
8. Subramaniam, C., 1982, Theme paper prepared for seminar on Indian Agriculture held on June 21 and 22, at Tamil Nadu Agricultural University, pub. by Rajaji International Centre, Institute of Public Affairs and Administration, New Delhi, p. 8.
9. Barbara, Adolph, 1995, What does it take to make a successful project"? Some findings from 13 watershed management projects in South India. ICRISAT, Socio-economics and Policy, Patencheru - 502 324, Andhra Pradesh, India.
10. Statement from Agriculture Minister published in the *Deccan Herald* paper, of 28th July 1996.
11. Sawanth, S.D., Irrigation and water use, 1991, page 93-116, in *Indian Agricultural Development since Independence*, Edt. by Dantwala, M.L., *op. cit.*
12. Common Wealth Secretariat 1992, Action to reduce poverty proposals for needed instructions developed by a Common Wealth Consultation on Rural Poverty alleviation, Colombo, Sri Lanka, 5-9, October, 1992, Food Production and Rural Development Division, Common Wealth Secretariat, London.
13. Srivastava, Druva and Haque, T., 1990, *Technological Assessment and Research Imbalances*. IARI, New Delhi.
14. Government of India, Census Report, 1981.
15. John, W. Mellor, 1975, The Impact of New Agricultural Technology on Employment and Income Distribution—Concepts and Policy, Cornell

University, *op. cit.*

16. Kessaba, 1989, Technology Systems for Small farmers: Issues and Options, Edt. book, Publ. West View Press, London.
17. *FAO Year Book on Agriculture,* 1994.
18. Nandapurkar, C.G., 1980, A study on entrepreneurship behaviour of small farmers unpublished Ph.D. thesis, *op. cit.*
19. Ekanthappa, A.S., 1987, Impact of selected schemes of IRDP on beneficiaries in Bangalore district. Unpublished M.Sc. thesis, Dept. of Agricultural Extension, UAS, Bangalore.
20. Ahluwalia, S.M., 1990, Policies for poverty alleviation. *Assian Development Review.* Studies on Asian and Pacific Economic Issues, published by Asian Development Bank, **8**(7) : 111-132.
21. Patrocinio Santos Villanueva 1966, Value of Rural Roads, pp. 775-776 in Raymond E. Borton, (Ed). *Selected Readings to Accompany Getting Agriculture Moving.* Vol. 2. Agricultural Development Council, New York.
22. Malgavkar, P.D., 1970, How small industries in Japan meet the challenges, paper presented in the souvenir brought out on the occasion of Inauguration of Technocrats Industrial Estate, Balanagar, Hyderabad, First week Aug. 1970, pp. 49-53.
23. Subbarao, K., 1991, "Agricultural Marketing" in Dantwala, M.L., (Ed). 1991, *Indian Agricultural Development since Independence, op. cit, pp.* 277-297.
24. Coombs, P.H. and Ahmed, M., 1974, "Attacking Rural Poverty—Report for World Bank, *op. cit.*
25. Report published in *Deccan Herald* dated March 3, 1995.
26. Government of India, 1985, Report of the committee to review the existing administrative arrangements of Rural Development and Poverty Alleviation Programmes (Chairman G.V.K. Rao), Ministry of Agriculture, Department of Rural Development, New Delhi.
27. Leonard, David "Conclusions," in Leonard, Dale Marshall, Jose Garzon, Stephen Peterson and Sven Steinmo, 1981, *Project on Managing Decentralization, op. cit.*
28. United Nations Rural Survey, 1997, quoted in *Deccan Herald, op cit.*
29. Narasimhan, Sakunthala, 1996, Failure of Poverty Alleviation, Published in *Deccan Herald, op cit.*
30. Sen, Amartya, 1998, Rural development without safety nets has no meaning. Statement made at the first press conference after getting his Nobel Prize, *Economic Times, op. cit.*
31. Hazare, Anna, 1997, *Ralegaon Siddhi—A Veritable Transformation.* Ralegaon Siddhi Pariwar Prakashan.

APPENDICES

APPENDIX-A

[Extracts from the paper "The value of rural roads" by Patrocinio Santus Villanueva (1966) from Raymond E. Borten (Ed). Selected Readings to Accompany Getting Agriculture Moving, Vol. II, published by Agricultural Development Council, New York]

THE VALUE OF RURAL ROADS

In an article entitled "Local Government : A Key to National Economic Advancement and Political Stability", A.B. Lewis wrote that "Economic development depends mainly on education and transportation". Recently, Raul Manglapus made a similar comment in his speech before the members of the Manila Lion's Club. It is possible that many people all over the world share the idea of these two men.

Roads are the major channels of transportation in this country. To the people in the barrio, land transportation is one means which directly affects their daily activities and yet is sadly wanting. To improve land transportation would mean, among other things, construction of roads, which would link the barrios to the main highways and centres like the market.

Since roads are constructed and intended for public use, it has always been assumed, at least in the Philippines, that the government is responsible for their construction, improvement and maintenance. The government, the National Government, maintains existing public roads and highway structures and constructs new ones. These roads are mostly national and provincial or city roads, although the Bureau may supervise the construction of municipal and other feeder roads.

In addition tc administering the national highways programme, the Bureau of Public Highways cooperates with the Presidential Assistant on Community Development (PACD) under the office of the President in the implementation of a self-help barrio road construction programme. For the latter project, the PACD has provided funds for the creation of a Self Help Barrio Road Section of the Bureau of Public Highways, and the organization of Barrio Road Construction Teams. Costs of moving heavy road equipment from the Bureau of Public Highways to areas of construction are also borne by the Presidential Assistant on Community Development. In critical dissident areas, the Armed forces of the Philippines through its corps of Engineers supply the technical services and road equipment.

While the National Government is fully aware of the big demands for more and better roads, it has been in a position to provide all barrios with roads. The majority of the barrios have not been served by roads. Public demands upon the National Government are too many and too varied to be adequately met by its present income. In view of this, the pace of road building has been rather slow and it will take a very long time before the 19,000 to 21,000 barrios in the Philippines will all benefit from a serviceable road system. Road studies in 1955 show that only nine per cent of all barrios were accessible by roads.

APPENDIX-B

[Paper by P.D. Malgavkar (1970) published in a Souvenir brought out on the occasion of the inauguration of Technocrats Industrial Estates, Balanagar, Hyderabad during the first week of August, 1970]

HOW SMALL INDUSTRIES IN JAPAN MEET THE NEW CHALLENGES

P.D. Malgavkar, I.M.P.
Principal Director, SIET Institute, Hyderabad

In the promotion and development of small industries in India the experience of other countries especially that of Japan is highly instructive and useful. In Japan, governmental policies actively encourage small industries and business to cooperate and if necessary, to merge so that their viability and competitive strength are increased. It may, therefore, be of interest to the technocrats to know more about this activity in Japan.

Co-operation

Under a law passed in 1949, cooperatives organized exclusively by medium and small enterprises were exempted from the application of Monopoly Law. Four types of cooperative organizations came to be set up under this law namely the common facility cooperative, the credit cooperative, the federation of cooperatives and the joint enterprise cooperative (Since then the Mutual Fire Insurance Cooperative and the Common Facility petty Cooperative have come into being). For several years now a realization that cooperation is one of the principal steps for the structural amelioration of medium and small scale enterprises has dawned and active encouragement is offered to the formation of cooperatives. Accordingly, a new organizational system for accelerating the cooperatives was founded in 1967 by partially revising the law on the formation of medium and small scale enterprises organization.

Behind the growing trend of closer cooperation in smaller Japanese enterprises was the high growth of Japanese economy, which stimulated demand. In order to meet the rising demand, they expanded their plants and equipment, improved their technological standards and adopted flow production system. Mass production enabled them to change over to the production of a few products in large quantities instead of a large variety of products in small quantities. They were required to optimize their sizes of enterprises and to meet this requirement, they stove for closer cooperation or *Kyogyo*.

The *Kyogyo* movement is, thus, directed to ensure, closer cooperation with a view to making smaller enterprises enlarge their size of enterprise and cope with large enterprises. The movement is most successful with smaller manufacturers capable of collectively mechanizing their plants and equipments. It has also influenced smaller service and mercantile enterprises which are in a position to collectively utilize their equipment and facilities. Their cooperation is usually advanced to the collective purchase of materials and to collective selling of products.

Modernization

By the year 1955, the protectionistic measures were gradually abolished and the economy was thrown open to foreign capital investment. The Japanese economy was thrown open to foreign capital investment. The Japanese economy has achieved unprecedented growth with technological innovation and modernization. This unprecedented growth resulted in labour shortages which brought forth far reaching effects in the medium and small scale industry. The labour shortage improved the rate of employment and stopped up modernization of employment practices, but it also increased wages.

Formerly, the ready availability of cheap labour was a valuable asset to the smaller Japanese industry. Now the small industries had to meet both labour shortage and high wages by management modernization.

Subsistence-level industries plagued with excessive competition and shortage of labour and funds were compelled to cooperate for collective production and selling, while industries with 100 to 199 employees cooperate for product standardization and the pooling of welfare facilities. Industries with 50 to 99 employees were most benefited by their affiliation with collective enterprises cooperatives. It may be assumed that smaller industries through the formation of cooperatives will have a size of capital and a number of employees adequate to face fair competition.

The chief motives for forming general cooperatives in the descending order are :

(a) Collective purchasing;
(b) Pooling of welfare facilities;
(c) Collective selling;
(d) Collective production;
(e) Product standardization, and
(f) Collective advertising and publicity.

Cooperatives were formed by food packers, food seasoning manufacturers, brewers, confectioners, food growers, leather tanners, rubber product manufacturers etc. Some cooperatives were formed to prevent large industries from encroaching on their members' interest. In the cooperatives formed for collective production and selling, member industries with less than 50 employees exceeded those with more than 51.

Participation in industrial estates

Participation by smaller industries in suburban estates is encouraged for cooperation promotion, for regional development and in order to avoid urban population concentration. According to the scheme, a group of small or medium scale industries desiring to participate in an industrial estate is required to organize a general cooperative to formulate an estate construction plan and to submit it to the Smaller Enterprises Agency, Ministry of International Trade and Industry, through the prefecture where the estate will be located. When the plan passes the scrutiny of the Agency, the cooperative is designated as eligible for subsidization. The prefectural government finances each designated cooperative in constructing its estate mainly with the subsidy granted by the central government. The prefectural government is also responsible for providing technical guidance for such a cooperative after its estate is completed. Manufacturing or a processing industry capitalized at less than 10,000,000 Yen or with less than 300 regular employees is eligible to participate in an industrial estate as per the Small Business Modernization Subsidization Law. By 1964, sixty eight industrial estates were nominated for subsidization, 39 of them for machinery and metal industries, seven for textile processing industries, three for sundry goods industry, 14 for wood working and lumbering industry, one for printing industry and four for miscellaneous industries. Among them are estates in which only sub-contractors to their respective parent industries are entitled to participate, such as sub-contractors for Toyota Motors Co., Mitsubishi Heavy Industries, Hitachi Ltd. and Hitachi Shipbuilding Co. In the estates specialization is advanced and in some, even the production of finished product is undertaken. There are many estates for machinery and metal industries because their growth is rapid and also because of the constraints on these industries to prevent air and water pollution and other public hazards. Little progress has been made by the estates in the pooling of equipment and facilities and this is one of their drawbacks. In contrast, the estates for lumber and wood working industries which are concentrated in lumber producing centres, have succeeded in pooling together their equipment and facilities. They are also keenly feeling the necessity of cooperation for management improvement. Estates for textile processing industries are broadly classified into those for ready made garments industries and those for tricot cotton making industries. The former include sewing industries as sub-contractors to readymade garments industries. A common problem bogging industrial estates is that it takes a long time to install equipment and facilities for collective use.

Merger of small enterprises

In the sixties, in order to adopt themselves to the changing structure, small enterprises stove for closer cooperation under government encouragement. As can be seen from Table I a similar was noticed in the rise of merger applications submitted by smaller enterprises and accepted by Fair Trade Commission, Prime Minister's Office, Government of Japan.

Table I : Merger applications submitted by Small Enterprises and accepted by Fair Trade Commission

Year	Number	Year	Number
1956	381	1961	591
1957	398	1962	715
1958	381	1963	997
1959	413	1964	864
1960	440	1965	894

Cooperation of smaller industries culminates in a merger which means complete cooperation by the forfeiture of independence. In 1962, out of the 715 mergers effected, 460 or 65 per cent involved smaller industries. Most of them took place between the parent industries and their sub-contractors, sales agencies and other affiliates. The mergers were motivated by (a) Poor management of small merged industries, (b) expansionist business policy of merging industries, (c) assumption that merger will benefit both the parties. A survey conducted by the small Business Finance Cooperation in 1963 indicated the effects of mergers as reduction in administration costs, increase of financial strength and more effective utilization of technological knowledge and experience.

APPENDIX-C

[Method followed by Anna Hazare in Ralegaon Siddhi village of Ahmednagar district of Maharashtra in establishing Village Grain Bank. Taken from the book "Ralegaon Siddhi—A Veritable Transformation" written by Anna Hazare(1997, pages 80-83].

GRAIN BANK

Q. **What is the modus operandi of the Grain Bank ?**

Due to the watershed development at Ralegaon Siddhi the agricultural production has gone up four to five times and the village has now become self-sufficient for foodgrains. About 70-80 per cent farmers benefited from the WSD. But those whose lands are on the heights could not get water. It would have been uneconomic to try to give them the required quantity of water. Despite the use of improved seeds, fertilizers, modern methods of agriculture etc. these 15-20 per cent farmers were unable to produce enough for their annual needs of foodgrains. They fall short by 3-4 months requirements. The village assembly considered as to what could be done to help out these people and it was decided that those farmers who had surplus grains and who sold the surplus, should spare some grain as per their capacity and collect such grains to help their needy brothers. The idea of the grain bank originated from this decision.

The idea caught on and people started depositing extra grain in the bank as per their ability. Starting with 34-40 quintals per year, the quantity increased to 200 quintals. The really needy are listed by the Village Assembly and are given their requirements. It is, however, not given free, for free things soon lose their value and create a bad habit of expecting everything free. The Government started doling out free benefits: soon the laziness grew amongst the people. The Village Assembly put a condition of returning five measures *(payalis)* extra within a year for every quintal of borrowed grain. There is an agreement on stamp paper to this effect and two guarantors are required in case of natural calamity some relaxation is given. But in every way, the transactions are carried out like they are carried out in any other bank dealing in money loans. If the crop is good and still the borrower does not return the loan, the guarantors are held accountable. But we are glad to record that such an occasion has not yet arisen and the people have honestly returned the loan along with the conditionality of giving back extra grain. Apart from meeting the urgent requirements of the needy, the grain bank serves the purpose of creating brotherhood and unity in the village. It sets a model of cooperation before the younger generation and also the desire to do something for others, a feeling of social commitment. That is why the grain bank has become an important facet of the comprehensive village development.

BIBLIOGRAPHY

Ahluwalia, S.M., 1990, Policies for poverty alleviation. *Assian Development Review.* Studies on Asian and Pacific Economic Issues, published by Asian Development Bank, 8(7) : 111-132.

Ahuja, Kanta, 1991, "Agricultural Labour and Rural Employment" Dantwala (Editor), *Indian Agricultural Development since Independence*, op. cit., pp. 367-398.

Alleviation, Colombo, Sri Lanka 5-9, October, 1992. Food production and Rural Development Division, Common Wealth Secretariat quoted by Joseph Mullen "Introduction—poverty rediscovered" in Joseph Mullen (Edt.) Rural Poverty Alleviation Aveberry, USA, Hongkong, Sydney, 1995.

Anna Hazare, 1997, *Ralegaon Siddhi—A Veritable Transformation,* Ralegaon Siddhi Pariwar Prakashan, Ralegaon Siddhi, Dist. Ahmednagar.

Anonymous (2000) "Government admits poverty reduction not enough", Report in the *Hindu Business Line* of November 14, 2000, p. 2.

Anonymous, 1980, Karnataka Cooperative Milk Producers Federation (KMF), mimeographal bulletin.

Anonymous, 1982, Sri Kshetra Dharmasthala Rural Development Project (SKDRDP), Belthangady, Dharmasthala.

Aziz, A., 1986, IRDP in Karnataka—An evaluation ISEC, Bangalore.

Balishter and Singh Roshan (1984), Role of lead bank in implementing IRDP in Bichpuri Block of Agra district, UP. *Agricultural Situation in India,* Vol. 41(1).

Barbara, Adolph, 1995, What does it take to make a successful project"? Some findings from 13 watershed management projects in South India. ICRISAT, Socio-economics and policy Patencheru - 502 324, Andhra Pradesh, India.

Bathrick, D.D., 1981, Agricultural Credit for Small Farm Development. Policies and Practices, West View Special Studies in Social-Political and Economic Development. West View Press, *op. cit.*

Bharathiya Vidya Bhavan, Bombay, 1966, *The Village Reconstruction.* M.K. Gandhi, Edt. and Pub. Hindorani.

Bhatty, I.Z. and Kulawant Madan (1982), "Delivery system in support of small farmers in the context of rural development Centre on Integrated Rural Development for Asia and Pacific, Comilla, Bangladesh, May 1982, pp. 82-83.

Census Report, 1991, Government of India, New Delhi.

Centre for monitoring Indian Economy, New Delhi, 1995, Data furnished on 19th Sept. 1995.

Chambers, Robert, 1993 Rural Development—putting the last first. Longman Scientific and Technical, New York, p. 44.

Chandra Kavate, M.S.,1985, Tardy implementation of IRDP, *Yojana*, Vol **29** (19), pp. 13-15,

Common Wealth Secretariat, London 1993, Action to reduce poverty, proposals for needful instructions developed by a Conmon Wealth Consultation onRural Poverty

Coombs, P.H. and Ahmed, M., 1974, *Attacking Rural Poverty* - Report for the World Bank prepared by the International Council for Educational Devel opment, Baltimore and London, John Hopkins Univ. Press.

Coombs, P.H. and Ahmed, M., 1974, *Attacking Rural Poverty, op. cit.*

Dantwala, M.L. and Barmeda, J.N. (1991), "Rural Development—Approaches and Issues". *op. cit.*

Dantwala, M.L. and Barmeda, 1991, Rural Development, approaches and issues in Dantwala (Ed.) *Indian Agriculture Development since Independence, op. cit.*, pp. 425-451.

Dantwala, M.L., 1978, Some neglected issues in employment, planning, *Economic and Political Weekly,* Vol. 13(6-7), Annl. No.

Dantwala, M.L., 1991, Agrarian Structure and Agrarian Relation in India in M.L. Dantwala (Ed.), *India's Agricultural Development since Independence* 1991, *op. cit.*, pp. 51-71.

Dantwala, M.L., 1991, S*trategies of Agricultural Development since Independence* in M.L Dantwala (ed) *Indian Agricultural Development since Independence,* Oxford & IBH Pub. Co. Pvt. Ltd.

Das, S.R., 1967, Tagore—A Pioneer in Village Reconstruction, *Kurukshetra,* A symposium, pp. 520, *op. cit.*

Department of Agriculture, Karnataka State, 1972, Block demonstration programme.

Desai Vasant, 1994, Fundamentals of Rural Development, Himalaya publication, Bombay, p. 19.

Desai, Vasant.,1991, Rural Development, Himalaya Publishing House, New Delhi.

Desai, D.K. and Hariprakash, 1974 Strategy for rural Development for Weaker Sections in Seminar on Rural Development for weaker sections, Seminar series XII, The Indian Society of Agricultural Economics, Bombay in collaboration with Centre for Management in Agriculture, IIM, Ahmedabad, p. 153-159.

Detailed Budget Speech of Union Finance Minister. Printed in *Economic Times* of 1st March 2000.

Devilaxmi, R.R., IRDP and Rural Women—the case of panchayats in Kerala,*Indian Journal of Ag. Economics*, Vol. **40**(3), pp. 269-270, 1985.

Dharia, Mohan, 1999, Freedom from Hunger—Agrarian Challenges, *Hindu* Paper, April 8, 1999.

Dhillon, D.S. *et al.* (1985), Monitoring and evaluation of IRDP. *Indian Journal of Extension Education*, Vol. 21 (1&2), pp. 48-52.

Druva, Srivastava and Haque, T., 1990, Technological assessment and research imbalances. IARI, New Delhi.

Economic and Political Weekly, 1993, Aug., 21—Table 8.

Economic and Political Weekly, 6-4-1985.

Ekanthappa, A.S., 1987, Impact of selected schemes of IRDP on beneficiaries in Bangalore district. Unpublished M.Sc. thesis, Dept. of Agricultural Extension, UAS, Bangalore.

Elizabeth Oughton (1995), Targetting Food Grains to the Rural Poor —A micro level study in India in Joseph Mullen (Ed.), *Rural Poverty Alleviation*, Avebury, USA.

Esakky, S., 1990, "The impact of IRDP on eradication of poverty among weaker sections in Tirunelveli district of Tamil Nadu", Unpublished Ph.D. Thesis, Dept. of Economics, *Ayyanad— Janice Ammal College.*

ESCAP 1985, The Rural Poor—Human capital for Nation building—A review of the EXCAP/FAO program on social benefits generated by projects Targeting the rural poor, Bangkok, UN.

Eshwara Prasad, Y., Ramanna, R. and Lalitha Achotha, 1997, Performance of IRDP in a Drought prone District of Andhra Pradesh, Pandey and Jalal (Eds.), *Rural Development in India : Issues and Policies,* Vol. II, Anmol Publications, Delhi, pp. 563-583.

FAO : Agriculture Production Year Book, 1994.

FAO : Regional Office for Asia and Pacific, 1993 : Farm Management Notes for Asia and Far East. Reg. Issue, 17.

Gaur, K.D. (1992), "Effectiveness of the Integrated Rural Development Programme (IRDP) in eradication of poverty in India" in K.D. Gaur (Editor). *Dynamics of Rural Development*, Mittal Publishers, New Delhi, 1992.

Ghosh, D.R., 1991, Making IRDP investment efficient, a district study, *Kurukshetra,* Vol. **40**(3), pp. 19-33.

Government of India (1988), Central Bureau of Health Intelligence, Ministry of Health and Family Welfare, *Health Information,* India.

Government of India (1988), Central Bureau of Health Intelligence, Ministry of Health and Family Welfare, *Health Information,* India.

Government of India (1989), Registrar General and Census Commissioner, India, "Household Literacy, Drinking Water and Toilet Facilities" - Occasional Paper No. 1.

Government of India (1991), Report of the Study Group of ICSSR and ICMR, "*Health to All*".

Government of India (1992), VIII Plan Document, New Delhi.

Government of India (1994), Planning Commission, Report of the Project Evaluation Organization.

Government of India, Report of High Powered Committee on Agricultural Policies and Programmes, 1990, Mimeograph report.

Government of India, 1958, Publications Division, *Jawaharlal Nehru on Community Development.*

Government of India, 1959, *Three Basic Institutions*, Ministry of CommunityDevelopment and Cooperation, New Delhi.

Government of India, 1985, Mid-term appraisal of the VIII Plan, 'Unpulished Report Quoted by *Deccan Herald* paper on July 29th 1995.

Government of India, 1985, Report of the committee to review the existing administrative arrangements of Rural Development and poverty alleviation programmes (chairman G.V.K. Rao), Ministry of Agriculture, Department of Rural Development, New Delhi.

Government of India, 1985, VII Five Year Plan, 1985-90, Vol. 2, Planning Commission, New Delhi.

Government of India, 1995, Budget speech of the Union Finance Minister delivered in Parliament on 16-3-1995 at the time of presenting the Union Budget for 1995-96, Budget speech reported by *Economic Times* paper dated 17th March 1995, p. 1.

Government of India, 1998, Address of the Union Finance Minister at the meeting of the Parliamentary Consultative Committee attached to the Finance Ministry on 17-12-1998, Reported in *Deccan Herald* on 18-12-1998.

Government of India, 2000, Union Finance Minister's Budget Speech for the year 2000-2001 delivered on 28-2-2000 and reported in *Economic Times* on 1-3-2000.

Government of India, 95th Report of Public Accounts Committee of the Lok Sabha, presented on 25-4-1995, reported by *Deccan Herald* paper on April 26, 1995.

Government of India, Agricultural Statistics At A Glance, 1998-99.

Government of India, *Census Report*, 1981.

Government of India, *Economic Survey* 1996-97, New Delhi.

Government of India, *Economic Survey for the Year 1998-99,* published by the Ministry of Finance.

Government of India, *First Five Year Plan.*

Government of India, Information released in Feb. 2001, which was reported by *Times of India* on 23-2-2001, page 1 & 9.

Government of India, New Delhi (1978), *4th Education Survey.*

Government of India, New Delhi, *5th Education Survey* (1986).

Government of India, Planning Commission : Mid-term appraisal of the VIII Plan reported by *Deccan Herald* paper dated July 20, 1995, p. 1.

Government of India, Planning Commission, VI Plan document, 1981.

Government of India, Planning Commission, New Delhi (1983), Draft Report of the Working Group on KVI.

Government of India, Planning Commission, VIII Plan document, 1992.

Government of Kerala : State Planning Board : Evaluation Division, Integratd Rural Development programme : An evaluation study, Trivendrum.

Haque, T., 1988, Role of technological change in improving the economic conditions of marginal farmers and landless labourers in India, paper presented to the seminar on Inter-relationships between Science and Technology for eradication of poverty, September 1-3, 1988, Convened by Indian Association.

Hari Kumar, S., IRDP succeeded, *Yojana,* Vol. 28(16), pp. 17-20, 1985.

Higgins, Benjamin, 1977, "Economic Development and cultural change Seamless web or Patchwork quilt", University of Ottawa, in Essays on Economic Development and cultural change in Honor of Bert. Hoselitz, Chicago, University of Chicago Press, pp. 99-100.

Hillary, Clinton, 1997, Statement made after visiting SEWA as reported by *The Times of India,* dated February 5, 1997.

Hillary, Clinton, 1998, Address at the Micro credit summit held at WashingtonDC, USA in February 1997 reported in *Deccan Herald.*

Hirevenkanagoudar, L.V. (1983), A Scientific Investigation of Impact of Dairy Development Programme of KDDC among small farmers, marginal farmers and agricultural labourers, Bangalore district, Karnataka, Unpublished Ph.D. Thesis, University of Agricultural Sciences, Bangalore, Dept. of Agricultural Extension.

IARI Extension Division, New Delhi : Proceedings of the National Conference and workshop on small farmers, held at New Delhi 1984-85.

India Planning Commission, Government of India : Report of the Team for the study of community projects and National Extension Service, Vols I and II, November, 1957 (popularly known as the Copp Team or the Balwantrai Mehta Team), published by the Government of India, Planning Commission.

Indira Gandhi National Open University (IGNOU), School of Continuing Education, Rural Social Services, August 1992.

Indira Gandhi National Open University (IGNOU), School of Continuing Education Development Programme—RDD-2 unit-3 education, p.52.

J. Paul Leagans, 1961, Extension Education for Community Development in Extension Education in Community Development, I Edn., Directorate of Extension, Ministry of Food and Agriculture, GOI, New Delhi.

Jain, S.C., 1986, Poverty alleviation programme in India : Some issues of micro-policy. *Indian Journal of Agricultural Economics*, Vol. 41(3), pp. 383-404.

Jain, T. (1991), "Poultry" in M.L. Dantwala (Editor), *Indian Agricultural Development since Independence*, *op. cit.* pp. 171-187.

Jazairy Idriss, 1989, "Foreword" in *Technology Systems for Small Farmers*, *op. cit.*

Kadian, R.S. and Kaushik, C.R., 1993, An impact study of institutional finance under IRDP in Kurukshetra district of Haryana, *Ag. Banker*, Vol. **16**(1).

Kamta Prasad (1985), *Planning for Poverty Alleviation.* Agricol. Publishing Academy, New Delhi, pp. 160-165.

Kareem, Abdul 1994, "Integrated Rural Development Programme in Kerala : An impact analysis". Unpublished Ph.D. Thesis, Dept. of Agril. Extension, UAS, Bangalore.

Kesseba, Abbas M. 1989, "Introduction" in *Technology Systems for Small Farmers*, Ed., Abbas M. Kesseba, Westview Press, USA and UK.

Kessaba, 1989, *Technology Systems for Small Farmers Issues and Options,* Edt. book, publ. West View Press, London.

Khalija Haq, 1995, "Poverty has a woman's face". *Our Planet*, 7(2) : 15-17.

Korten, Frances E and Sarah Young "The Mothers Clubs of Korea" *Managing Community Based Population Programmes*, Kuala Lumpur. International Committee on the Management of Population Programmes.

Krishnappa, A.M. *et al*. 1996, "Watershed Development in Karnataka"— Agricultural College, Hebbal, Bangalore Golden Jubilee 1946-1996, Alumni Association, UAS, Bangalore.

Kutti Krishnan, B.C., 1984, A case study of IRDP in Kerala Village, *Indian J. of Ag. Economics,* Vol. **39**(3), pp. 256-259.

Leonard, David, "Conclusions" in Leonard, Dale Marshall, Jose Garzon, Stephen Peterson and Sven Steinmo, 1981, Project on managing decentralization, *op. cit.*

Leonard, David; Dale Marshall; Jose Garzon; Stephen Peterson and Sven Steinmo, 1981, Linkages to Decentralized Units, Mimeographed paper, Project on managing decentralization, University of California, Berkeley, USA.

M.K. Gandhi, *Harijan,* 18-1-1948.

M.K. Gandhi, *Harijan,* 10-11-1946.

M.K. Gandhi, *Harijan,* 28-7-1946.

M.K. Gandhi, *Harijan,* 5-6-1937.

M.K. Gandhi, *Harijan,* 9-11-1947.

Malgavkar, P.D., 1970, How small industries in Japan meet the challenges, paper presented in the souvenir brought out on the occasion of Inauguration of Technocrats Industrial Estate, Balanagar, Hyderabad, First week Aug. 1970, pp. 49-53.

Malik, R.S.; Punia, P.K.; and Deeppunia, 1986, Achievements, accelerators and barriers in TRYSEM, *Khadi Gramodyog*, **36**(6).

Malyadri, P., 1985, Success of IRDP Myth or Reality: A study, *Kurukshetra,* Vol. **33**(11), pp. 17-20.

Mellor John, W., 1975, "The Impact of new Agricultural Technology on employment and Income distribution—concepts and policy", occasional paper No. 81, Employment and Income Distribution Project, Dept. of Agril. Economics, Cornell University, USA.

Morss, E.R.; Hatch, J. K.; Mickelwait, D. R.; and Sweet, C.F., 1975, Strategies for small farmers development : An empirical study of rural development projects—Executive summary, Development Alternatives, Inc., Jefferson Place, Washington D.C., USA, May, 1975. Mimeo publication.

Mosher, A.T., 1978, An introduction to agricultural extension, Agricultural Development Council, New York, USA.

Mukerji, B., 1961, *Community Development in India,* I Edn. Orient Longmans, Bombay.

Muniraju, A., 1976, A study on extension participation of farmers in Bangalore District of Karnataka State, Unpublished M.Sc. thesis, Dept. of Extension, University of Agricultural Sciences, Bangalore.

Muzumdar N.H. and Menon, K.A., 1991, Saving and capital formation in Agricultural Sector, A review in M.L. Dantwala (Ed.), *Indian Agricultural Development since Independence, op. cit.,* pp. 207-242.

Nandapurkar, C.C. (1980), "A scale for Entrepreneurial behaviour of small farmers". Unpublished Ph.D. Thesis, Dept. of Agril. Extension, University of Agricultural Sciences, Bangalore.

Narayanaswamy, B.K., 1994, Management services for small farmers development, Unpublished Ph.D. thesis, Department of Agricultural Extension, University of Agricultural Sciences, Bangalore.

Navajeevan Publishing House, 1966, *Village Industries* by M.K. Gandhi, Compiled by R.K. Prabhu.

Navajeevan Publishing House, Ahmedabad, 1956, *Rebuilding Our Villages* by M.K. Gandhi.

Navajeevan Trust, Ahamedabad, 1968, *The Selected Works of Mahatma Gandhi,* **6**, Voice of Truth.

Office of the Registrar General, Government of India, "Vital Statistical Division Report".

Official reappraisal of Agricultural Sector made in 1995 as reported in *Deccan Herald* paper, dated April 30, 1995.

Padamanabhan, M. and Swaminathan, H.L., 1994, Rural development report—Rural employment, National Insitute of Rural Development, Hyderabad (AP), p. 1.

Pande, G.C. and Pandey, P.C., 1991, Drought Prone Areas and Rural Development—A review of policy and programme in Pandey and Jalal (Eds.), *Rural Development in India,* Vol. 1, *op. cit.*, pp. 129-148.

Patrocinio Santos Villanueva 1966, Value of Rural Roads pp. 775-776. in Raymond E. Borton, (Ed). *Selected Readings to Accompany Getting Agriculture Moving,* Vol. 2. Agricultural Development Council, New York.

Planning Commission, Government of India : Information furnished from time to time.

Planning Commission, Government of India, 1985, *The 7th Five Year Plan,* 1985-1990.

Planning Commission, Government of India, 1992, *The 8th Five Year Plan,* 1992-1997.

Prathap Reddy, K. and Buchanan, K., 1992, Impact of Integrated Rural Development Programme on Rural poor—A micro study in K.D. Gaur (Ed.) *Dynamics of Rural Development, op. cit.* pp. 35-49.

Rajagopalachari, 1952, Gram Kalyan, October, 1952, *Kurukshetra,* A symposium, pp. 6, *op. cit.*

Rajendra Prasad, 1952, The Yajna Broadcast from All India Radio, Delhi, October 2, 1952, *Kurukshetra,* A symposium, pp. 1, *op. cit.*

Ramdas Reddy, J., 1987, "TRYSEM in a drought prone area", *Khadi Gramodyog,* **33**(4).

Rao, G.V.K., 1979, "Employment expansion among agricultural labour and small farm households— An Indian experience", paper presented at the ILO Seminar organised at the University of Agricultural sciences, Bangalore on Agricultural Labour Employment.

Rao, V.M. and Deshpande, R.S., 1991, Agricultural production — pace and pattern of growth in M.L. Dantwala (Ed.). *Indian Agricultural Development since Independence, op. cit.* pp. 75-92, 1991.

Rath, N., Lokanatha, Garibi Hatao,1985, Can IRDP do it?, D.R. Shah (Ed), *Alternatives in Rural Development*, Sterling Publishers, New Delhi,

Rathi, V. and Sharada, M.K., 1992, Impact of IRDP on the rural poor, *Agricultural Situation in India,* Vol. 47(2), pp. 117-119.

Ravi Varma, R., 1967, Ramrajya and Community Development, *Kurukshetra,* A Symposium Publications Division, Government of India, pp. 30.

Report published in *Deccan Herald* March 3, 1995.

Report published in the *Economic Times* Chennai edition dated 15th November 2000, pp. 3, under the title "Poverty the key word as Wolfensohn makes rounds".

Report published in the *Hindu Business Line,* dated Nov. 14, 2000, page 2 under the caption "Government admits poverty reduction not enough".

Roy Kartik, C. and Tisdell Clement, A. and Rajkumar Sen (Eds.), 1992, *Economic Development and Environment : A Case Study of India.* Oxford University Press, Delhi.

Roy Kartik, C. and Tissdell Clement, A., 1992, :Gandhi's concept of development and Nehru's central planning [Roy Kartik C., *et al.* (Eds.), *Economic Development and Environmental, op. cit].*

Narasimhan, Sakuntala, 1996, "The failure of poverty eradication", *op. cit.*

Narsimhan, Sakunthala, 1996, "The failure of poverty eradication" a review report on the national consultation of rural development held at Delhi in October, 1996, published in *Deccan Herald,* dated 10-11-96

Sarawgi, A.A., *et al.* (1986), Financing by State Bank of India, Agricultural Development Branch in Patan Block of Jabbalpur District of M.P. under IRDP, *Indian Journal of Agricultural Economics*, Vol. **21**(4), pp. 669.

Satish Verma and Rajendra Singh (1991) 'Self employment scheme— An evaluation in Pandey and Jalal (Eds.) *Rural Development in India— Issues and policies, op. cit.,* pp. 43-63.

Sawant, S.D. (1991), "Irrigation and Water Use" in M.L. Dantwala (Editor), *Indian Agricultural Development since Independence, op.cit.* pp. 93-107.

Sen, Amartya, 1998. Address at the first press conference on 15th October, 1998 after getting the Nobel Prize, published in *Economic Times* on 16th October, 1998.

Sen, Amartya, 1998. Globalization without safety nets for poor is bsurd. Press report published by the *Deccan Herald* paper on 18th December 1998.

Sen, Amartya, 1998, Address at the International Press Conference after receiving the Nobel Prize, *op. cit.*

Sen, Amartya, 1998, Rural development without safety nets has no meaning. Statement made at the first press conference after getting his Nobel Prize, *Economic Times, op. cit.*

Shivalingegowda, N.S., 1995, An analysis of poverty alleviation programmes in Bangalore Rural District of Karnataka, Unpublished Ph.D. Thesis, Dept. of Ag. Extn., Univ. Agril. Sci., Bangalore.

Siddhu, B.S. and Singh, A.J. (1991), "Technological Change in Agriculture" in M.L. Dantwala (Editor), *Indian Agricultural Development since Independence, op. cit.* p. 129.

Sidhu, D.S. and Singh, A.G., 1991, Technological change in Indian Agriculture in M.L. Dantwala (Ed.). *India's Agricultural Development since Independence, op. cit.,* pp. 117-136.

Singh, B.N.P. (1994), India's rural development through industrialization. in A.S. Bhalla and A.K.N. Reddy (eds). *The Technical Transformation of Rural India, Intermediate Technology,* Pub. ILO, London.

Singh, S.K., 1989, "TRYSEM and rural employment generation", *Kurukshetra*, **37**(7).

Special article in weekly magazine *Sudha* titled "Shree Shakthi" written by Srikanth and published in March. 1998.

Sripathi, K.P. 1994, Let industrialization be focussed on JRY : A case study of D.K. district, *Kurukshetra*, **42**(5) : 11-14.

Sripathy (1994), Training of Rural Youth for Self-Employment. *Kurukshetra*, Vol. **37**(7) : 124-127.

Srivastava, Druv and T. Haque,1990, "Technology, Agricultural Growth and Regional Imbalances", IARI, New Delhi

State Bank of India (1989), Evaluation of Seetu Scheme State Bank of India. *Monthly Review*, Vol. 28 No. 5, May 1982, pp. 255-275.

Statement by the Honourable Union Minister of State for Planning and Programme Implementation made in Lok Sabha in answering the question on June 3, 1998 and published by *Deccan Herald* paper on June 4, 1998, p. 6.

Statement from Agriculture Minister published in the *Deccan Herald* paper, on 28th July 1996.

Subbarao, K., 1991, "Agricultural Marketing" in Dantwala, M.L., (Ed). 1991, *Indian Agricultural Development since Independence, op. cit, pp.* 277-297.

Subbaraydu, C.; Sambashiva Rao, B.; and Narayana, E.V., 1991, "Impact of IRDP on income and employment through milch cattle distribution scheme" in Pandey and Jalal (Eds.), *Rural Development in India — Issues and Policies,* Vol. 1, *op. cit.*, pp. 28-29.

Subramaniam, C., 1982, Position paper presented to the seminar on Indian Agriculture held on June 21-22, 1982 at Tamil Nadu Agricultural University, Coimbatore, Published by Rajaji—International Centre for Public Affairs, New Delhi.

Sundaram, K., 1984, Registrar General's population projections, 1981-2001. An appraisal and an alternative scenario, *Economic and Political Weekly*, Vol. 19(34), Aug. 25.

Sundaram, T.R., Role of agriculture in the Indian National Economy, pp. 17-49, in the *Indian Agricultural Development since Independence*, Edt. by Dantwala, 1991, *op. cit.*

Swaminathan, M.S. 1983, "Agricultural Progress—Key to 3rd World Prosperity—3rd World Lecture 1983. 3rd World Foundation Monograph–71, 3rd World Foundation, London.

Swaminathan, M.S., 1985, Achieving rural urban Harmony in Agricultural Development, Guest hectare series No. 3, Institute of Rural Management, Anand, Gujarat.

Taylor, Carl, *et al.*, 1965, "Steps in Local Group Action" *op. cit.*

Taylor, Carl, 1956, A critical analysis of India's community development programme. Issued by the Community Projects Administration. Government of India.

Tendeler, Judith, 1979, New Directions for Rural Roads, Washington, DC : Agency for International Development, Office of Evaluation.

Times of India dated February 23, 2001, pages 1&9.

Tiwari, R.H. and Kanwar, P.C., 1983, IRDP—Can it improve rural income distribution? *Kurukshetra,* Vol. **24** (6), pp. 7.

UN Economic and Social Commission for Asia and Pacific, Annual survey, 1997, Released on April 16, 1997, Published by the *Deccan Herald* on April 17, 1997.

UNCTAD Report, 1997, Published in *Deccan Herald*, September 27, 1997.

United Nations : Department of Public Information, 1995, Platform for Action : Beijing Declaration, page 38.

United Nations Economic and Social Commission for Asia and Pacific, 1985, *The Rural Poor— Human Capital for Nation Building,* Bangkok.

United Nations Economic and Social Commission for Asia and the Pacific, 1985, *The Rural Poor : Human Capital for Nation Building, op. cit.*

United Nations Population Fund Report dated 19-10-1999 published in *Deccan Herald* dated 20-10-1999.

United Nations Rural Survey, 1997, quoted in *Deccan Herald, op cit.*

Vallabh Reddy, G.P., 1985, "TRYSEM programme —A study in Madhya Pradesh", *Kurukshetra*, **33**(12).

World Bank 1998, Global Competitiveness Report of the World Economic Forum released on June 18, 1999 and reported in *Deccan Herald* Paper on June 19, 1999.

World Bank Study Report, 1997, Quoted by *Deccan Herald* Paper dated April 28, 1997.

World Bank, 1975, Rural Development— Sector policy paper, Washington, D.C., U.S.A., pp. 3-4.

World Bank, 1994, *Poverty,* World Bank, Washington, D.C., USA.

World Bank, 1995, *Gender and Poverty in India,* New Delhi.

INDEX